# Untangling
# DATA-BASED
# Decision Making

## A Problem-Solving Model
## to Enhance MTSS

JASON E. HARLACHER    JON POTTER    ADAM COLLINS

**MARZANO** Resources

555 North Morton Street
Bloomington, IN 47404
888.849.0851
FAX: 866.801.1447

email: info@MarzanoResources.com
MarzanoResources.com

Visit **MarzanoResources.com/reproducibles** to download the free reproducibles in this book.

Printed in the United States of America

**FSC**
www.fsc.org
FSC® C012681
The mark of responsible forestry

Library of Congress Cataloging-in-Publication Data

Names: Harlacher, Jason E., 1977- author. | Collins, Adam (Psychologist), author. | Potter, Jon, author.
Title: Untangling data-based decision making : a problem-solving model to enhance MTSS / Jason E. Harlacher, Adam Collins, Jon Potter.
Other titles: Problem-solving model to enhance multi-tiered systems of support
Description: Bloomington, IN : Marzano Resources, [2024] | Includes bibliographical references and index.
Identifiers: LCCN 2023043522 (print) | LCCN 2023043523 (ebook) | ISBN 9781943360789 (paperback) | ISBN 9781943360796 (ebook)
Subjects: LCSH: Education--United States--Data processing. | Multi-tiered systems of support (Education) | School management and organization--United States--Decision making.
Classification: LCC LB1028.43 .H27 2024  (print) | LCC LB1028.43 (ebook) | DDC 371.200973--dc23/eng/20231128
LC record available at https://lccn.loc.gov/2023043522
LC ebook record available at https://lccn.loc.gov/2023043523

**Production Team**
*President and Publisher:* Douglas M. Rife
*Associate Publishers:* Todd Brakke and Kendra Slayton
*Editorial Director:* Laurel Hecker
*Art Director:* Rian Anderson
*Copy Chief:* Jessi Finn
*Production Editor:* Miranda Addonizio
*Copy Editor:* Mark Hain
*Proofreader:* Charlotte Jones
*Text and Cover Designer:* Laura Cox
*Acquisitions Editor:* Hilary Goff
*Assistant Acquisitions Editor:* Elijah Oates
*Content Development Specialist:* Amy Rubenstein
*Associate Editor:* Sarah Ludwig
*Editorial Assistant:* Anne Marie Watkins

# Acknowledgments

As a new school psychologist fresh out of graduate school, it didn't take long to see how fragmented systems were in schools. How can we expect educators and students to succeed when they face barriers in the system each day? Seeing the state of schools ignited a desire to improve the systems in schools, and in turn, outcomes for all students. As my career progressed, I was assigned to a district team to coach other schools. After working several years as a school psychologist and then returning to graduate school to earn my doctorate, I took a job at the state level, building systems and coaching schools. I now work at the national level building systems and coaching schools, districts, and state departments. This path has spanned nearly two decades, and what I've learned is that data use is the key to improving schools.

You can train on technical information, you can provide resources, you can have engaging presentations . . . but what ultimately improves schools is teaching people to use data (the right data) to make decisions. In my work, I've seen people start with data first, poring over mounds of them. They stare at screens and pages of them, flipping through them, developing questions, and making "Oh, look at that" comments as they comb through it.

This is the wrong direction.

Rather, people should start with their question first and *then* select the right data to answer it. *Question to data* rather than *data to question*. This book illustrates how to do that.

Data-based decision making and the problem-solving model are my passions. They tie together all my education, training, and work. To get to the point I am now, I learned from incredible colleagues, professors, and friends. I have to thank all of them for their guidance, support, and hours of conversation. To the late Ken Merrell for being an amazing adviser and constant source of calm during chaotic graduate years. To Tami Sakelaris, Nicole Kattelman, and Trish Shaffer for their humor, support, and drive to make things better during my doctoral internship.

To Rebecca (Briggsy!) Carver and Aaron Barnes for their nerdy school psych talks, binging on shows (*LOST!*), and knowing that the right decisions come from the right data. To Heidi Mathie Mucha for long lunches during our internship years where we conversed about school systems (and cinnamon bears!). And to Adam Collins and Samantha Lyon for being sources of planning and structure that informed our work. And of course, I must thank my coauthors, Jon Potter and Adam Collins, for letting me drag them through this writing process!

I've always been driven to use the problem-solving model and data. I hope this book can help you do so too.

*—Jason*

Throughout my life and career, I have had the opportunity to learn from some wonderful people and be a part of some amazing teams. These experiences have shaped me in how I think about the world, and how to make it better. I never wanted to be an educator when I was a kid. And then I grew up and had the opportunity to be around some incredible educators, and I saw the impact they were making for kids each and every day. It is because of the people in my life that I am able to write this book, so I would like to take this opportunity to thank them.

Thank you to my graduate advisers, Roland Good and Ken Merrell, for mentoring me and introducing me to the problem-solving model. They helped me understand that the goal of problem solving is not to fix problems inherent in our students. Rather, the goal is to fix the problems that our school systems face, the problems that don't allow educators to excel and children to flourish.

Thank you to my colleagues at the Oregon Response to Instruction and Intervention (ORTIi) project who have had an immeasurable impact on how I think about the field of education. That includes Erin Lolich, Dean Richards, Lisa Bates, Tammy Rasmussen, and Christie Rivas for giving me the opportunity to join the project in its very infancy. I learned so much from being the new guy on the team and getting to learn from such incredible, dedicated educators. It includes Jenice Pizzuto, who continually provided positive perspective and eternal excitement in doing this work of improving school systems. It includes Shelby DiFonzo, who was my go-to for everything related to special education (and also anything related to Oregon Ducks football and '90s hip-hop). It includes Beth Ferguson, who was my podcast buddy, so knowledgeable about effective reading instruction and yet always looking to learn more. It includes David Putnam, who led the ORTIi project for over a decade. Your impact on me and on Oregonian students has been immeasurable. It includes Brad Thorud, who kept the project moving forward through some rough and rocky times. And it includes Jamie Maier, who always provided the project with tech support, a different perspective, and a whole lot of levity.

Thank you to the teachers, specialists, and administrators in all the school districts that I have had the privilege of working with as part of the ORTIi project.

You welcomed me into your schools to problem solve with you and your teams. You allowed me to listen to your challenges and to do my best to be a small part of the solutions. Through each meeting and each conversation, you have helped to refine the problem-solving process described in this book, making it more manageable for adults and more meaningful for kids. I am so grateful for each and every educator I got the chance to talk with and learn from (even the teacher who disparagingly referred to me as "Mr. Scientist Guy" due to my fondness for data and using it to make decisions). This book would not have been possible without each and every one of you.

Thank you to my two coauthors, Jason and Adam, for inviting me to collaborate on this book. I'm grateful for the opportunity to contribute to such a wonderful and well-needed resource for educators. I sincerely hope that all the shared experience that we have put into this book will be helpful in improving the lives of students and educators.

And last, and most importantly, thank you to my wife, Ashley. You have supported me through the ups and downs. You have heard my frustrations and celebrated my successes. You have listened attentively whenever I talked about education, even when you had no idea what I was talking about. And you have supported me in writing this book, giving me time to do so even as we were in the middle of having our second child, which is no small feat. And for that, and for everything else, I am grateful.

*—Jon*

The use of data, both big data and street data, is necessary for our schools to become the fully realized bastions of hope and opportunity for which we as educators strive. At the heart of my career is the prevention of bullying. I have met those in the field of education who will tell you that bullying is a rite of passage and just part of growing up. I have also met those who see the real damage it can do to students, families, teachers, and the community. Luckily, the latter far outweigh the former. But it raises the question, How do we better understand those educators who do not see value in spending school hours improving social-emotional learning skills, while also changing their hearts and minds?

One answer, which you will find in this book, is data. We can use data to find trends, warning signs, and potential solutions. After implementing effective solutions, we can show how strong academic and social-emotional improvements are making the lives of our students better. In other words, we can attempt to change minds. In some cases, though, we must also use data to change hearts. These data come from the voices of our students and families: the children who fake being sick so that they don't have to go to school and face their tormentor. The parents who see their teenagers frustrated every day coming home because they just can't seem to get it right in their mathematics class. Centering these voices in our solutions to problems furthers educational equity. Plus, sharing their very real stories may even help change some hearts and minds.

Thank you to my coauthors, Jason and Jon, for your constant support in my contributions to this book. And to think I probably would have never met Jon if it weren't for COVID-19 lockdowns and online video games. As for Jason, there is no one who has done more for me professionally just by being a good person and friend. Even if you are a Bears fan.

Finally, thank you to those who have taught me the most about using data in the real world: my family. I remember when sleep training our oldest child, I told my wife, Kelly, about all the research studies and data collected on the amount of time to let your kid cry before going in to comfort them. What I didn't tell her, because I didn't know, is that when it's *your* child, you have a *physiological* response to their crying. Five minutes feels like five lifetimes. Thank you, Kelly, for making sure I remember that balance is just as important as strict adherence to guidelines. You are the glue that keeps it all together. And to my children, thank you for always reminding me that data are only a single snapshot in time. Each day is another chance to start a new, positive trend.

—*Adam*

Marzano Resources would like to thank the following reviewers:

Benjamin J. Kitslaar
Principal
West Side Elementary School
Elkhorn, Wisconsin

Paula Mathews
STEM Instructional Coach
Dripping Springs ISD
Dripping Springs, Texas

Jennifer Rasmussen
Literacy Specialist and Instructional
Service Director
CESA 4
West Salem, Wisconsin

Katie Saunders
Kindergarten Teacher
Bath Community School
Bath, New Brunswick, Canada

Christie Shealy
Director of Testing and Accountability
Anderson School District One
Williamston, South Carolina

Visit **MarzanoResources.com/reproducibles** to download the free reproducibles in this book.

# Table of Contents

*Reproducibles are in italics.*

# About the Authors

**Jason E. Harlacher, PhD,** is a senior researcher with American Institutes for Research and the director for the Center on Multi-Tiered System of Supports (MTSS Center; mtss4success.org). Jason began his career working with youths in a day treatment center, which sparked his passion for using data to create safe and effective school environments. Since then, he has worked at the state, district, and school level, having held roles as a school psychologist, district-level technical assistance provider, adjunct professor, and state-level consultant. With over eighteen years in education, he presents across the United States on topics related to classroom management, data-based decision making, and MTSS. He is an award-winning author, with titles that include *Bolstering Student Resilience: Creating a Classroom with Consistency, Connection, and Compassion* and *An Educator's Guide to Schoolwide Positive Behavioral Interventions and Supports.*

Jason earned a bachelor's degree in psychology from Ohio University, a master's in school psychology from Utah State University, and a doctorate in school psychology from the University of Oregon.

**Jon Potter, PhD,** is a senior technical assistance consultant with American Institutes for Research. Jon has worked in education for more than sixteen years, supporting school districts in developing and sustaining MTSS. As an RTI implementation coach for the Oregon Response to Instruction and Intervention Project, he supported school districts across the state of Oregon in improving systems of reading instruction for all learners. He presents across the United States on topics related to data-based decision making, developing positive school cultures that can sustain systems change, and translating the science of reading into effective classroom practices.

Jon earned a bachelor's degree in psychology from the University of Denver, and a master's degree in special education and a doctorate in school psychology from the University of Oregon.

**Adam Collins, PhD,** is the founder of Envision Zero Bullying and author of *Effective Bullying Prevention: A Comprehensive Schoolwide Approach*. He has over fifteen years of experience researching and implementing bullying prevention best practices at the school, district, and state levels. He serves on the board of directors and is the co-vice chair of programming for Act to Change, the only national nonprofit working to end bullying for Asian American and Pacific Islander (AAPI) youth. Adam serves as the statewide bullying prevention manager at the Colorado Department of Education, where he spearheaded the creation of Colorado's first statewide bullying prevention model policy and now leads a multimillion-dollar grant-funded bullying prevention program.

Adam earned a bachelor's degree in psychology from the University of Kansas and a doctorate in school psychology from the University of Nebraska–Lincoln.

# Introduction

Take a look at the following three problems and try to solve them. Write down your answers before you turn the page.

1. A bat and a ball cost $1.10 in total. The bat costs $1.00 more than the ball. How much does the ball cost?

   _____ cents

2. If it takes 5 machines 5 minutes to make 5 widgets, how long would it take 100 machines to make 100 widgets?

   _____ minutes

3. In a lake, there is a patch of lily pads. Every day, the patch doubles in size. If it takes 48 days for the patch to cover the entire lake, how long would it take for the patch to cover half of the lake?

   _____ days

Did the answers jump out at you? It should be 10, 100, and 24, right? Would you be surprised to learn that the correct answers are actually 5, 5, and 47? If you missed one, don't feel too bad, as 83 percent of people get at least one incorrect. In fact, when Shane Frederick (2005) developed this cognitive reasoning test and administered it to almost 3,500 participants, one-third of people didn't get any of the questions correct. Only 17 percent of participants got all three questions right!

The correct answers seem obvious after you read them. Perhaps you realized where you made your mistake and you thought, "Oh, I just didn't process that" or "I was reading it too fast." You likely made a quick decision on some of your answers, which resulted in an incorrect response. How could this happen when all the information was there to get the right answer?

To understand how this occurs, we have to consider the difference between intuition and deliberation. *Intuition* is our ability to make judgments or choices without conscious reasoning. It's the feeling we get that guides our choices. *Deliberation* is the conscious and slower reasoning in which we take into account various sources of information before making a choice (Kahneman, 2011; Mega, Gigerenzer, & Volz, 2015; Myers & Twenge, 2021; Psychology Today, n.d.). Intuition can save us time and allow us to pull up information quickly when evaluating a choice, but it can also lead us astray (as you may have experienced with the questions earlier). Intuition is helpful, particularly when we draw on previous experiences we have in our mind about certain events or situations. For example, we may have a frame of reference or schema of what style of clothing to wear for a wedding reception, thus making the choice to wear a suit and tie or a formal dress a quick and easy decision. But when making higher-stakes decisions, intuition can be detrimental; for example, when making decisions about a large purchase, an investment, or with students and their instruction. Our decision making can be quick and intuitive, which is subject to errors and misjudgments, or it can be slow and deliberate, which allows us time to think through choices and be accurate (Kahneman, 2011).

It's ironic that we may make faulty or inaccurate decisions, as data and information are all around us—literally at our fingertips. It's the speedometer in our car, the daily balance in our bank account, the number of steps on our fitness tracking device, our GPS telling us which route to take, and the reviews on websites for products. It's push notifications from our cell phones, internet search results, and beeps and alerts from medical instruments. Data are so abundant that they flood us and we can feel buried, unable to decide which information we should use for our decision. In fact, *analysis paralysis* is a phenomenon in which people freeze when making a decision because the amount of data is overwhelming (Schwartz, 2005). (Ever go to stream a movie, only to spend an hour browsing all the choices?) As educators, we have seen that too much data can actually make it harder to make a decision. As a practicing school psychologist many years ago, Jason was sharing evaluation results with a parent regarding her child's reading scores. He was so prepared, showing her the scores and results of not one, not two, but three different reading assessments! Surely with all that information, they would get an accurate view of the student's reading ability and could make the right decision! After proudly sharing scores from three different assessments, the parent looked at Jason and said, "Well, which one is right? This one says he's doing well, this one is a little low, and this one here is way low. I can't tell which one is right."

She had a point. All those data and they weren't closer to knowing the answer to their question. Jason had just led a meeting that was "data rich but information poor" (Fuchs & Kern, 2014; Slotnik & Orland, 2010).

Our goal with this book is to help educators so they never find themselves in a similar situation. We offer a way to identify and use data deliberately to make decisions. We want educators to use relevant data that are easy to gather, easy to access, and easy to interpret. The data we use should guide decisions and directly answer the questions we have. More pointedly, we want to ensure educators can perform high-quality *data-based decision making*, which is defined as the use of relevant and helpful data to make valid and impactful decisions that benefit students (Deno, 2016; McIntosh & Goodman, 2016).

Educators use data daily in their profession. But educators are increasingly working within best practices and a tiered system in their school, known as a multitiered system of supports (MTSS). Thus, educators need to not only use data but also to use it within MTSS. We'll get into MTSS in greater depth in chapter 1 (page 15), but to briefly explain, it is a schoolwide prevention framework in which data are used in an iterative manner to match and monitor the level of support students receive (Jimerson, Burns, & VanDerHeyden, 2017). Its key components consist of the following (Collins & Harlacher, 2023; McIntosh & Goodman, 2016).

- A *continuum of supports* to serve the diverse needs of students
- A *comprehensive assessment system* to gather data
- *Teaming structures* to guide implementation and support students
- The use of *data-based decision making* to drive the work

Educators use data across the continuum of supports within MTSS, which are organized into tiers. *Tier 1* is universal or core instruction that all students receive, *Tier 2* is additional time provided with standardized interventions, and *Tier 3* is individualized supports for students with intensive needs. However, the types of data educators use and the questions they ask vary between the tiers. At lower tiers (Tier 1), educators make more systemic decisions about schoolwide performance and gradewide performance of students. At upper tiers, educators make decisions about groups of students (Tier 2) and decisions about individual students (Tier 3). As such, educators could benefit from clear and friendly guidance on not only using data effectively but also using data within the framework of MTSS.

To assist educators, we have written this book that outlines the use of data for each tier within MTSS. It is our hope that we can share with educators how to make deliberate, high-quality decisions that benefit students. Educators throughout all levels of the school will find this book useful, but before we share how to use this book and its chapters, let us outline a few tenets of data use that underpin the book.

## First Tenet of Data Use: Be Objective

Data should be accurate, reliable, and valid; in short, they need to be objective. This is nothing new we're telling you, as the use of subjective data or invalid data can give us misleading or faulty information. However, we must also make sure that we interpret data objectively, not just that data are objective in and of themselves. We all have our perceptions that are true and important to use. However, if we rely on our perception too much, the view we have may be inaccurate or biased. Take a look at figure I.1 and decide which line is longer.

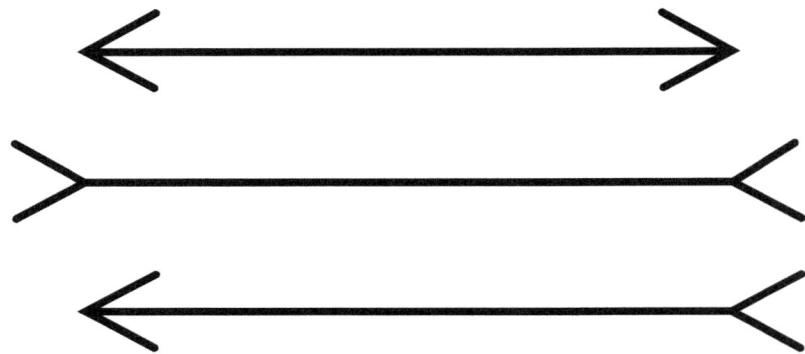

*Source: Müller-Lyer, 1889.*

**Figure I.1: Line perceptions.**

You may be surprised to learn that all three lines are the same length. This is one small example of how our perceptions can fail us. In this example, the data are objective because all three lines are the same length, but our interpretation can be led astray by the orientation of the arrows in the image. In education, we want to be aware of our subjective interpretation of information because our perceptions or biases can mislead us. For example, has someone ever cut you off in traffic? Certainly they did so because they're bad drivers, right? But what do you say when *you've* cut someone off? We're sure you don't call yourself a bad driver and instead argue that it's the situation that made you do it. ("I was in a hurry and didn't see them!") That's the *fundamental attribution error*: our mistakes are because of the situation, but others' mistakes are because of who they are personally. With students, sometimes we may fall victim to the fundamental attribution error when we think they are acting out or refusing to learn material because of their personality (for example, "They're just not a good student."), rather than understanding that the situation or stressors may be causing them to feel unsafe or be emotionally dysregulated (Harlacher & Whitcomb, 2022; Myers & Twenge, 2021).

It doesn't take much to form a view of a person that impacts our judgment or decision making. In fact, one single word about a person's personality can influence our overall view of him, her, or them. A famous study by Harold Kelley (1950) demonstrated this well. In the study, a college class was surprised with an unexpected guest lecturer. Before the lecture began, the students received a paper with a note from their professor sharing his apology for suddenly not attending. It read:

> Mr. _____ is a graduate student in the Department of Economics and Social Science here at MIT. He has had three semesters of teaching experience in psychology at another college. This is his first semester teaching Ec 70. He is 26 years old, a veteran, and married. People who know him consider him to be a rather warm person, industrious, critical, practical, and determined. (Kelley, 1950, p. 119)

Half of the class received the note with the preceding description. The other half received a note that was exactly the same, but the last sentence now read: "People who know him consider him to be a rather *cold* person, industrious, critical, practical, and determined" [emphasis added] (p. 119).

When asked to evaluate the lecturer after class, the students who received the "warm" note rated the lecturer higher on fifteen different personality traits compared to students who received the "cold" note, even though it was the *exact same lecture*! They rated the speaker as more intelligent, more considerate, more humorous, more good-natured, more modest, and more sociable (among other traits). One tiny word painted the view students had of a person (is he a *warm* person or a *cold* person?), a finding that stood true over thirty-five years later (Widmeyer & Loy, 1988).

These findings continue to be validated, including in how our perceptions and the information we're given about students can impact our views of them. Rachel Fish (2017) examined teachers' perceptions of students. Fish (2017) had teachers read different vignettes about low-income male students who showed signs of either academic difficulties, behavioral difficulties, or giftedness, respectively. After reading the vignette, teachers were asked to rate how likely they would offer various supports to the student, such as providing extra time for assignments or reducing the difficulty of their assignments. They also asked how likely they were to refer the student for testing for a learning disability, for an emotional or behavioral disorder, or for giftedness. The wording of the vignettes was designed to evoke racial perceptions by varying only one word—the name of the student (for example, Jacob, Demetrius, or Carlos). Fish (2017) discovered that teachers were more likely to refer a student with a White-sounding name (Jacob) for giftedness or for a learning disability compared to a Black-sounding name (Demetrius) or a Latino-sounding name (Carlos). These findings highlight how personal perceptions and biases can affect a teacher's decision making.

It's important to know that biases are common and normal, but we need to be aware of them so they don't unduly influence our decision making. We've summarized a few common misperceptions and biases in table I.1. As you read the table, consider whether there are any misperceptions you have seen in your role as an educator.

**Table I.1: Common Misperceptions**

| Misperception | Description | Example |
|---|---|---|
| Availability Heuristic | Favoring information that is more readily or recently available | Believing a student is doing well in mathematics because of a recent assessment, despite the abundance of assessments showing poor growth in mathematics |
| Confirmation Bias | Using information that aligns with your views and ignoring evidence to the contrary | Administering a learning-styles assessment and ignoring research that learning styles are not instructionally relevant |
| Fundamental Attribution Error | Attributing one's own behavior to the situation, but attributing others' behavior to their personality | Believing a student is arguing with you because many have described the student as a "problem student" |
| Hindsight Bias | Perceiving a past event as more predictable than it was | Believing you should have known an intervention would be ineffective |
| Illusory Correlation | Believing two variables or events are related even though they aren't | Blaming the principal for district policies because the principal communicates the policy |
| Sunk Cost Fallacy | Continuing with a choice or decision, even though the costs outweigh the benefits | Continuing to implement an instructional strategy, despite its limited impact |

*Source: Merrell, 2016; Myers & Twenge, 2021; Ruhl, 2021.*

## Second Tenet of Data Use: Focus on What's Alterable and Relevant

Our second tenet is to focus on what's alterable and relevant. To explain this tenet, first let us clarify our frame of reference for how we believe students learn. We operate from an assumption that all students can succeed and learn in school. For students to succeed, we believe that the instruction, curriculum, and environment must all be aligned to achieve positive student outcomes (Christ & Arañas, 2014; Harlacher, Potter, & Weber, 2015). When a student is not learning or succeeding in school, then there's a breakdown somewhere within the instruction, curriculum, and environment. Consequently, we measure this dynamic to determine where that breakdown is occurring.

When we attempt to gather information to understand where the breakdown is occurring, we measure variables that are relevant, alterable, and tangible, such as the number of opportunities to respond or the explicitness of the instruction. We won't measure variables that are abstract, inalterable, or less relevant, such as cognitive processing or the student's birth order. For example, if students are not demonstrating schoolwide expectations for engagement in class (let's say they're coming to class unprepared), we're going to ask if they've been effectively taught the expectations for arriving to class (*an instructional question*). We're going to ask if they understand the lessons used to teach that expectation (*a curriculum question*). We're also going to ask if the classroom is supportive of the instruction. For example, have they received prompting for the expectation or reinforcement when they do use that expectation (*an environment question*)? We can also ask if there are student characteristics (*learner questions*) that may impact their learning, such as a vision or hearing need that may affect how instruction is provided. All of these questions can be measured in tangible ways (for example, we can examine the lesson plans used and observe the instruction provided). By gathering information on the instruction, curriculum, and environment, we can then understand how it may interact with the student (the learner) to lead to positive outcomes. Take a look at table I.2 for a list of information that is more relevant versus less relevant as it relates to the interaction between the instruction, curriculum, and environment to produce positive outcomes for the learner.

**Table I.2: Examples of Data Gathered to Assist Data-Based Decision Making in MTSS**

| Relevant Information | Less Relevant Information |
| --- | --- |
| • The types of practices used for instruction<br>• The number of opportunities to respond during instruction<br>• The scope and sequence of the curriculum<br>• The mastery of student skills relative to the items taught in the curriculum<br>• The explicitness of schoolwide expectations<br>• The quality and number of relationships the student has<br>• Learner characteristics that impact learning (hearing, vision, energy level, medical conditions, and so on) | • Cognitive processing scores (such data make high inference assumptions)<br>• Student's siblings or familial order (this information doesn't impact instruction)<br>• Student's state test scores from several years ago (data are not recent)<br>• Leveled reading assessments that assign students a reading level (such assessments have poor predictability, reliability, and instructional utility)<br>• Published norm-referenced tests (they often are not instructionally relevant and may be invalid data because of cultural biases or poor administration) |

## Third Tenet of Data Use: A Team Is Mightier

The third and final tenet of using data is to not go about it alone. We suggest using data within the context of a team. Certainly one person can examine data and make effective decisions, but our recommendation is to use data as part of a team's decision-making processes. It can be difficult for one person to have all the resources, time, and expertise to use all the pieces well within data-based decision making (McIntosh & Goodman, 2016). For that reason, a team can offer a way to share responsibility within data-based decision making.

Being part of a team also diversifies viewpoints when interpreting data and can lead to a deeper analysis of facts and information. For example, Samuel R. Sommers (2006) examined mock juries that were racially homogeneous (all White) or racially diverse (33 percent non-White). Sommers (2006) discovered that racially diverse groups examined more case facts, made less factual inaccuracies, and spent more time in deliberation compared to the homogeneous group. Further, the diverse juries were more likely to correct factually inaccurate statements, such as when someone misstated the population of a city. We mentioned biases earlier, so having a group of different people (with different perspectives, such as in Sommer's study) can help combat biases that may influence a single person. Such findings extend to educational settings, as data teams in schools can build teacher confidence in use of data, improve collaboration and trust among staff, and increase one's knowledge related to data use (Hallam, Smith, & Wilcox, 2015; Hubers et al., 2018; Schildkamp, Poortman, Ebbeler, & Peters, 2019; Serviss, 2022). With a variety of team members, educators can make decisions that consider different viewpoints and take into account developmental and cultural considerations (Harlacher & Rodriguez, 2017).

In this book, we describe the use of data-based decision making within MTSS. To do so, we offer the types of decisions different teams may make across the tiers. In figure I.2, we provide a brief summary of the teams we'll discuss in chapters 3 through 6. The exact name of each team may vary within your school, but we describe a schoolwide or leadership team that is focused on the overall health and function of the school in chapter 3 (page 73). We then describe teams at the Tier 1 core level that focus on grade levels or departmentwide goals in chapter 4 (page 113). We discuss a team for Tier 2 and Tier 3, respectively, which focus on identifying students who need additional support in chapters 5 (page 151) and 6 (page 185).

## A Note About Practices in the Book

Throughout this book, we'll mention the names of certain interventions or assessments as we describe MTSS and the problem-solving model (which can be abbreviated to PSM). Other times, we'll use generic terms or nondescript terms to describe an assessment or intervention. Additionally, education often makes frequent uses of abbreviations, so we have included a list in table I.3 (page 10) to help make some

| Team | Example Names | Purpose | Example Questions They Ask |
|---|---|---|---|
| Leadership Team | Schoolwide team, MTSS team, admin team | Examine schoolwide trends and resolve any equity concerns | • Are at least 80 percent of our students successful with core supports alone?<br>• Do we have equitable outcomes for all students? |
| Tier 1 Team | Grade-level team, department-level team, professional learning community, core review | Ensure all students meet grade-level standards or expectations | • Are at least 80 percent of our students achieving grade-level standards?<br>• Who's the core working for?<br>• Who's it not working for? |
| Tier 2 Team | Intervention team, Tier 2 support | To review and provide supports to students who need supplemental or targeted support | • Which students are at risk?<br>• Who is Tier 2 working for?<br>• Who is it not working for?<br>• Which students are not achieving sufficient growth? |
| Tier 3 Team | Intensive team, intervention team, individualized problem-solving team, instructional assistance team | Review and provide supports to students who need intensive support | • Which students need intensive supports?<br>• Who is Tier 3 working for?<br>• Who is Tier 3 not working for?<br>• Which students are not achieving sufficient growth? |

**Figure I.2: Example of teams within MTSS.**

of the more common acronyms and abbreviations clear. Although readers may encounter some of these in other sources, and they are encouraged to use them in their own practice as necessary, we do keep the use of abbreviations in this text to a minimum to ensure clarity and ease of reading.

The mention of a practice is not an endorsement on our end; we are simply offering examples from our work experience and the literature to enhance and contextualize the problem-solving model. We intentionally use reading, mathematics, writing, and social-emotional-behavioral examples for both the elementary level and secondary level throughout the book. In doing so, we hope our readers see the flexibility and applicability of the problem-solving model. It's our intention that readers provide the specific content area when using the model at their sites. As such, it's helpful to think of a content area as you read this book.

**Table I.3: Glossary of Terms and Their Acronyms**

| Acronym | Description | Definition |
|---|---|---|
| CBM | Curriculum-based measurement | A set of standardized procedures used to assess student progress in academics |
| DBDM | Data-based decision making | The use of data to make decisions that ultimately benefit student achievement and well-being |
| ICEL | Instruction, curriculum, environment, learner | The four domains that educators can assess when examining student needs |
| MTSS | Multitiered system of supports | A framework that organizes and aligns the multiple systems, practices, and assessment procedures within a school to create greater overall efficiency and effectiveness |
| ODR | Office discipline referral | A data source that documents a student's behavioral incident, including the type of behavior, and when and where the incident took place |
| OTR | Opportunity to respond | A teaching strategy that provides a chance for a student to respond to an academically oriented task, such as posing a question or problem to solve; the opportunity to respond enables teachers to acknowledge or provide corrective feedback based on the student's accuracy of response |
| PBIS | Positive behavioral interventions and supports | A framework for implementing evidence-based practices in a tiered approach to support students' behavioral, academic, social, emotional, and mental health needs |
| PLC | Professional learning community | An ongoing process in which teams of educators within a school or district meet regularly to share expertise, improve teaching skills, and better support the needs of students |
| PSM | Problem-solving model | A heuristic that educators can use to identify and solve problems by gathering and analyzing both fidelity and outcome data |
| RIOT | Review, interview, observe, and test | The four assessment methods for gathering information on students |
| RTI | Response to intervention | A preventive systems approach to improving schoolwide and individual achievement through tiered supports provided in response to student need |
| SOP | Standards of practice | Common agreements across a school or district on what will be taught (curriculum), how it will be taught (instruction), and the learning supports that will be provided (environment) |

With this understanding in mind, we know that educators have questions about the selection of practices. We'll talk about selection in chapter 2, but here we offer a list of reputable websites that our readers can access to find lists of evidence-based practices and evidence-based interventions (see table I.4). It's important to pair use of the problem-solving model with evidence-based practices. The model provides the method with which to make decisions (the *how* of data-based decision making). But it's important to have background knowledge of evidence-based practices (the *what* of data-based decision making) within a content area to ensure your decisions are impactful. Without this knowledge of evidence-based practices, users may run the risk of perpetuating poor practices (which in turn lead to poor student outcomes).

**Table I.4: Websites That List Effective and Evidence-Based Practices**

| Website | Link |
|---------|------|
| Best Evidence Encyclopedia | https://bestevidence.org |
| Center on Instruction | www.centeroninstruction.org |
| Evidence-Based Intervention Network | https://education.missouri.edu/ebi |
| National Center on Intensive Intervention Tools Charts | https://intensiveintervention.org/tools-charts/overview |
| What Works Clearinghouse Practice Guides | https://ies.ed.gov/ncee/wwc/practiceguides |

## How to Use This Book

This book is a user-friendly, practitioner-focused application of data-based decision making within MTSS. We recommend that all readers begin with part 1 by reading chapters 1 and 2, in which we lay the foundations of MTSS and data-based decision making. In chapter 1, we define MTSS and discuss each of its components. We also share resources for finding more information and ideas for implementation. In chapter 2, we lay out precisely what data-based decision making is and define the four-step problem-solving model as the method for making data-based decisions. We outline each step and illustrate its use in schools.

Readers can then choose to read the chapters that are most relevant to them.

Part 2 focuses on decision making for systems. School leaders and administrators will find great use in chapter 3, which applies the problem-solving model to schoolwide issues. We illustrate how educators can use the problem-solving model to answer questions at a schoolwide or systemic level, such as, *Are at least 80 percent of our students reaching benchmark* or *Do we have any inequity among student outcomes?* In chapter 4, we outline applying the problem-solving model to the Tier 1 or core instruction. General education teachers will find this chapter helpful, as we share how they can work as part of a grade-level or department-level team to identify where their core instruction is working and where it can be strengthened.

Part 3 focuses on decisions for students. In chapter 5, we turn our attention to targeted supports and interventions (Tier 2). Here we show the reader how to identify students who need additional support and how to efficiently select an appropriate intervention for those students. We discuss progress monitoring as well. Chapter 6 is similar, but our attention is on intensive supports and individual students' needs (Tier 3). We apply the problem-solving model to students who need the most intensive support.

In chapters 3 through 6, we illustrate and apply the problem-solving model across different content areas, and we offer worksheets that you can print and use in team meetings for making data-based decisions. All worksheets are available at **MarzanoResources.com/reproducibles** in downloadable electronic versions. Within each of those chapters, we also discuss how to structure one's team for that particular tier and offer activities to do before, during, and after each meeting.

Finally, we end the book with an epilogue. We review key concepts and offer tips and advice for implementation of the problem-solving model based on our experience and the extant literature. As we mentioned at the start, data are all around, but they can flood us and leave us without helpful information. This conclusion is our attempt to ensure you become data rich *and* information rich.

# PART 1

# Foundations of Data-Based Decision Making

# CHAPTER 1

# Overview of Multitiered System of Supports

Our central focus within this book is on data-based decision making (sometimes abbreviated as DBDM) and how it can be used across different levels of support. Before digging into data-based decision making, we first discuss its backdrop: MTSS. In doing so, we provide foundational knowledge and lay the framework and context within which data-based decision making occurs. For additional information on MTSS, we recommend *Integrated Multi-Tiered Systems of Support: Blending RTI and PBIS* (McIntosh & Goodman, 2016) and *Practical Handbook of Multi-Tiered Systems of Support* (Brown-Chidsey & Bickford, 2015).

## What Is MTSS?

A *multitiered system of supports* is a framework that organizes and aligns the multiple systems, practices, and assessment procedures within a school to create greater overall efficiency and effectiveness (Collins & Harlacher, 2023; McIntosh & Goodman, 2016). It is based on the philosophy that all students can learn, and that educators can adjust alterable variables within the instruction, curriculum, and environment to improve outcomes for all students. It is a proactive and prevention-based schoolwide framework in which data are used in an iterative manner to match and monitor the level of support students receive (Jimerson et al., 2016). Further, it is designed to improve the overall quality of the school in that it aims to have most students (for example, at least 80 percent) meet grade-level standards with core instruction and supports alone. In doing so, critical resources and supports can be sufficiently allocated for students who need more than just core support to reach grade-level standards. As such, it's a systemic model designed to improve the overall effectiveness of the school, as well as a system to improve outcomes for each individual student (McIntosh & Goodman, 2016; Sugai & Horner, 2006).

Historically, MTSS grew out of two parallel school reform movements: (1) response to intervention (RTI) and (2) positive behavioral interventions and supports (PBIS; Freeman, Miller, & Newcomer, 2015; Harlacher, Sakelaris, & Kattelman, 2013; McIntosh & Goodman, 2016; Jimerson et al., 2016). As the name implies, RTI was the response (no pun intended) to four concerns that developed in education (Harlacher et al., 2013; Jimerson et al., 2016; McIntosh & Goodman, 2016).

1.  A need to improve academic outcomes among students, particularly those with disabilities (for example, 37 percent of fourth-grade students scored below the basic level in reading and 25 percent in mathematics on the National Assessment of Educational Progress; National Center for Education Statistics, 2022a; 2022b)

2.  Over-classification of students with disabilities

3.  Concern over a lack of data use and lower-quality instructional practices

4.  The siloed nature of classrooms, which contributed to variance in the curricula and practices used by teachers

Simultaneously, schools were implementing PBIS to address discipline inequity among student racial groups; for example, Black students are three times more likely to be suspended than White students (U.S. Department of Education Office for Civil Rights, 2014) and zero-tolerance approaches disproportionately impact students of color and students with disabilities (Alnaim, 2018; APA Zero Tolerance Task Force, 2008)

Although the exact components that define MTSS vary across organizations, researchers, or state departments, MTSS generally comprises four components (Collins & Harlacher, 2023; Jimerson et al., 2016; McIntosh & Goodman, 2016).

1.  A *continuum of supports* used to meet student needs that increases in intensity

2.  A *comprehensive assessment system* to gather the data needed for decision making

3.  *Teaming structures*, including a leadership team, to guide overall implementation and additional teams to meet the specific needs of students

4.  The use of *data-based decision making* to make changes and match students to supports

As illustrated in figure 1.1, these four components work collectively with each other, as teams meet and use data from the assessment system to engage in problem solving and match students to supports along the continuum of supports. In doing so, they use a data-based problem-solving process. We describe the components of MTSS next before discussing implementation of MTSS.

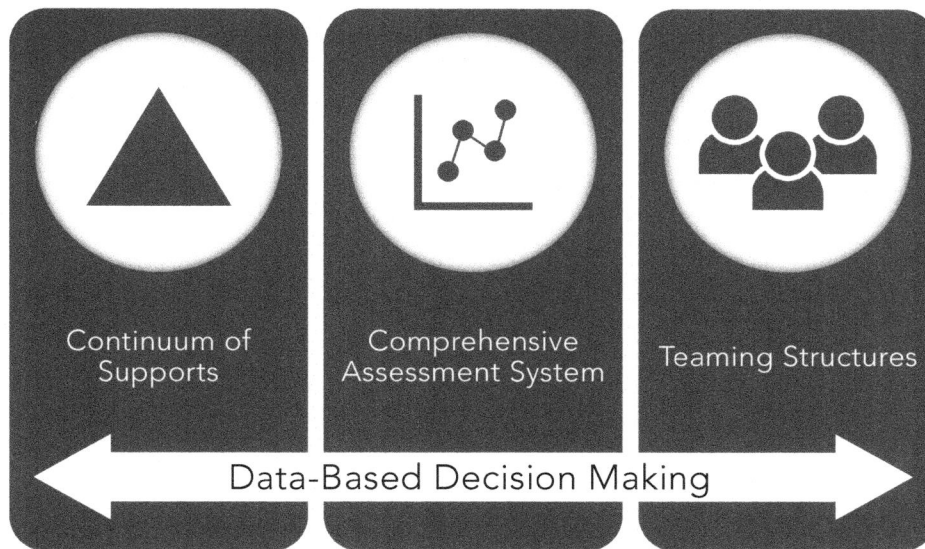

**Figure 1.1: Illustration of MTSS and its components.**

### What Is the Evidence for MTSS?

Research has shown the use of MTSS to be effective through individual components as well as holistically (Burns, Appleton, & Stehouwer, 2005; Jimerson et al., 2016). As it relates to effective teaming and data-based problem solving, research has repeatedly demonstrated that the use of problem-solving teams to develop solutions is an effective approach (Burns & Symington, 2002; Chaparro, Horner, Algozzine, Daily, & Nese, 2022; Horner et al., 2018; Marston, Muyskens, Lau, & Caner, 2003). Moreover, using a comprehensive assessment system to gather data for decision making is a long-standing, effective way to support student learning (Deno, 2005; 2016; Fuchs & Fuchs, 1986; Klute, Apthorp, Harlacher, & Reale, 2017). As a whole, MTSS has also been shown to be effective at improving academic and behavioral outcomes (Burns et al., 2005; Jimerson et al., 2016; Marchand-Martella, Ruby, & Martella, 2007; Sailor, Dunlap, Sugai, & Horner, 2009; Stewart, Benner, Martella, & Marchand-Martella, 2007; Solomon, Klein, Hintze, Cressey, & Peller, 2012) for both elementary and secondary levels (Greenwood, Kratochwill, & Clemens, 2008; Jimerson et al., 2016; Sailor et al., 2009).

### Continuum of Supports

As illustrated in figure 1.2 (page 18), the use of a *continuum of supports* organizes the school into layers of instruction and interventions, called tiers, that increase in intensity. Educators use these multiple tiers to then match students to a corresponding level of support. There are three levels of supports: Tier 1 or core instruction, Tier 2 or targeted supports, and Tier 3 or intensive supports.

3–5 percent of students receive intensive, individualized support.

10–15 percent of students receive targeted group support.

All students receive universal instruction and support. This level of support meets at least 80 percent of students' needs.

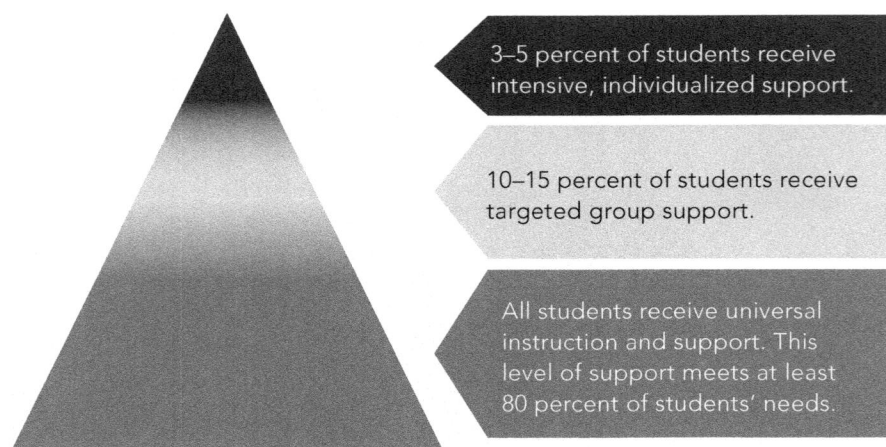

**Figure 1.2: Continuum of supports.**

Educators use outcome and fidelity data to ensure overall effectiveness of academic and behavioral supports, as well as to identify students who need additional support. The goal is to ensure that core instruction, or Tier 1, meets the needs of at least 80 percent of the students. Approximately 15 percent of students will receive targeted, or Tier 2, supports, which are designed to fill skill gaps or to address acute issues students may experience. Tier 3, or intensive, supports are provided to 3 to 5 percent of students; these supports are designed for students with ongoing, intensive needs (Collins & Harlacher, 2023; McIntosh & Goodman, 2016).

As Kent McIntosh and Steve Goodman (2016) pointed out, these tiers represent levels of prevention, not groups of students. Further, because the tiers refer to levels of support and not students, there is no such thing as "a Tier 2 student" or "Tier 3 students." In fact, it's important to note that students' needs are met across the tiers, regardless of any classification they may carry (for example, special education or talented and gifted). It may be tempting to view students as the tier of support that they receive, but students are rounded individuals, have complex needs, and may receive core instruction alone for one content area (for example, reading) and Tier 2 and Tier 3 supports for other content areas (for example, mathematics and behavior).

### Tier 1

All students receive Tier 1 supports, which makes Tier 1 perhaps the most vital in MTSS. These supports are universal in that everyone receives them and they should be sufficient to meet the academic and behavioral needs of at least 80 percent of students (Harlacher et al., 2015; McIntosh & Goodman, 2016). In this tier, all students receive an academic and behavioral curriculum that is aligned horizontally (that is, all classrooms in a grade level follow the same pacing and teach the same standards) and vertically (that is, the beginning lessons of one grade level pick up where the previous grade level ends; Harlacher et al., 2015; McIntosh & Goodman, 2016; Stoiber & Gettinger, 2016). In addition, educators use explicit instruction, differentiation, and an evidence-based curriculum for all students in Tier 1 (McLeskey et al., 2017; Stoiber & Gettinger, 2016).

Along with a core curriculum, staff implement high-leverage practices and evidence-based practices. High-leverage practices are effective at improving student performance *across* grade and content levels (McLeskey, Maheady, Billinglsey, Brownell, & Lewis, 2022). Whereas high-leverage practices are effective across content areas, evidence-based practices are shown to be effective for a *specific* content area. For example, modeling is an effective practice across multiple content areas, but the use of repeated readings is a specific evidence-based practice to improve reading fluency (Dowhower, 2006; International Literacy Association, 2018). Moreover, research suggests that combining high-leverage practices and evidence-based practices may lead to even greater academic and behavioral gains for students (McCray, Kamman, Brownell, & Robinson, 2017). In table 1.1, we provide a brief glossary of key terminology for Tier 1.

**Table 1.1: A Glossary of Terms for Tier 1**

| Term | Definition |
|---|---|
| Core curriculum | The curriculum used by staff during Tier 1 |
| Differentiation (differentiated instruction) | Matching evidence-based strategies and instruction to the individual needs of learners |
| Evidence-based curriculum | A curriculum that has evidence that it leads to positive student outcomes |
| Evidence-based practices | Practices or instructional strategies related to positive student outcomes for a specific content area (repeated readings of text is an effective strategy for improving reading fluency) |
| Explicit instruction | Directly modeling skills and guiding students in use of those skills before they use them independently (that is, I do, we do, you do) |
| High-leverage practices | Practices or instructional strategies related to positive student outcomes (for example, modeling is an effective strategy across numerous content areas) |

The following list includes commonly used high-leverage practices related to improving student achievement (TeachingWorks, n.d.; see https://bit.ly/3JNsY30 for a detailed description of each one).

- Building respectful relationships
- Leading a group discussion
- Explaining and modeling content
- Eliciting and interpreting
- Attending patterns of student thinking
- Implementing norms and routines for discourse
- Coordinating and adjusting instruction
- Establishing and maintaining community expectations
- Implementing organizational routines
- Setting up and managing small-group work
- Communicating with families
- Learning about students
- Setting learning goals
- Checking student understanding
- Selecting and designing assessments
- Interpreting student work
- Providing feedback to students
- Analyzing instruction to improve it

In addition, a list of high-leverage practices effective for students with disabilities has four pillars: (1) collaboration, (2) assessment, (3) social-emotional and behavioral, and (4) instruction. Each of the four pillars includes specific, actionable approaches for supporting student learning and should be part of teacher preparation programs (Ball & Forzani, 2011; see https://highleveragepractices.org to learn more).

Your teams should have a clear definition of Tier 1, including common agreements on the time teachers spend on Tier 1 supports, the skills they teach during Tier 1 instruction (for example, the components of your core reading curriculum), and the common instructional strategies they use during teaching (for example, modeling and guided practice). If a school does not have these core features of Tier 1 in place, establishing them should be the priority before engaging in the Tier 1 problem-solving process. Attempting to engage in the problem-solving process without these key features will likely lead to frustration and false starts.

### Tier 2

Tier 2 supports are for those students who need additional time or exposure to Tier 1. This typically represents 10–15 percent of the student population (Anderson & Borgmeier, 2010; Stoiber & Gettinger, 2016). Tier 2 supports are targeted, as they are focused on a small set of skills, are provided to small groups of students (though they are not always provided in a small-group setting; Hawken, Crone, Bundock, & Horner, 2021), and are designed to offer more opportunities to practice and reinforce correct responses for students. Further, Tier 2 supports are standardized interventions in that each student receives the same intervention for their area of need, and the intervention has standard processes and conditions under which it's provided. Educators use standardized interventions and processes at Tier 2 because when they do so, 70–80 percent of students respond and no longer need intervention support (Hawken et al., 2021; Vaughn et al., 2011; Vaughn, Wanzek, & Murray, 2012). In turn, more extensive assessment and resources can be reserved for Tier 3 supports (Harlacher et al., 2015; McIntosh & Goodman, 2016).

Of note, we view Tier 2 supports as consisting of *evidence-based interventions*, which are sequenced or packaged interventions with core features that utilize both high-leverage practices and evidence-based practices. For more on this, see the National Center on Intensive Intervention's (n.d.c) "Levels of Intervention and Evidence" (visit https://bit.ly/41fIP1H). When an evidence-based intervention isn't available for a given content area, educators can provide an intervention that consists of high-leverage practices and evidence-based practices for certain content areas (for example, explicit instruction during which students learn vocabulary words, using a chunking strategy to teach reading comprehension, and so on). The Institute of Education Sciences and the Center on Instruction offer practice guides that outline effective practices for specific content areas (table I.4, page 11, provides links). Many core curricula offer supplemental materials that can be used for Tier 2 as well.

Tier 2 is additional time provided beyond the time allotted for Tier 1 for groups typically between three and eight students (Harlacher et al., 2013; McIntosh & Goodman, 2016). Students receive additional intervention sessions three to five times per week for anywhere from twenty to sixty minutes or more, with students in secondary settings receiving lengthier intervention sessions (Harlacher et al., 2013; Harlacher & Rodriguez, 2017; McIntosh & Goodman, 2016). Behavioral interventions at Tier 2 vary in how they are delivered but can include social-emotional learning and social-skills groups, mentoring, or use of a check in–check out intervention (Harlacher & Rodriguez, 2017). After approximately ten to twenty weeks, schools use data to consider the provision of Tier 3 supports for students not making adequate progress in Tier 2 (Hawken et al., 2021; Vaughn et al., 2012).

### Tier 3

The third tier of supports is provided to roughly 3–5 percent of students who have the most significant needs (Harlacher et al., 2013; McIntosh & Goodman, 2016). Whereas Tier 2 is focused on efficiency and providing a standardized intervention, Tier 3 focuses on individualized supports for a student (Harlacher et al., 2013; McIntosh & Goodman, 2016; Zumeta-Edmonds, Gandhi, & Danielson, 2019). Educators provide students receiving Tier 3 with supports based on their unique data profile, strengths, and areas of need. This means that Tier 3 supports typically require more in-depth diagnostic assessments so that educators can tailor interventions to the specific student. Accordingly, Tier 3 supports build off the intervention educators provide in Tier 2 by intensifying and individualizing that support by adjusting factors within the instruction, curriculum, environment, or a combination (Zumeta-Edmonds et al., 2019).

Generally speaking, educators can intensify interventions from Tier 2 to Tier 3 by increasing the dosage of the intervention (for example, more time or smaller group size), adding additional instructional practices to improve explicitness (for example, increasing opportunities to respond or amount of corrective feedback), modifying the curriculum (for example, adjusting scope and sequence of skills or increasing practice time), or improving the environment (for example, increasing praise or reteaching routines). Additionally, schools may add wraparound services and behavioral or social-emotional support for students at Tier 3 (Coffey et al., 2018; Hunter, Elswick, & Baylot Casey, 2018). In figure 1.3, we offer a brief preview of some basic ways to intensify supports from Tier 2 to Tier 3. In chapter 6 (page 185), we provide more in-depth information on intensification of supports.

| Factor | Description | Example |
| --- | --- | --- |
| Instruction: Dosage | The total amount of time and strength of the support provided | Increasing the number of interventions sessions in a week from three to five |
| Instruction: Delivery or explicitness | The actual delivery of instruction and amount of explicitness | Increasing modeling, opportunities to respond, and corrective feedback provided to students |
| Curriculum | The collection of skills and the sequence in which those skills are taught | Adjusting the sequence of skills taught to match the student's background knowledge |
| Environment | The setting within which the instruction occurs | Ensuring a 5:1 praise-to-redirect ratio |

**Figure 1.3: Instructional factors to modify to intensify supports and examples.**

It is through these multiple levels of instruction that MTSS creates greater efficiency for schools (Dunlap et al., 2010; Zumeta-Edmonds et al., 2019). By focusing on robust and effective Tier 1 supports, schools reduce the number of students needing Tier 2 or Tier 3 supports. To be clear, Tier 2 and Tier 3 supports are *in addition to* core instruction, *not in replacement of* core instruction. However, educators will need to coordinate intensive supports and make decisions on an individual basis regarding how to supplement or supplant some of a student's Tier 1 time with Tier 3 supports. Sometimes, educators will make the mistake of supplanting all or the majority of a student's Tier 1 with Tier 3, which inadvertently leads to further skill gaps because of critical missed instructional time in Tier 1 (Harlacher et al., 2013; 2015). By prioritizing efficiency over individualization at Tier 2, teams can allocate more expertise, time, and resources to Tier 3 and to those students who need the most intensive time, assessment, and attention (Hawken et al., 2021; Zumeta-Edmonds et al., 2019). Working in tandem, the multiple levels of instruction provide a clear structure for educators to best meet student needs.

### Comprehensive Assessment System

A comprehensive assessment system refers to the procedures used to collect different types of data needed for data-based decision making within MTSS. Generally speaking, there are four types of data gathered for decision making in MTSS: (1) universal screening data, (2) diagnostic data, (3) progress-monitoring data, and (4) fidelity data (Christ & Arañas, 2014; Hosp, Hosp, Howell, & Allison, 2016; McIntosh & Goodman, 2016). As illustrated in figure 1.4, a comprehensive assessment system includes collecting all four types of data and ensuring accurate collection of those data (National Center for Intensive Intervention, n.d.b; Taylor, 2009).

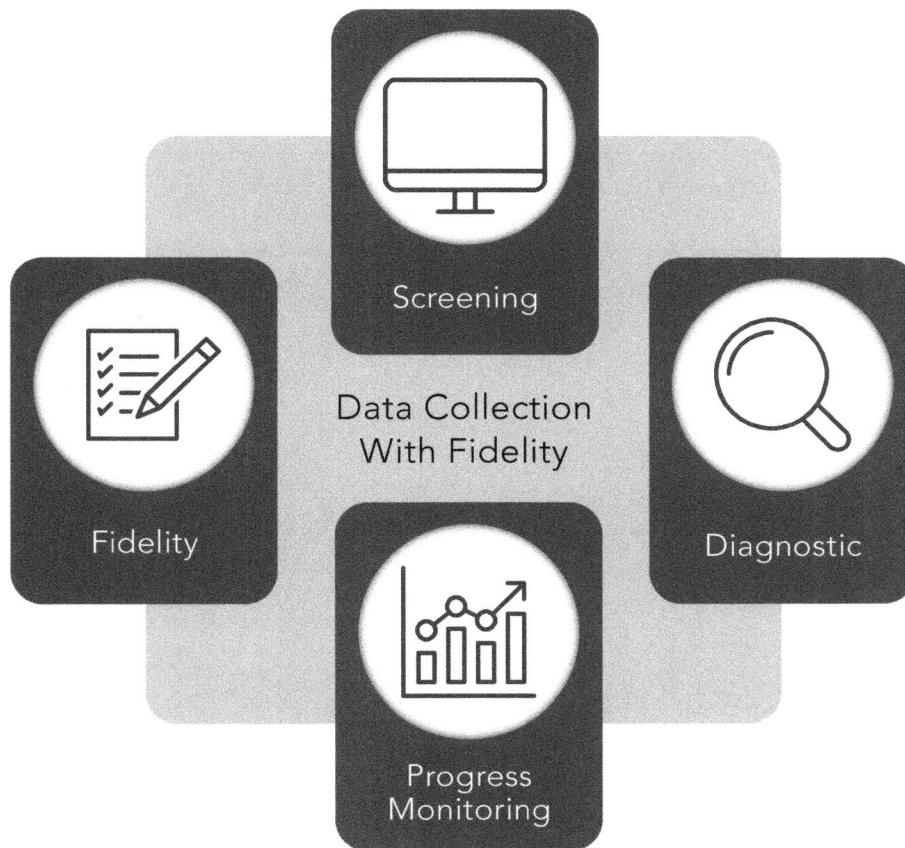

**Figure 1.4: Illustration of comprehensive data system.**

#### Screening Data

Screening data are used to identify a student's current level or standing relative to socially valid criteria, such as grade-level benchmarks (Christ & Arañas, 2014). Screening assessments are brief, general indicators of a student's mastery of certain skills. For example, educators can use Oral Reading Fluency, which is a one-minute probe where students read aloud and the educator records the number of correct words. This provides an overall measure of reading skill (Christ & Arañas, 2014; McIntosh & Goodman, 2016).

In the early grades and elementary school (that is, preK–6), educators will commonly screen students for basic skills in language, literacy concepts, reading, writing, and mathematics, as well as general indicators for social, emotional, and behavioral functioning. Educators can screen for those same skills in later grades (that is, grades 7–12), but often, secondary students are screened for their level of school engagement or their risk for school dropout (Marken, Scala, Husby-Slater, & Davis, 2020). We typically recommend using validated screening tools with high sensitivity and specificity to identify students' risk level. However, schools can also use other data sources to identify students who may need additional support, such as pre-existing data (for example, referrals or attendance) and parent or teacher nomination. In table 1.2, we offer a list of screening tools that are commonly used at elementary and secondary levels.

**Table 1.2: Examples of Screening Tools**

| Academic | Social, Emotional, Behavioral |
|---|---|
| <ul><li>Acadience (acadiencelearning.org)</li><li>AimswebPLUS (app.aimswebplus.com)</li><li>Dynamic Indicators of Basic Early Literacy Skills (DIBELS; 8th ed., University of Oregon, n.d.; (http://dibels.uoregon.edu/dibels8)</li><li>FastBridge (www.renaissance.com/products/fastbridge)</li><li>Measures of Academic Progress (MAP; www.nwea.org/the-map-suite)</li><li>Star Assessments (CBM, Reading, Mathematics, Early Literacy, Spanish; www.renaissance.com/products/star-assessments)</li></ul> | <ul><li>Behavior Assessment System for Children (BASC-3, 3rd ed.; Reynolds & Kamphaus, 2015)</li><li>BASC-3 Behavioral and Emotional Screening System (BESS; Kamphaus & Reynolds, 2015)</li><li>Early warning indicators (such as attendance, office discipline referrals, and course grades)</li><li>Strengths and Difficulties Questionnaire (SDQ; Youth in Mind, 2022; www.sdqinfo.org/a0.html)</li><li>Student Risk Screening Scale (SRSS; Drummond, 1994)</li></ul> |

Educators can use screening data for a few reasons, one of which is to identify those students needing additional supports to meet academic, social-emotional, and behavioral goals. In this situation, all students get the screening measure and those who fall below the criterion receive further assessment to ensure they are actually at risk, a process called *risk verification* (Bailey, Colpo, & Foley, 2020). We dig into how to do risk verification in chapter 2 (page 41). Risk verification is important because it ensures the validity of a student's risk status and enables schools to accurately identify those who need interventions.

Another use of screening data is to evaluate the health of core instruction, both for the overall school level and for individual grade levels. In this situation, educators can examine the total percentage of students who scored in the low-risk range for their grade level to see if they meet the 80 percent threshold for effective core instruction. This calculation can be done for all students in the school and for each grade level. Some screening measures consist of a single score, whereas others may be composed of several different subtests that assess different important areas. For example, consider the Acadience screener. Acadience Learning (2021) is an education company that offers assessment tools. In the area of reading, the Acadience screener comprises multiple assessments examining a range of early literacy skills, including phonemic awareness, phonics, fluency, and reading comprehension (Good et al., 2019). These multiple assessments are combined to create a composite score, giving the most comprehensive indicator of overall risk level. This composite score is what you would use to determine the percentage of students who are at low risk. You can think of the composite score as a combination of multiple indicators of overall health, similar to the multiple indicators you would receive at a yearly checkup with a health provider. Each year, your doctor will typically take your blood pressure, temperature, and weight. They look at all these tests together to determine whether there is a low level of risk for current or future health problems or if there is reason for concern with one or more of your numbers.

One final note about screening tools is that certain grade levels may use the results of non-screening assessments to actually screen students. For example, teachers may examine the previous year's state test scores, which are summative exams, to identify which students may be at risk. Although the state test is neither brief nor designed as a screener, teams can access certain scores as a quick screening source or risk-verification source (Harlacher & Rodriguez, 2017). That said, we encourage teams to use validated screening tools whenever possible because of their high predictability of risk level.

### Diagnostic Data

Diagnostic data identify students' strengths and areas of need (Harlacher & Rodriguez, 2017; Hosp, 2008; McIntosh & Goodman, 2016). This information then informs the type of instruction or intervention they may receive. Whereas screening assessments are often brief measures that take only a few minutes, diagnostic assessments are lengthier and more comprehensive. For example, a doctor would take your temperature as a general indicator of overall health. If that indicator suggested a problem (for example, your temperature was above 98.6 degrees), then additional diagnostic data are used to determine why your temperature is high (for example, conducting a blood panel or doing a full health exam). Similarly in education, screening assessments are used to check a student's educational "health," and diagnostic assessments are reserved for exploring students' needs when their educational health is at risk. For example, a student may be screened using a mathematics

## Can a Screener Be Diagnostic?

Screeners typically measure a small number of skills that are most predictive of future success and easiest to measure. They are not a comprehensive assessment of every skill a student needs to be successful. While this allows us to collect screening data rather efficiently, it does not always provide all the information we need to inform our next steps. When a student is flagged as at risk, we won't always necessarily know *why* (which is the purpose of a diagnostic assessment).

You can gain some diagnostic information from a screener, but you will want to maintain a balance between the time it takes to administer the screener and the depth of information you receive from it. Depending on the tool your team uses, you may have sufficient data to determine a general priority skill to target (for example, phonemic awareness to phonics or fluency to reading comprehension), or you may have more general screening information that does not allow for much problem analysis. If this is the case, you can choose to use a follow-up diagnostic assessment, such as a phonics survey or mathematics computation error analysis, to further identify or target instruction toward a priority skill. If you determine that further diagnostic assessment is needed, you should only conduct that assessment with those students who are below the benchmark. You could also supplement your existing screener with other important measures it lacks, such as adding measures of vocabulary or oral language.

computation probe to determine whether they're at risk, and if they are, educators can then administer a mathematics diagnostic tool, such as a mathematics facts inventory, to determine why they're at risk (that is, what exact computation needs does the student have?). Because of the fundamental differences between screening and diagnostic assessments, the information and questions you can answer are different. That is, screening assessments give you an overall big picture of students' risk, whereas diagnostic assessments provide the nuanced information on the skills students have mastered versus have not mastered. We offer common diagnostic tools and data sources in table 1.3.

### Progress-Monitoring Data

Progress monitoring is a type of formative assessment. *Formative assessment* refers to the use of data and information to evaluate the extent to which students are meeting learning objectives or whether they are learning the taught content (Christ & Arañas, 2014; Klute et al., 2017; McIntosh & Goodman, 2016). Formative assessments are critical sources of data within MTSS, particularly for staff as they adjust interventions and instruction to ensure students master the content. When teaching, staff use formative assessment to guide their in-the-moment adjustments, but when providing interventions and determining whether students are benefiting from those interventions, more technically adequate and rigorous assessment methods are needed. Accordingly, this is when educators use progress monitoring.

**Table 1.3: Examples of Diagnostic Data Tools and Sources**

| Academic | Social, Emotional, Behavioral |
|---|---|
| • Acadience Reading Diagnostic (http://acadiencelearning.org/acadience -reading/diagnostic)<br><br>• CORE's Assessing Reading: Multiple Measures<br><br>• Error analysis in a content area<br><br>• Measures of Academic Progress (nwea.org)*<br><br>• Phonics Inventory (www.hmhco.com/programs /phonics-inventory)<br><br>• Primary Spelling Inventory (www.pearson.com /en-us/campaigns/words-their-way.html)<br><br>• Single-skill worksheets or assessments<br><br>• SpringMath (springmath.org)<br><br>• Star Phonics (renaissance.com/products/star -phonics) | • Direct Behavior Rating (http://dbr .education.uconn.edu)<br><br>• Functional Assessment Checklist for Teachers and Staff (FACTS; Anderson & Borgmeier, 2007)<br><br>• Functional Behavioral Assessment (Crone & Horner, 2015)<br><br>• Interviews with key personnel or with student<br><br>• Strengths and Difficulties Questionnaire (www.sdqinfo .org/a0.html)*<br><br>• Student Risk Screening Scale (Drummond, 1994)* |

* Depending on which scores are analyzed, these measures can serve as diagnostic measures.

*Progress monitoring* is the formal measurement of a student's skill using a validated tool (McIntosh & Goodman, 2016). Educators use progress-monitoring data to assess a student's growth toward an identified goal, which usually corresponds to a particular benchmark or grade-level criterion (Hosp, 2008; Hosp et al., 2016; McIntosh & Goodman, 2016). This requires the use of psychometrically sound (reliable and valid) tools that are brief to use, standardized, sensitive to growth, and have various forms so that teachers can administer them repeatedly over time (Hosp, 2008; Hosp et al., 2016). By *reliable*, we mean the measurement is accurate and consistent; by *valid*, we're referring to tools that measure what they purport to measure (Marzano, 2018). In using progress monitoring, educators can keep an active eye on a student's growth over time. Additionally, because progress-monitoring tools are reliable and valid, their use ensures accurate measurement of a student's skills and a reliance on objective data (versus subjective). Further, established progress-monitoring tools and frequent measurement are related to effective decision making and positive student outcomes (Fuchs & Fuchs, 2007; Klute et al., 2017; McIntosh & Goodman, 2016).

One challenge with progress monitoring is choosing an effective tool to use. For elementary-aged students, educators have a plethora of tools to choose when measuring basic skills. However, progress monitoring for older students is more challenging because of a decrease in tools appropriate for their grades and because older students may have mastered basic skills (thus making the use of some progress-monitoring tools less applicable). In such cases, educators may choose to use key early warning indicators, such as course grades, attendance, and office behavior referrals (Marken et al., 2020); targeted curriculum-based measurement probes (for example, algebra probes; Hosp et al., 2016); or even common formative assessments to progress monitor. In table 1.4, we provide examples of data and tools to use when progress monitoring.

### Fidelity Data

Educators use fidelity data to measure how well a practice, assessment tool, plan, intervention, or instructional strategy is implemented as intended (Collins & Harlacher, 2023; McIntosh & Goodman, 2016). This ensures that the results of a plan are not simply the artifact of poorly administered interventions or assessments. Generally speaking, fidelity data are gathered by directly observing the practice, having someone report on it, or examining permanent products associated with the practice (for example, examining lesson plans; Harlacher & Rodriguez, 2017). There are pros and cons to each approach, which we summarize in table 1.5.

## *Teaming Structures*

The third key component of MTSS is having clear teaming structures. Schools will need a leadership team to guide implementation and ensure the overall health of the school's instruction. In addition to the leadership team, additional teams are needed to ensure a high-functioning MTSS. Grade-level or department-level teams examine the effectiveness of their core instruction, and student-level teams will examine data to identify and monitor students who need additional interventions (for example, Tier 2, Tier 3). The exact teaming structures in school will vary depending on the size of the school, but generally, there are a leadership team, grade- or department-level teams, a Tier 2 team, and a Tier 3 or individual student team. In figure 1.5 (page 30), we illustrate this team set up and briefly describe each.

At the leadership team level, a representative group of grade-level staff, administrators, specials staff, and family members (in some instances) takes on the responsibility of ensuring the effective implementation of the MTSS framework. This team is responsible for designing what MTSS will look like in a school, including what practices, curricula, assessments tools, interventions, and instructional strategies will be used. In addition, they make decisions about when and how to gather data, create rules for evaluating interventions, and outline a protocol for providing support to students (for example, a protocol outlines who gets what support and when; Barnes & Harlacher, 2008; McIntosh & Goodman, 2016). Further, the leadership team ensures the necessary support systems and infrastructure are put in place to support the components of MTSS. That is, the leadership team provides training and coaching to staff on MTSS, ensures effective two-way communication, and follows selection procedures for choosing which practices or

**Table 1.4: Examples of Data Sources for Progress Monitoring**

| Content Area | Progress-Monitoring Tools |
|---|---|
| Reading | Acadience Reading (acadiencelearning.org/acadience-reading/k-grade6/)<br><br>aimswebPlus (pearsonassessments.com)<br><br>Course grades<br><br>Dynamic Indicators of Basic Early Literacy Skills (DIBELS; 8th ed., http://dibels.uoregon.edu/dibels8)<br><br>FastBridge (www.renaissance.com/products/fastbridge)<br><br>Star CBM Reading (www.renaissance.com) |
| Mathematics | Acadience Math (acadiencelearning.org/acadience-math/k-grade6)<br><br>aimswebPlus (pearsonassessments.com)<br><br>Course grades<br><br>FastBridge (www.renaissance.com/products/fastbridge)<br><br>Star CBM Math (www.renaissance.com) |
| Social, Emotional, Behavioral | Behavior Assessment for Children (BASC; 3rd Ed., pearsonassessments.com)<br><br>Direct behavior observation<br><br>Direct Behavior Rating (dbr.education.uconn.edu)<br><br>Office discipline referrals |

**Table 1.5: Examples of Data Sources for Fidelity**

| Fidelity Tool | Pros | Cons |
|---|---|---|
| Observation | Direct documentation of behavior | Time consuming, harder to observe certain phenomena |
| Self-Report | Efficient, can gather information on a variety of behavior | Subject to bias, particularly if items are not objectively defined |
| Permanent Products | Efficient, do not require additional time to gather | May not provide a direct measure in some situations |

| Team | Example Names | Purpose | Example Questions They Ask | Members |
|---|---|---|---|---|
| Leadership Team | Schoolwide team, MTSS team, admin team | Examine schoolwide trends and resolve any equity concerns | • Are at least 80 percent of our students successful with core supports alone?<br>• Do we have equitable outcomes for all students? | Administration, district personnel, and school staff, including regular and special education teachers and support personnel |
| Tier 1 Team | Grade-level team, department-level team, core review team, collaborative team | Ensure all students meet grade-level standards or expectations | • Are at least 80 percent of our students achieving grade-level standards?<br>• Who's the core working for?<br>• Who's it not working for? | General education teachers, other personnel as needed |
| Tier 2 Team | Intervention team, Tier 2 support | Review and provide supports to students who need supplemental or targeted support | • Which students are at risk?<br>• Who is Tier 2 working for?<br>• Who is Tier 2 not working for?<br>• Which students are not making sufficient growth? | General education teachers, administrators, and support personnel such as school psychologist, counselor, or interventionists |
| Tier 3 Team | Intensive team, intervention team, individualized problem-solving team, instructional assistance team | Review and provide supports to students who need intensive support | • Which students are most at risk?<br>• Who is Tier 3 working for?<br>• Who is Tier 3 not working for?<br>• Which students are not making sufficient growth? | Administration, district personnel, and school staff, including regular and special education teachers and support personnel |

**Figure 1.5: Example of teams within MTSS.**

assessments to use (McIntosh & Goodman, 2016). Finally, the team engages in an iterative process to evaluate how well implementation is going, which includes identifying and solving barriers to implementation. The leadership team is responsible for designing and implementing MTSS, but it also evaluates its impact on the overall functioning of the school. It examines data related to the overall effectiveness of the instruction and supports across the schools, as well as identifying and resolving any disparity or equity issues that may exist or arise over time (Harlacher et al., 2015; McIntosh & Goodman, 2016). Using a teaming structure has several benefits, including the disbursement of responsibilities, which avoids staff burnout, improved sustainability, and increased capacity for the school to continuously improve student outcomes (McIntosh & Goodman, 2016).

Tier 1 or grade-level teams consist of staff who focus on the overall effectiveness of grade-level instruction and on using a screening process to identify students needing additional supports. This team also provides input on the health of the entire Tier 1 system at the school through ongoing monitoring and evaluation of classroom instruction and supports. When this team identifies that the core instruction is not meeting the needs of at least 80 percent of students, it is tasked with developing a plan to address such issues (Harlacher et al., 2015).

Whereas the leadership team focuses on the effective implementation of MTSS and the grade-level team focuses on the health of their grade-level's core instruction, student-level teams are typically responsible for monitoring and supporting students receiving Tier 2 and Tier 3 supports. Student-level teams use data to identify students who need additional support, develop intervention plans, support the implementation of the plans, and determine the effectiveness of the plans. Clear entry and exit criteria for Tier 2 and Tier 3 supports are used in combination with data to decide when students should have supports intensified or faded (Harlacher et al., 2015; Zumeta-Edmonds et al., 2019). To ensure teams can function well, we describe effective team functioning next, as well as the use of a team audit to ensure schools have the right teaming structures.

### Effective Teaming Practices

In order to achieve its goals efficiently, each team should use effective teaming practices. These include, at a minimum, four practices: (1) clear roles, (2) accountable norms, (3) a standardized agenda format, and (4) clear communication (Schildkamp et al., 2019). If you have ever been on a team that does not have clear roles and responsibilities, you understand why they are essential. It's like being on a sports team without knowing who is playing point guard or quarterback. Having clear roles and responsibilities ensures that team members know what they are supposed to do and who to turn to when questions arise. Some of the most common roles on a team are the facilitator (who runs the meeting and ensures the agenda is followed), note taker (who documents the broad discussions and decisions made during the meeting), and the active participant (everyone who is a member of the team). It's important to note that this last role specifically defines how team members engage during meetings. They are not passive observers—their responsibility is to speak up and share their thoughts and perspectives to make sure all voices at the table are heard.

The second effective teaming practice is to have *accountable norms*. By this, we mean that the norms are not just the result of an activity during one of the first meetings; rather, team members agree to abide by the norms and to be held accountable if they fall short of living up to them. When teams have accountable norms, it creates a safer environment for members to share their perspectives, ask questions, and develop stronger interpersonal connections.

One of the easiest ways for school-level teams to create norms is by using the three to five schoolwide expectations already in place at their site. For example, what does it look like to be respectful, responsible, and safe during the team meeting? Another option is to take time during the first meeting to jointly develop the team norms through an activity. For example, you could have team members think of the best team they have been on. This could be a sports team, educational team, or any other type of team. Then, each member writes down the characteristics that made that team successful. Next, have members think of the *worst* team they have ever been on and write down the characteristics that made it the worst. As a larger team, members can then go through translating the characteristics they brainstormed into norms.

Having a standardized agenda format leads to more efficient meetings. Agendas serve the purpose of getting everyone on the same page regarding what topics they will discuss and for how long, as well as what decisions they need to make during the meeting. Additionally, agendas provide the space for meeting minutes so that documentation of the results of the meeting is available to all members. Figure 1.6 offers an example of a standardized agenda.

The final effective teaming practice is clear communication. Internally, this means team members have identified communication channels for team members to easily access the meeting agenda and minutes. One of the simplest ways to do this is by storing digital agendas on the cloud (for example, Google Drive). When this is the case, team members can find out the decisions that were made even if they were not able to attend the meeting. Externally, clear communication structures enable the team to inform families, students, and other staff about decisions. Using two-way communication channels also allows those outside of the team to provide feedback that the team can then use as data to improve their work (Center on MTSS, 2022a; McIntosh & Goodman, 2016).

### Team Audit

Often, schools may have too many overlapping teams within their building conducting parallel work. For example, a school may have a bullying prevention team

| Members present: Jon, Jason, Adam | | Date: 9/8 | | |
|---|---|---|---|---|
| **Agenda Item** | **Notes** | **Action Step** | **Person Responsible** | |
| 1. Screening select | We selected a screening tool from the two options discussed. Staff will need training, which we'll discuss next time. | n/a | | |
| 2. Communication with parents | We discussed a process to share screening results with parents. We will email parents one week prior to screening, and then will email results of screening. | Draft emails to send out | Adam | |
| 3. | | | | |
| 4. | | | | |
| **Did we follow the norm?** | | **Average team rating** | | |
| Professional (arrive on time, complete action steps) | | 1   2   3   4   5 | | |
| Stay engaged (attentive, respect toward self and others) | | 1   2   3   4   5 | | |

**Figure 1.6: Example team agenda.**

*Visit **MarzanoResources/reproducibles** for a free reproducible version of this figure.*

## Creating Norms

To create norms, use this simple activity or one similar to it.

1. Meet together as a team.

2. On a single piece of paper (or sticky note), have each team member individually write down one trait of a high-functioning or high-quality team. Examples include *staying engaged, arriving on time, reading the minutes before each meeting,* and *letting others finish before speaking.*

3. Each person can write three to five traits, using one sticky note per trait.

4. Place the notes on a whiteboard or table so everyone can read them.

5. As team, group together into categories based on commonalities or themes (for example, *be on time* and *be ready* could be grouped; *focus on the task at hand* and *give attention to each agenda item* could be grouped).

6. Identify a label for each category (for example, *be on time* and *be ready* could be labeled *professionalism; focus on the task at hand* and *give attention to each agenda item* could be labeled *engagement*).

7. Once each category is labeled, reduce them down to no more than five. These five or fewer can be your team norms. Revise and reword each category as needed.

and a behavior team that inadvertently address similar issues (Collins & Harlacher, 2023; McIntosh & Goodman, 2016). To identify the right people and teams within MTSS, one helpful activity for schools is to conduct a team audit. A team audit enables educators to ensure they have efficient and effective teams. Educators use a team audit to identify all the critical teams for MTSS within their school, and then they can analyze the gathered information to adjust the number of teams in their school. To conduct a team audit, educators can use a template modeled after the example in figure 1.7. Educators list all the teams related to MTSS or to a particular topic or grade level (for example, all the teams that handle behavior in schools or all the teams that are related to fifth-grade students). Once all the teams are listed, educators analyze the purpose, data used, and personnel involved. They look for gaps in purposes related to MTSS, as well as redundancy or overlap. From there, they can reduce, combine, or add teams to ensure they have the right teams for MTSS.

| Team<br>Team, initiative, project, group, or committee | Purpose (Outcome)<br>Why does the group meet? | Data<br>What data are used to inform decisions? | Target Group<br>All students? Some? Few? Grade level? | Staff Involved<br>Who is responsible for the team or initiative? |
|---|---|---|---|---|
| Academic team | To review and identify standards for school grades | Analysis of current curriculum and summary of standards per grade | K–3 | Leo, Eliza, Arlo, Jasper |
| Instructional team | Identify expected practices to use in core instruction | State testing and screening data by grades | K–3 | David, Johnny, Alexis, Moira |
| Student study team | Review and support students receiving Tier 3 | Progress-monitoring data for individual students | K–5 | Janine, Gregory, Ava, Melissa, Barbara |

**Figure 1.7: Example team audit.**

*Visit **MarzanoResearch.com/reproducibles** for a free reproducible version of this figure.*

Within the preceding example, the first two teams listed (academic team, instructional team) have similar purpose in that they're reviewing and examining instructional practices and curricula. They are involved with improving overall instruction in the schools, so these teams could be combined to continue to analyze core instruction, as well as to take on the role of leading MTSS implementation (that is, the leadership team role). The student study team can continue to function as is, as it aligns with the Tier 3 team listed in figure 1.5 (page 30).

### Data-Based Decision Making

Driving the MTSS framework is the effective use of data to make decisions. In fact, a key purpose of MTSS is to create an information-rich school that uses data on a regular basis to make decisions (Collins & Harlacher, 2023; McIntosh & Goodman, 2016). Consequently, the last component is *data-based decision making*, which we describe as the use of data to make decisions that ultimately benefit student achievement and well-being (Harlacher et al., 2015; McIntosh & Goodman, 2016). It's a systematic process that schools can apply to individual students, groups of students, or systemic and schoolwide issues (Collins & Harlacher, 2023; Harlacher et al., 2015). Arguably, data-based decision making is the engine of MTSS, as it creates an iterative loop between the supports within the tiers and the analysis of data to evaluate the effectiveness of the tiers. We discuss data-based decision making in depth in chapter 2 (page 41), but it is the cumulative component of MTSS that ties the other components together and can be used to inform implementation. Further, as we've referenced earlier and in the introduction (page 1), data-based decision making is easier when done within a team. Consequently, although we devote a whole chapter to data-based decision making and how it can be structured, we discuss how teams can use data-based decision making at each tier in the later chapters of the book.

## Implementing MTSS

If you have ever been on a team attempting to install the MTSS framework in a school or district, you know how difficult it can be. Effective implementation of MTSS requires supportive systems and structures for schools and educators. As its name implies, multiple systems must be organized into one cohesive approach to improve student outcomes. Given the fact that a poorly implemented MTSS framework means poor data-based decision making, the rest of this chapter focuses on how to effectively implement MTSS in schools. That is, a school may design strong tiers of support, select the best assessment tools, and set clear meeting times for their teams, but they'll need supportive systems and infrastructure to effectively engage in the *work* of MTSS (Barnes & Harlacher, 2008; McIntosh & Goodman, 2016; Sugai & Horner, 2006). Infrastructure broadly includes four parts.

1. Professional development, including training and coaching

2. Two-way communication

3. A process for the selection of practices

4. Supportive logistics, such as scheduling, sufficient time to review data, and equitable allocation of resources

### Professional Development

For staff to engage in MTSS and data-based decision making, they will likely need professional development. If the staff are expected to use certain assessment tools, instructional practices, and curriculum, they will need both training and coaching to do so (Joyce & Showers, 2002). The training, however, is not just limited to using practices or tools but should also include building staff's understanding of and capacity in content areas (for example, science of reading, functions of behavior, or cognitive load theory).

In addition, we suggest that sites not only identify the initial and ongoing training needed for staff to implement a given practice but also provide ongoing or job-embedded coaching. Staff can be trained, but educators will be more likely to implement MTSS over time if they have follow-up support and coaching (Freeman, Sugai, Simonsen, & Everett, 2017). Schools may need to be creative with identifying the coaching support for sites, such as accessing district coaches, modifying job descriptions to include coaching, partnering with local universities, or adjusting staff teaching assignments or duties to have time for coaching. Schools should also plan to train new staff each year and temporary staff when they are at their school.

### Two-Way Communication

Communication is a critical piece because teams need to disseminate and share the decisions they make with other staff and with families. Schools should have a clear communication plan or method to disseminate information, such as regular emails, social media postings, newsletters or notes home, or weekly announcements (Center on MTSS, 2022a). Further, schools need to have a feedback loop to ensure that staff, families, and the community can provide feedback to the leadership team on MTSS. Examples include offering brief surveys on a monthly or quarterly basis, having a general email account for people to contact the team or school, and holding focus groups to gather input (Feuerborn, Wallace, & Tyre, 2013; Swain-Bradway, Pinkey, & Flannery, 2015).

### Process for Selecting Practices

Part of MTSS is making decisions about what instructional strategies, interventions, and assessment tools to use (McIntosh & Goodman, 2016). To that end, leadership teams will need to identify and agree on a process for choosing which practices to implement, as well as which practices to stop implementing. A selection process is important because having an evidence-based practice is just one factor to consider when implementing MTSS. Educators should ensure they use practices that are not only evidence based but also contextually relevant and culturally appropriate for their students; using a structured selection process can ensure this.

We suggest using either the FAIR Test from the National Center on Systemic Improvement (McGuire, Peterson, & Kuchle, 2021) or the Hexagon Tool from the National Implementation Research Network (Metz & Louison, 2018) for a selection process. When using a selection process, teams can access the tool and rate the practice using the tool's questions or factors. For example, in figure 1.8, when using the FAIR Test, teams can answer each question related to a given practice. After discussion, the team can then decide if they should use or discontinue that practice.

| Question |
| --- |
| What practice (intervention, assessment tool, strategy) are we discussing? |
| **For that practice, ask:** |
| Is it feasible?<br>• Are there sufficient training, coaching, time in the schedule, and resources to implement the practice with fidelity? |
| Is it acceptable?<br>• Does the practice align with the values and priorities of the school and students? |
| Is it impactful?<br>• Are there strong evidence and empirical support for use of the practice? |
| Is it relevant?<br>• Does the practice meet the needs of our staff, students, and families? |

**Figure 1.8: Questions to ask when using the FAIR Test.**

### Supportive Logistics

We use *supportive logistics* to refer to the nuances and day-to-day structures that can support staff and schools with MTSS. For example, leadership teams may need to modify schedules to allocate enough time not only for interventions but also for teams to meet and examine data. Administration may need to adjust resources, such as allocating funding toward professional development or adjusting people's roles to allow them to provide coaching (Center on MTSS, 2022b). In table 1.6 (page 38), we offer a list of supportive logistics for MTSS.

## Stages of Implementation

The final area of MTSS implementation to consider is the stages of implementation, which we summarize in figure 1.9 (page 39). As described by Dean Fixsen, Sandra Naoom, Karen Blase, Robert Friedman, and Frances Wallace (2005), implementation is a process, not an event. In general, this process is divided into four stages.

The first stage is *exploration*. During this stage, school leaders form a team, or assign an existing team, to gather data to determine the extent of the need they have identified. For example, if a school believes that there are concerns with student behavior, school leaders may form a team and begin to examine the number of office discipline referrals, suspensions, and attendance. This team goes through the beginning of the problem-solving process and works together to select a practice that addresses the concern. Often, that work falls to the leadership team discussed in figure 1.5 (page 30), but there is flexibility with the actual people completing this task (for example, a subcommittee of the leadership team may gather data and

**Table 1.6: Supportive Logistics for MTSS**

| Logistic | Description |
|---|---|
| Schedules | The master schedule has sufficient time for each tier, including time for staff to meet in teams, to analyze data, and to administer assessment tools. |
| Funding | There are available monetary resources for materials, stipends, substitute coverage, and other needs for MTSS. |
| Communication Pathways | There are two-way communication structures and means of disseminating information. Leadership is able to share information with staff, students, and families, but it also has avenues to receive feedback. |
| Instructional Materials | The assessment and instructional materials used are evidence based and are culturally and contextually appropriate for the needs of the students. |
| Roles | Staff are available and assigned specific roles to support implementation of MTSS, such as team member, interventionist, or internal coach. |
| Alignment | The staff understand why MTSS is being implemented and how it supports and aligns with key priorities and initiatives of the school. |
| Buy-In and Understanding | Leadership actively builds buy-in and understanding among staff by frequently meeting with staff, orienting new staff, and regularly gathering feedback. The staff support implementation and understand the spirit of MTSS (that is, it's how business is done in their school and they support all students). |

the needed information, or non-members of the leadership team may be asked to assist with the task).

The second stage of implementation is *installation*. School leaders purchase or adopt the selected practice. It's during this stage that much of the professional development for staff takes place for the chosen practice. Leaders create or align data systems to support the use of data-based decision making once they implement the practice. The third stage is known as *initial implementation*. During this stage, staff members begin the actual implementation of the practice they have selected and trained for in previous stages. There will be inevitable barriers and concerns that arise during this stage, which is where data-based decision making comes in to support continuous improvement. In the final stage, *full implementation*, staff describe the practice as "how we do business" in the school. Sustaining and ensuring that the expected outcomes of the practice are in place becomes the ongoing goal.

| Stage | Description | Example Activities |
|---|---|---|
| Exploration | A site determines a need for change and identifies MTSS and certain practices to implement. | A team reviews data and finds low student reading outcomes and over-identification of students in interventions. The team determines a need to improve its instructional practices, so it selects a literacy curriculum to implement at Tier 1. |
| Installation | A site gathers resources and provides training to staff to implement MTSS and its practices. | A team provides training to its staff on using the Tier 1 curriculum. It also secures data sources and processes for examining effectiveness of the curriculum. |
| Initial Implementation | The site implements practices for MTSS; specifically, it introduces the practice, which is used with students for the first time. The focus is on fidelity of implementation. | The curriculum is initially used with students. A team gathers data on fidelity of implementation, along with student outcome data. The team examines fidelity and outcome data and uses the results to continuously improve implementation. |
| Full Implementation | The site uses the practice with fidelity throughout the school. The focus is on ensuring it achieves its desired outcomes. | Staff members understand how to deliver the curriculum and the adjustments they can make to ensure it is effective for individual students. They analyze data consistently to ensure effective implementation and outcomes. |

**Figure 1.9: Stages of implementations.**

## Summary

By now, one can see how MTSS provides the infrastructure and systems to support data-based decision making. We have described data-based decision making as the engine that drives and connects all the components of MTSS together. As you'll see in the subsequent chapters, educators gather data as part of the day-to-day functioning of a school (that is, the comprehensive data system component). As teams analyze the data and work through problem solving, they will identify a plan, which entails adjustments or modifications to instruction and interventions (that is, the continuum of supports component). All these decisions and implementation of plans are made easier and more feasible with the assistance of a team (that is, the teaming structures component). As schools ensure the right teaming structures are in place, build their continuum of supports, and gather sufficient data with their comprehensive assessment system, all those components are tied together with data-based decision making, therein making it possible for schools to create an iterative, responsive MTSS. With figure 1.10, we offer a summary of the components of MTSS.

In the next chapter, we'll go into much greater depth on what data-based decision making is and how it works with all four steps of the problem-solving model.

| Component | Description |
|---|---|
| Continuum of Supports | |
| *Tier 1* | • Educators provide universal supports to all students, including differentiated instruction and a research-based curriculum. <br> • There are common agreements for time, instructional materials, and instructional strategies. |
| *Tier 2* | • Educators provide standardized interventions to groups of students, though they do not always do so in a group setting. <br> • Tier 2 includes more explicit instruction and more practice with skills relative to Tier 1, as well as a school-home connection. |
| *Tier 3* | • Educators provide intensive, individualized supports that address skill gaps and remediation. <br> • Tier 3 includes the most explicit instruction with the most practice with and feedback on skills. <br> • Tier 3 offers connections to community supports and explicitly engages families. |
| Comprehensive Assessment System | • Educators coordinate and use assessments to gather the critical data needed for decision making. <br> • Educators gather screening, diagnostic, progress-monitoring, and fidelity data. |
| Teaming Structures | • Designated teams ensure effective implementation of MTSS and monitor achievement of desired goals. <br> • A leadership team designs what MTSS looks like, develops and trains staff on MTSS, and evaluates the effectiveness of MTSS overall. <br> • Grade-level teams evaluate core instruction and, in conjunction with additional teams, regularly review student data to identify and monitor those who need additional support. |
| Data-Based Decision Making | • Educators use data to make decisions related to high-valued outcomes. <br> • Educators use the four-step problem-solving model to make decisions about supports. <br> • Educators make decisions about the effectiveness of the system (for example, Are at least 80 percent of students meeting grade-level standards?). <br> • Educators also make decisions about individual students (for example, Is this student benefiting from the current instructional plan?). |

**Figure 1.10: Summary of the components of MTSS.**

# CHAPTER 2

# Defining Data-Based Decision Making

As we discuss in the introduction (page 1), the use of data is key for ensuring one's misperceptions and biases don't override accurate decision making. By using reliable and valid data, educators can make sure their decisions regarding students are the most beneficial for the student. To make effective data-based decisions, particularly within an MTSS framework, we advocate for the use of the four-step problem-solving model. The problem-solving model is a *heuristic*, or practical method, that educators can use to identify and solve problems by gathering and analyzing both fidelity and outcome data (Deno, 2016). In this chapter, we expand on the four steps of the model, which are (1) *problem identification*, (2) *problem analysis*, (3) *plan identification and implementation*, and (4) *plan evaluation*. A simpler way to think about these four steps is (1) identify, (2) analyze, (3) implement, and (4) evaluate. We offer a brief summary of the problem-solving model in figure 2.1 (page 42).

For this book, we have chosen to use this four-step model for data-based decision making for a few reasons. First, the problem-solving model simplifies the data-based decision-making process by outlining four steps with a clear purpose and question asked during each step. Second, the problem-solving model creates efficiency within a school system. In education, it's not uncommon for educators to feel stressed or pressured to urgently address every issue that arises (Bottani, Duran, Pas, & Bradshaw, 2019; Stoiber, 2014). As working school psychologists, we experienced frantic calls and emails asking us when we would be at the school next. We would shift our schedule and arrive at the school as soon as possible, only to be told, "Oh, that's not critical anymore." What was urgent would quickly evaporate, resulting in undue stress and a waste of resources. To avoid jumping from one

| Step | Action | Description | Key Question |
|------|--------|-------------|--------------|
| 1 | Problem Identification | The use of data, typically screening or indicator data, to identify and verify that a problem exists | Is there a problem? (What is the problem?) |
| 2 | Problem Analysis | The use of diagnostic data to analyze the instruction, curriculum, environment, and learner to identify hypotheses as to why a problem exists | Why is it occurring? |
| 3 | Plan Identification and Implementation | The selection and implementation of a plan to solve the problem based on the hypothesis generated during problem analysis | What can we do about it? |
| 4 | Plan Evaluation | The analysis of fidelity and outcome data to evaluate the extent that the plan is working | Did the plan work? |

**Figure 2.1: The steps of the problem-solving model.**

issue to the next or focusing our attention on one thing only to find it less critical relative to other issues, the problem-solving model is built on prioritizing concerns within the first step. Part of step 1 is determining whether a problem exists and whether it's large enough to prioritize, as opposed to selecting a problem out of urgency or because it *feels* important to solve. The model quantifies issues in education and allows educators to select those that are objectively worth time and energy to solve (Pluymert, 2014).

A third reason for choosing the problem-solving model is that it's applicable at all levels within MTSS: the individual student level, the group level, and the school-wide level (Harlacher et al., 2015; McIntosh & Goodman, 2016). Within MTSS, teams analyze data and ask questions related to the overall health of the school (Do we have at least 80 percent of our students meeting standards?), as well as group-level questions (Is Tier 2 effective overall?) and the individual level (Is this student at risk? Is this student achieving sufficient growth?). As such, educators can apply the four steps of the model across all levels and tiers within MTSS, making the problem-solving model an adaptable and flexible method (Gimpel Peacock, Ervin, Daly, & Merrell, 2010; Harlacher et al., 2015). Because of the problem-solving model's versatility, educators can learn one method for using data and then apply it to all levels within a school.

Finally, we have built data-based decision making within this book around the problem-solving model because it is an evidence-based model with a long record of efficacy. The problem-solving model grew out of Stan Deno's (1985, 2003, 2016) pioneering work as he searched for an effective method to identify and monitor valid goals for students with disabilities. Deno (1985, 2003, 2016) developed curriculum-based measurement because many of the assessments used to evaluate progress for students receiving special education were inadequate. They often measured intra-individual characteristics (for example, aptitude or personality traits) that were removed from the curriculum or unrelated to learning, didn't accurately assess the skills students were being taught, and weren't amenable to timely decisions (Deno, 2016; Merrell, Ervin, Gimpel Peacock, & Renshaw, 2022). The use of curriculum-based measurement provided a method for schools to regularly assess and monitor student growth, drew a stronger connection between instruction and assessment (Merrell et al., 2022; Ysseldyke & Christenson, 1988), and contributed to data-based decision making in education (Filderman, Toste, Didion, Peng, & Clemens, 2018; Fuchs, Fuchs, Hamlett, & Stecker, 2021; Hamilton et al., 2009; McIntosh & Goodman, 2016; Stecker, Fuchs, & Fuchs, 2005).

Since Deno's (1985, 2003, 2016) work, researchers have added to the literature on the problem-solving model, illustrating the use of data and instructional decision making as effective processes at the elementary school level (Donegan, Wanzek, & Al Otaiba, 2020; Vaughn et al., 2003), middle school level (Filderman et al., 2018; Parker, Van Norman, & Nelson, 2018; Vaughn et al., 2011), high school level (Filderman et al., 2018; Shih Dennis & Gratton-Fisher, 2020), and for students with disabilities or intensive needs (Jung, McMaster, Kunkel, Shin, & Stecker, 2018). Further, the problem-solving model and the use of a structured problem-solving process are evident in other iterations of data-based decision making, such as the plan-do-study-act cycle (Langley, Nolan, Norman, & Provost, 2009; Shakman, Wogan, Rodriguez, Boyce, & Shaver, 2020), team-initiated problem solving (Chaparro et al., 2022), and professional learning communities (DuFour, DuFour, Eaker, Many, & Mattos, 2016). These processes have the tenets of the problem-solving model within them (for example, defining a problem, developing a plan, monitoring that plan, and adjusting the plan based on the data) and have documented their use of improved systemic or student outcomes (Doğan & Adams, 2018; Newton, Horner, Algozzine, Todd, & Algozzine, 2012; Tichnor-Wagner, Wachen, Cannata, & Cohen-Vogel, 2017). At the schoolwide or systemic level, seminal articles from Roland H. Good, Jerry Gruba, and Ruth A. Kaminski (2002) and Mark R. Shinn (2008) illustrated how curriculum-based measurement and the problem-solving model are used to evaluate the overall health of a school. Since then, numerous books and case studies have illustrated the use of a structured problem-solving approach to benefit students, entire schools, and districts (Glover & Vaughn, 2010; Greenwood et al., 2008; Jimerson et al., 2016; Sailor et al., 2009). The use of the problem-solving model and data to inform instruction has been utilized at the individual and systemic level since the mid-1980s in education and has resulted in positive gains for staff and students (Burns et al., 2005; Jimerson et al., 2016; Sailor et al., 2009).

We must also note that regardless of your plan or supports, the power of the problem-solving model is the monitoring and adjusting it brings. There is no perfect plan, curriculum, framework, or instructional strategy that will meet the needs of all learners at all times. Even the most effective instructional systems tend to drift over time and become less effective. People who have created exercise or diet plans may notice the same pattern. This lack of sustainability can happen for a variety of reasons. Sometimes one gets tired of following the plan, as it requires a high level of continued discipline and effort. Sometimes competing life obligations (for example, family, work, or an active social life) make it hard to devote one's continued time and energy to the plan. Sometimes one reaches the initial goals and pulls back their efforts, leading to a drop off in sustainability. People are simply more likely to spend more time on initial planning and less time on checking in periodically to see how the plan is going. Ultimately, many of the factors that make diet and exercise plans successful are the same factors that will make school-improvement plans effective. In addition to solid initial planning, schools need a system of ongoing check-ins to examine their plans and tweak them when needed. That's the ultimate power of the problem-solving model.

## Steps of the Problem-Solving Model

As we indicated, the model includes four steps, each of which corresponds to a key question. Educators ask the key question for that step and then analyze data to answer it. Four steps, four key questions (see figure 2.2): rather than wading through numerous questions or mounds of data, the problem-solving model allows educators to anchor a key question to each step.

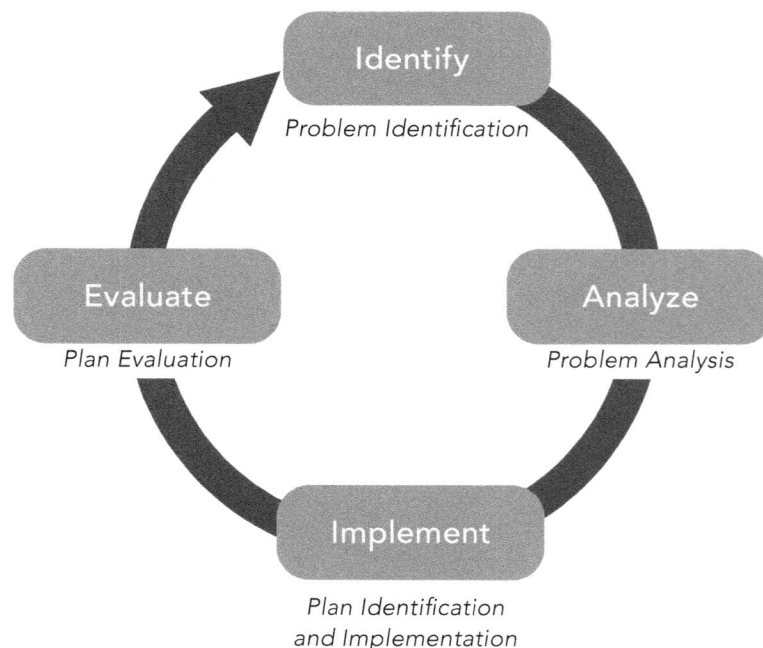

**Figure 2.2: Illustration of the problem-solving model.**

### *Problem Identification*

When you go to the doctor's office for a visit or annual exam, a doctor or nurse usually records your height, weight, and blood pressure and perhaps asks you a few questions about how you're feeling. The medical provider is gathering data on general indicators of your health to determine whether there are any signs of a problem. Accordingly, the medical provider compares the observed performance (such as your temperature) to the expected or desired performance (in this case, 98.6 degrees Fahrenheit). If your temperature is too high or too low, they may take your temperature again to ensure it wasn't a fluke, but having a large gap between the observed and expected performance signifies that there is a problem worth investigating. This is the focus of problem identification: quantifying the problem with a gap analysis and determining whether it warrants exploring further (Harlacher et al., 2013, 2015; Pluymert, 2014). The formula for a problem would be as follows:

**Observed Performance – Expected Performance = Problem?**

#### Gap Analysis

Educators begin problem identification with a question to determine whether a problem exists. The questions can focus on an individual student (for example, *Is this student at risk for poor mathematics outcomes?*), groups of students (for example, *Which students in grade 8 are at risk for school dropout?*), or a system within a school (for example, *Is core instruction working for the majority of students?*). In asking a question, educators compare the observed performance to an expected performance. They then quantify the magnitude of the gap to determine whether the gap indicates there's a problem and whether it's large enough to spend time solving. This is commonly referred to as a *gap analysis* (Harlacher et al., 2013).

For example, an expectation for a student in the third grade may be to read ninety words per minute accurately. A student who reads eighty-eight words per minute is only two away from the expectation, so this may not be considered a problem. On the other hand, a student who is reading fifty-five words per minute would have a gap of thirty-five words per minute, and this would be a clear problem worth solving. By quantifying problems in step 1, educators eliminate ambiguity around issues of concern. In this example, instead of describing the problem as "the student has issues in reading," the problem is defined as "the student is reading fifty-five words per minute and the student should be reading at least ninety words per minute." This provides clarity on the problem. By conducting problem identification, educators can assess and quantify a student's performance or other indicators of concern in schools, which allows them to determine both the existence and severity of a given problem (Deno, 2013; Harlacher et al., 2015; Pluymert, 2014). In figure 2.3 (page 46), we offer some educational examples of gap analyses to define problems.

Screening assessments are a critical part of step 1, as they offer efficient means to gather information with large groups of students. Screening assessments measure broad outcomes or general indicators for a given content area, thus allowing

| Variable | Observed Performance | Expected Performance | Gap | Decision |
|---|---|---|---|---|
| Writing | 37 correct writing sequences | 46 correct writing sequences | –9 correct writing sequences | Problem (conduct risk verification) |
| Attendance Rate | 88 percent of school days attended | 92 percent of school days attended | –4 percent days attended | Not a problem |
| Student Risk Screening Scale: Externalizing | 8 (raw score, classified in moderate risk) | 0–3 raw score (low risk) | +5 raw score | Problem (conduct risk verification) |
| Reading | 105 words read correct | 90 words read correct | +15 words read correct | Not a problem |

**Figure 2.3: Example gap analyses.**

educators to determine whether students are at risk for poor learning outcomes (Albers & Kettler, 2014; McIntosh & Goodman, 2016). Using screening data, educators can quantify the level of risk a student may have by comparing their performance to certain thresholds. Typically, educators can identify students as scoring within a *low-risk range* (that is, they don't need additional support beyond universal instruction), a *some-risk range* (that is, they likely need some additional support that lasts ten to twenty weeks), or within a *severe-risk range* (that is, they need longer-term support that is very individualized and intensive; McIntosh & Goodman, 2016). With universal screening data, however, educators can do more than identify which students need additional support. As mentioned in chapter 1 (page 15), they can also determine the overall health of their school, as educators can aggregate the percentage of students at risk and evaluate whether at least 80 percent of their students are benefiting from core instruction compared to those who likely need additional support (Harlacher et al., 2015; McIntosh & Goodman, 2016). Thus, screening data are beneficial for both evaluating core instruction and for identifying which students need additional support.

In table 2.1, we illustrate common assessments used in step 1 of the problem-solving model and their corresponding risk thresholds. Although the actual language to indicate a certain level of risk may vary among screening tools, educators will need a list of data sources and corresponding thresholds to conduct problem identification (that is, step 2 of the model). Table 2.1 categorizes thresholds across low-risk, some-risk, and severe-risk categories. The publishers of a given screening tool typically define these thresholds; for example, Acadience Learning (2021) validates risk status through its statistical research. Some standards are guided by national percentiles and guidelines, such as office discipline referrals (Harlacher & Rodriguez, 2018; PBISApps, n.d.).

**Table 2.1: Example Screening Assessments and Example Thresholds**

| Measure | At Criterion | At Risk | |
| --- | --- | --- | --- |
| | Low Risk | Some Risk | Severe Risk |
| Acadience (DIBELS Next) | At Benchmark, Above Benchmark | Below Benchmark | Well Below Benchmark |
| FastBridge | On Track | Some Risk | High Risk |
| Student Risk Screening Scale | Low Risk | Moderate Risk | High Risk |
| Strengths and Difficulties Questionnaire | ≤ 11 | 12–15 | 16+ |
| Office Discipline Referrals (Major) | 0–1 | 2–5 | 6 or more |
| Absences | 5 per semester | 6–9 per semester | 10+ per semester |
| Tardies | 3 per semester | 4–9 per semester | 10+ per semester |
| Suspensions | 0 | 1 | 2 |
| Course Grades | 2.5 GPA or higher | 2.0 GPA or lower | 1 or more Ds or Fs |

Note: The language for low risk, some risk, and at risk within each cell is based on each screening tool's risk classification (for example, Acadience Learning uses *below benchmark*, whereas FastBridge uses *some risk* to indicate a similar level of risk status). When numbers are shared, these are based on national norms or evidence-based guidelines.

Educators can also develop thresholds by using local research and analysis of local norms, which may be useful for attendance thresholds or course grades (Marken et al., 2020). We encourage teams to use the predetermined thresholds that accompany screening tools, but when such thresholds are not available, we recommend using national guidelines (for example, Hasbrouck & Tindal, 2017). Teams can also determine thresholds by conducting their own statistical analysis to find what thresholds predict poor learning outcomes for their context (Marken et al., 2020; Stewart & Silberglitt, 2008).

If a student scores within the some-risk or severe-risk range, educators then conduct risk verification to ensure the student really is at risk. Screening measures cast a large net and will likely identify some students who are not actually at risk (that is, false positives). To ensure that students who receive support are in need of that support, educators use risk verification (Bailey et al., 2020; Center on MTSS, n.d.).

### Risk Verification

To conduct risk verification, educators take the screening score and then analyze at least two additional data sources in conjunction with it (Bailey et al., 2020; Center on MTSS, n.d.; Pierce & Jackson, 2017). For example, if a student scores below benchmark on a screening assessment in mathematics, the teacher or team would then verify the risk status by examining course grades and a different mathematics assessment. If two of the three scores show the student at risk, then educators would conclude the student is in fact at risk and needs intervention. If the two additional scores are within normal limits or indicate low risk for a student, they would conclude the student is not at risk. In cases such as the latter, educators may want to keep an eye on a student who they deemed not at risk during risk verification (for example, they may administer a screening assessment again in a few weeks to monitor the student). Of note, educators can readminister the original mathematics screener with a different probe (that is, screeners often come with multiple worksheets or probes that measure the same skills to allow for re-administration or more frequent administration). Thus the three scores can be the original screener, the readministered screener, and then an additional data source.

Screeners often overidentify students, so risk verification is an important step for ensuring students who receive intervention are the ones in most need of those interventions. As figure 2.4 shows, two students can score at risk on a given intervention, but only one is actually in need of the intervention. Student A would not need intervention because two of the three total data sources show low risk. However, student B would be slotted for intervention because there are two at-risk scores on the data sources.

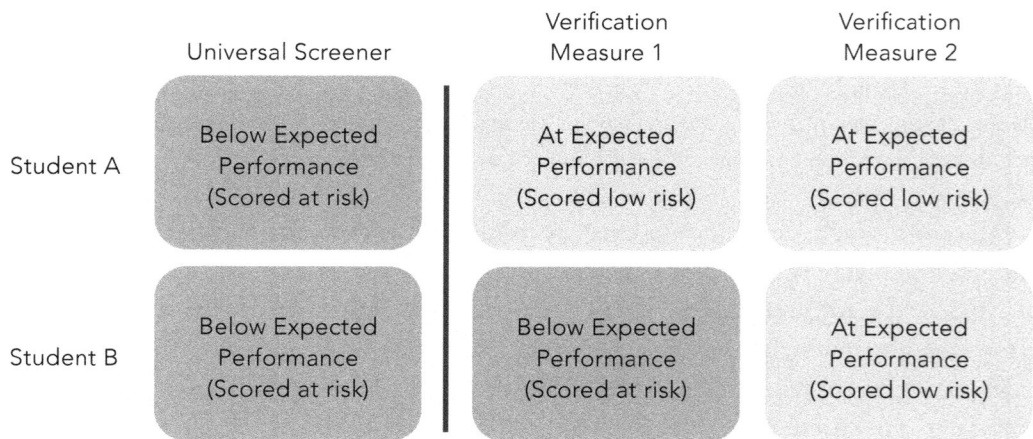

| | Universal Screener | Verification Measure 1 | Verification Measure 2 |
|---|---|---|---|
| Student A | Below Expected Performance (Scored at risk) | At Expected Performance (Scored low risk) | At Expected Performance (Scored low risk) |
| Student B | Below Expected Performance (Scored at risk) | Below Expected Performance (Scored at risk) | At Expected Performance (Scored low risk) |

**Figure 2.4: Comparing risk verification between two students.**

Following risk verification, educators have a list of students who need additional support. They can then proceed to identify why those students are at risk and what intervention they may need during step 2 of the problem-solving model. If educators were examining schoolwide issues, such as the overall health of core instruction or disparities among subgroups of students, educators would still conduct a verification process to ensure that their initial problem is actually valid. For example, if a team analyzes data regarding the number of students who are proficient on an end-of-unit reading assessment and find that only 35 percent of students scored proficient, they would still want to verify the accuracy of those data. Here, they could calculate the percentages again to make sure there wasn't a mistake or they could compare the results to similar data sources, such as a district benchmark. They could also administer a new end-of-unit assessment and analyze those scores. The overall message is to ensure your initial red flag is a legitimate issue before you proceed to step 2 of the problem-solving model. Additionally, it's important not to dismiss data that don't align with your perception. Rather, educators will want to explore or verify initial indications of a problem (remember that perceptions can be misguided at times). By the end of step 1, educators should agree that the problem exists, that it's worth solving, and to have a quantified magnitude of the problem.

### *Problem Analysis*

In step 2, problem analysis, educators analyze information to understand the context of the problem, all with the intention of forming a hypothesis as to why the problem is occurring. For example, a medical provider would gather additional information about your health and administer more extensive tests, such as gathering a blood panel, taking X-rays, asking about your diet and exercise habits, ordering diagnostic scans, or some combination of these. Analyzing the data these tests generate allows the medical provider to prescribe a treatment based on the cause of the problem. Given how expensive and time consuming such medical tests can be, it's easy to see why you would want to be sure there's a problem before investing a lot of resources. Imagine the waste of time and energy if medical providers gave every patient they saw a CAT scan and full blood panel (not to mention the toll on the patient)? Now consider an education setting where time, energy, and resources are limited. By ensuring problems are valid and worth solving in step 1, we can ensure our time and energy in step 2 are well spent.

#### Alterable Variables

As we discussed in the introduction (page 1), the focus of problem analysis is on alterable variables, or those variables that educators can influence (Christ & Arañas, 2014; Collins & Harlacher, 2023). In fact, the focus during problem analysis is not necessarily the learner. Rather, it's the *interaction* among the instruction, curriculum, and environment, and the extent to which that interaction supports the learner, as illustrated in figure 2.5 (page 50). Instead of intra-individual characteristics, data-based decision making within the problem-solving model assumes that learning is the result of the interaction among the instruction, curriculum, and environment (Harlacher et al., 2013; Howell & Schumann, 2010). Therefore, when

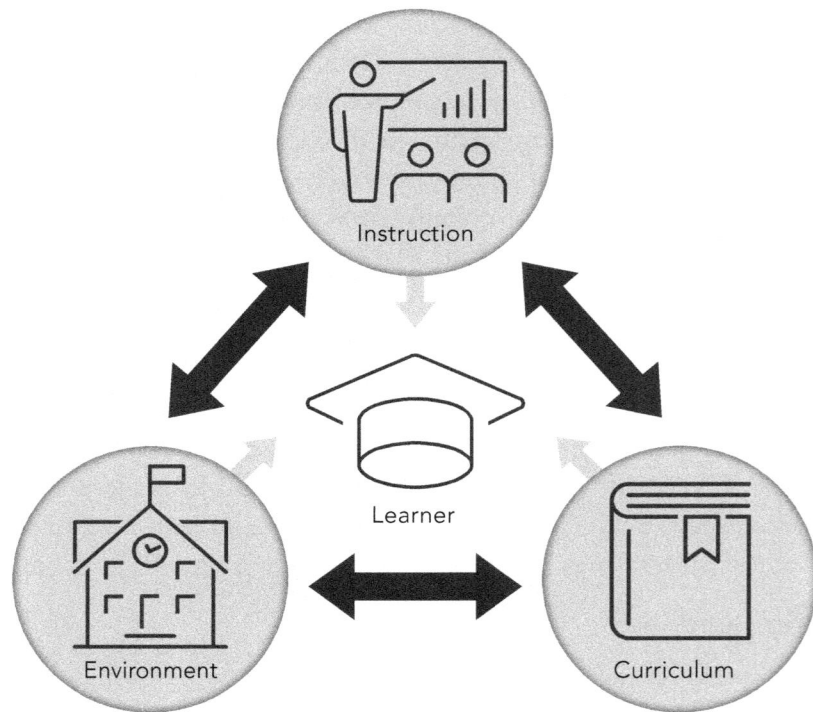

**Figure 2.5: Illustration of factors that impact learning for students.**

learning doesn't occur, it's due to a breakdown among the instruction, curriculum, and environment in relation to the learner's (or learners') needs (Harlacher et al., 2013). By focusing on alterable variables within the instruction, curriculum, and environment (such as the use of corrective feedback or the scope and sequence of the content), educators have power and volition to solve the identified problems. If educators identify variables outside of their control as causes for the problem (such as the student's learning history or lack of certain resources), then they effectively cannot solve the problem. Imagine how deflating it would be to recognize a problem and then not identify any way to solve it!

Within problem analysis, educators gather additional data, in part, by using diagnostic assessments. *Diagnostic assessments* are comprehensive assessments educators use to tease apart global skills into discrete skills, thus allowing them to pinpoint which skills students have mastered and not mastered (Christ & Arañas, 2014; McIntosh & Goodman, 2016). For example, a screening assessment in reading only tells an educator if the student is on or off track for reading competency. The educator can use diagnostic assessments, however, to pinpoint which reading skills the student has mastered, including phonemic awareness, phonics, fluency, vocabulary, and reading comprehension (Christ & Arañas, 2014; Harlacher et al., 2015). As another example, imagine that the check engine light turns on in your car. This is a big red flag that a problem exists. To diagnose why the check engine is on, you would need the help of various diagnostic tools and procedures. Perhaps you would pop the hood and connect a battery assessment or a computer scan to check that certain processors are working correctly. You may also do a *visual diagnostic scan* and look for loose cables or whether any hoses are disconnected. Educators can use diagnostic assessments to understand the context and nuances of the instruction provided to students, the curriculum used, and the environment within which the instruction occurs (Christ & Arañas, 2014).

### RIOT/ICEL

Although it's common to think diagnostic assessments are used to diagnose skill strengths and weaknesses in students, we also view them as part of assessing the learning environment and other characteristics related to student learning. For example, educators can observe instruction during a lesson to assess the overall level of explicitness used, or they can interview students or teachers to assess effective classroom management practices. To gather these data, we advocate for the use of the RIOT/ICEL framework, a method for organizing data collection (Christ & Arañas, 2014; Harlacher et al., 2013). *RIOT* is an acronym that stands for the assessment methods used: review, interview, observe, and test. *ICEL* is an acronym that stands for the assessment domains: instruction, curriculum, environment, and learner. Table 2.2 summarizes the definitions of RIOT and ICEL.

**Table 2.2: RIOT and ICEL Defined**

| Area | Definition, Description |
|---|---|
| **RIOT** | |
| Review | Review of records, products, and previously collected data |
| Interview | Interviews with those close to the problem, such as teachers, parents, or students |
| Observe | Observation (direct and informal) to measure variables |
| Test | Tests or assessments to gather more information |
| **ICEL** | |
| Instruction | How the students are taught, including level of explicitness, opportunities to respond, dosage, and use of evidence-based practices |
| Curriculum | What is being taught or the focus of the instruction, such as scope and sequence, materials used, pacing, and amount of review |
| Environment | Where the instruction and learning take place, including classroom expectations, amount of structure and routines, use of reinforcement, seating arrangement, and so on |
| Learner | Who the recipient of the learning or instruction is, including their previous learning history, study habits, mastery of skills, and impairments |

RIOT is organized from the least invasive and time-consuming methods to more invasive and time-consuming ones (for example, the review of records may involve a few minutes of looking at the student's attendance and behavior referrals, whereas administering an assessment would take more time and energy). ICEL is intentionally organized to begin with instruction, curriculum, and environment before the learner because educators have the most control over those areas. This isn't to say the learner is not important, but one must understand how the learner's needs inform the characteristics for instruction, curriculum, and environment to support the learner. Additionally, placing the learner at the end helps educators avoid falling into the trap of solely blaming the learner for the problem.

Together, the use of RIOT and ICEL forms a matrix that indicates variables that educators can assess. Consequently, educators can use the RIOT/ICEL matrix to guide their data collection and generate hypotheses (Christ & Arañas, 2014; Harlacher et al., 2013; Hosp, 2008). In figure 2.6, we offer a RIOT/ICEL matrix that has common variables to measure, including hypotheses that educators can formulate related to each assessment domain (for example, within instruction, they can generally ask if the instruction is evidence based, explicit, and intense enough for a given student, group of students, or across the school).

Rather than assessing every possible area related to student learning, educators can use the matrix to guide their hypotheses about why the problem exists. To use the RIOT/ICEL matrix, educators identify an initial hypothesis and then gather information to either confirm or disconfirm that hypothesis. The results of that analysis will then lead them to other cells of the matrix. For example, a team may have an initial hypothesis that the instruction is not explicit enough for the student. Team members can then observe the instruction and review lesson plans to determine the amount of explicit instruction the student is receiving. During the observation, team members may learn that although the instruction is explicit, they wonder if there's a mismatch between the skill being taught and the student's skills (that is, does the student have the background knowledge or necessary skills to engage with the curriculum?). They would then proceed to compare the student's skill mastery to the current curriculum (thus moving to the Review Curriculum cell). As such, the team will "bounce" around the cells of the matrix until it has found an accurate hypothesis. Educators should start with the most likely hypothesis for the problem, given the information gathered thus far on the student or students. If there is no agreed-on place for educators to start, we recommend starting with examining instruction. Instruction is perhaps the most direct domain that an educator has control over and one that can highly influence students' performance. Once educators have a reasonable hypothesis and data to confirm it or highly suggest it's the most likely hypothesis, they can proceed to step 3 and craft a potential solution for the problem.

| | Instruction | Curriculum | Environment | Learner |
|---|---|---|---|---|
| **General Hypothesis** | *Is the instruction evidence based, explicit, and intense enough?* | *Does the curriculum match the needs of the students?* | *Does the environment support learning in a positive, proactive way?* | *Do the instruction, curriculum, and environment consider the learners' characteristics?* |
| **Review** | ▪ Permanent products or lesson plans for previous strategies and interventions used; instructional demands; differentiation provided; types of responses by students<br>▪ Previous instruction for practices or interventions used | ▪ Lesson plans for skills taught in relation to students' mastery of skills; scope and sequence of skills; learning objectives relative to student skills; massed versus distributed practice; juxtaposition of examples used for concepts | ▪ Lesson plans for extent to which behavioral expectations were taught<br>▪ Seating charts or arrangement for access to materials, board, sound in room | ▪ Products or gradebook for comparing students' scores to classroom average or others in group<br>▪ Records for health history; attendance; office discipline referrals; previous test results and patterns<br>▪ Previous instruction for response and change in skills |
| **Interview** | ▪ Teacher for intended versus actual use of strategies; perceptions of use of strategies<br>▪ Peers for perception of tasks and instruction | ▪ Teacher for adherence to curriculum, pacing, lessons, and so on; alignment of core with interventions and of needs of students | ▪ Teacher for teaching of expectations and routines; use of classroom management strategies<br>▪ Students for perception of climate, structure, and routines | ▪ Perception of needs and skills; perceptions between classes or core versus interventions<br>▪ Family report of social-emotional and behavior history |
| **Observe** | ▪ Lessons for adherence and use of evidence-based practices<br>▪ Task demands; completion of tasks by students; opportunities to respond and accuracy of responses; focus of instruction compared to students' mastery of skill along instructional hierarchy | ▪ Fidelity to content and lesson plans<br>▪ Alignment of objectives, use of curriculum, content covered between classrooms, settings, and so on; clarity of learning objectives | ▪ Physical environment<br>▪ Interactions among students and among student and staff and the teacher<br>▪ Feedback (error correction and praise) provided | ▪ Behavior patterns (antecedents, behaviors, responses)<br>▪ Student engagement with content |
| **Test** | ▪ Administer fidelity checklists or measures of instructional practices<br>▪ Manipulate instructional practices or demands and measure effect on students' responses | ▪ Determine readability of texts, assignments, and so on in relation to student reading level<br>▪ Manipulate difficulty of material or manner in which it's presented to measure effect on students' responses | ▪ Administer classroom environment scales<br>▪ Compare students' performance between settings or classrooms | ▪ Direct assessment to determine students' mastery of skills along instructional hierarchy<br>▪ Administer and examine diagnostic data for students<br>▪ Conduct error analysis to determine error patterns<br>▪ Direct behavior rating to quantify behaviors of concern |

Note: To read this table, look at the assessment method on the far left (review, interview, observe, test) and read each cell with that assessment method as the sentence starter (for example, look at the Review and Instruction cell to read as, "Review permanent products or lesson plans for previous strategies and interventions used").

*Source: © 1998 by Heartland Area Education Agency 11. Adapted with permission. All rights reserved.*

**Figure 2.6: RIOT/ICEL matrix and examples of ways to assess variables.**

*Visit **MarzanoResearch.com/reproducibles** for a free reproducible version of this figure.*

Although we think of RIOT and ICEL as largely helpful for individual problem solving (Christ & Arañas, 2014), it can be used for systems and groups of students during problem analysis. In subsequent chapters, we'll discuss in depth how RIOT and ICEL are used in those situations, but in figure 2.6 (page 53), we identify variables that educators can consider for both individual students, groups of students, or the entire school system. For example, a team member may observe instruction to determine whether there is a sufficient rate of opportunities for students to respond during a lesson. This information can be recorded for an individual student (for example, Is student A getting enough opportunities to respond?), groups of students (for example, Are there sufficient opportunities to respond for all students receiving intervention A?), or instruction in general (for example, Are there sufficient opportunities to respond during core instruction?). An observer can record any level for these opportunities to respond, but the question and observation are generally the same.

### Instructional Hierarchy

As part of problem analysis and analyzing the learner, particularly for individual student problem solving, educators should assess the student's mastery of skills as they pertain to the instructional hierarchy, sometimes referred to with the acronym *IH* (Brown-Chidsey & Bickford, 2015; Burns, 2021; Burns, VanDerHeyden, & Zaslofsky, 2014; Daly & Martens, 1994; Daly, Lentz, & Boyer, 1996; Haring, Lovitt, Eaton, & Hansen, 1978). The *instructional hierarchy* is a framework for understanding how students develop a given skill and includes four stages: (1) acquisition, (2) proficiency, (3) generalization, and (4) adaptation, as shown in figure 2.7.

As students initially use skills, they perform the skill slowly and with errors. During the *acquisition* stage, educators provide students instruction that models the skill and immediate, specific feedback on the skill (ideally provided after each use of the skill). As students develop accuracy with the skill, educators enter the *proficiency* stage by shifting instruction to focus on building fluency and speed with the skill. In this stage, educators provide instruction with accurate practice, including high-rate practice and frequent response to build proficiency. They provide feedback on reaching standards for fluency. During the third stage, *generalization*, educators can shift the focus to using the skill in new settings or environments. Here, instruction centers on performing the skill in new or different settings. Generalization is not something that can naturally develop, per se; rather, educators should plan for it and provide opportunities for it (Ardoin & Daly, 2007; Burns, 2021). During the final stage, *adaptation*, educators will teach students to grasp the core concepts or essence of the skill and be able to apply it to new and novel situations. By adjusting the instruction and feedback given to students based on the instructional hierarchy, educators can assist students as they go from an inaccurate, laborious use of the skill to a proficient use of the skill in new and novel settings.

| Stage | Description | Goal | Focus of Instruction | Feedback Given |
|-------|-------------|------|----------------------|----------------|
| Acquisition | Skill is laborious and inaccurate. | Achieve accuracy of skill. | Focus on accurate use of skill with model-lead-test format. | Provide immediate feedback. Focus on accurate use of skill and close approximations of it. |
| Proficiency | Skill is accurate but slow. | Achieve accuracy and fluency with skill. | Focus on more fluent use of the skill, meeting standards for fluency. | Provide feedback for reaching standards and fluency. Feedback can be delayed or less than one on one. |
| Generalization | Skill can be performed accurately in instructional setting or performed inaccurately in noninstructional setting. | Perform skill in new settings or contexts. | Focus on performing skill in new or noninstructional settings. | Provide feedback on use in different contexts. |
| Adaptation | Skill is performed across settings, but with limited flexibility or rigid application. | Adapt skill in novel or new settings. | Focus on identifying and using the core concepts of the skill or novel use of the skill. | Provide feedback on trying applications of the skill in new ways and in novel settings. |

**Figure 2.7: The instructional hierarchy and its stages.**

*Visit **MarzanoResearch.com/reproducibles** for a free reproducible version of this figure.*

As an example, imagine when you first learned to drive. You had to mentally focus on all the details—hands on the wheel in the nine and three position, eyes on road, pressure on the brake or gas, music off, and so on. Your working memory was actively processing all the stimuli coming at you. You were probably jerky with your movements, perhaps forgetting at times to use your turn signal. You were in the acquisition stage of driving on the instructional hierarchy. Over time, you developed fluency for driving; you no longer had to actively think about the pressure of your foot on the pedal or how to depress the brake, and you used your turn signal without even thinking about it. As you felt more proficient with driving, you then freed your working memory to think about other things, such as talking to someone in the car or the directions for your destination. More so, once you developed proficiency with driving, you could then sit in a new car and begin to apply driving skills to that car, even though the setting was different. (You know that feeling when you sit in a rental car or a friend's car for the first time?) Your driving skills progressed through acquisition to proficiency to generalization (and if you applied your driving skills to a motorcycle or a boat, then to the adaptation stage). With academic skills, students follow a similar trajectory. Each step is sequential and builds on the previous, and thus mastery of each step is necessary before proceeding to the next stage of the instructional hierarchy (Burns, 2011, 2021; Parker & Burns, 2014).

As illustrated in figure 2.7 (page 55), the use of instruction and feedback within the instructional hierarchy is strategic and intentional. Instruction changes across the stages to match what the student needs at that time, and feedback is used relative to the student's mastery of the skill, which also shifts as the student learns the skill. Typically, instruction focuses on the first three stages of the hierarchy for students receiving interventions (Burns, 2021). In exploring hypotheses and conducting problem analysis, educators can thus consider if the focus of instruction matches the student's skill development (that is, Is there a match between the focus of instruction and the skill development along the instructional hierarchy?), as well as the use of feedback. Here, one can see how understanding the learner's characteristics affects the instruction, curriculum, and environment provided to the student (or learner). In fact, Matthew K. Burns (2021) and other researchers have conducted considerable research showing the value of the instructional hierarchy and improved outcomes by matching the focus of an intervention to the student's skill development within the instructional hierarchy (Daly et al., 1996; Parker & Burns, 2014; Szadokierski, Burns, & McComas, 2017).

### Plan Identification and Implementation

Once there is an understanding of the problem and why it's occurring (that is, there is a reasonable hypothesis for the problem), educators can develop and implement a plan in step 3, plan identification and implementation. This step entails identifying four items.

1. A plan

2. A goal

3. A progress-monitoring tool to assess progress toward that goal

4. A fidelity measure to ensure the plan is implemented as intended

The general principle behind why a problem exists is because there's a breakdown somewhere within the instruction, curriculum, and environment that is causing the problem or impacting student learning. Accordingly, the general structure for plans is to modify or adjust factors within instruction, curriculum, and environment to resolve the problem. For example, if students in a core classroom aren't learning a given skill because the curriculum is not evidence based, then part of the plan would be to adjust the curriculum and use an evidence-based curriculum. Plans are therefore structured to address changes within instruction, curriculum, and environment.

Further, plans often involve identifying a skill that educators need to teach, reteach, or strengthen to resolve the problem (such as mathematics fact fluency, decoding multisyllabic words, or schoolwide expectations). For example, Tier 1 plans revolve around identifying a skill that most students need to have retaught or strengthened. At Tier 2, educators identify a skill that matches the instructional need for students and provide interventions to teach or strengthen that skill. Thus, we can think of *plans* as modifying instruction, curriculum, and environment to support learning of that skill. This is a general structure for plans that will vary across the tiers in terms of explicitness and nuance. We'll provide more context in subsequent chapters. In figure 2.8, we offer general questions for thinking about plans by anchoring them around a skill to be taught and adjusting instruction, curriculum, and environment to support it.

There are several considerations when identifying and implementing a plan, including professional learning. To ensure educators can evaluate the extent to which a plan worked or did not work, they will also need to identify a goal, a way to measure progress toward that goal, and a way to measure fidelity of the plan (Harlacher & Whitcomb, 2022; Simonsen et al., 2021). They will also need to measure the fidelity of assessments (National Center on Intensive Intervention, n.d.b). We cover each of these topics in the following sections.

| Domain | Question |
|---|---|
| Learner (Skill) | What skills do educators need to target, teach or reteach, or strengthen? |
| Instruction | How will educators modify the instruction to support learning those skills? How can the instruction be more explicit, more evidence based, or more intense to support learning? |
| Curriculum | How can educators adjust the curriculum to ensure the learner can access it? |
| Environment | How can educators make the environment more positive and proactive to support learning? |
| Learner (Characteristics) | How can educators modify the instruction, curriculum, and environment to support specific learner needs? |

**Figure 2.8: Questions to use when developing plans.**

### Professional Learning for Staff

One consideration when developing plans is the professional learning that staff may need to implement the plan. For example, if a school defines bullying as a schoolwide problem, the staff may need training to implement certain practices and strategies that would decrease bullying. For effective professional learning, we know that training is needed, but also that follow-up support and coaching are just as critical (Joyce & Showers, 2002; McIntosh & Goodman, 2016). Educators may need to secure certain training and coaching for staff, but they'll also want to make sure the training and coaching are effective. They may gather data on whether staff receive the training well, use fidelity data to judge whether the training is translating to use of the strategy, administer surveys on how useful and user-friendly the staff perceive the strategies they've been trained on, or a combination of all three (see the National Implementation Research Network; nirn.fpg.unc.edu).

### Goal Identification

Goals are necessary because they anchor educators around evaluating whether or not a plan was effective (Harlacher et al., 2013). To identify goals, we recommend a clearly written and easily measurable goal statement. To accomplish this, goals should have four parts (Simonsen & Myers, 2015).

1. Who is performing the skill?

2. What is the skill being performed?

3. Where, by when, and under what conditions should the skill be performed?

4. What are the criteria for the skill, such as to what extent or how much should the skill be performed?

By including all four of these parts, the goal is measurable and observable. In figure 2.9, we outline several examples and nonexamples of goal statements.

| Example | Nonexample |
| --- | --- |
| Alex (*who*) will score at least 18 points (*criteria*) on a mathematics concepts and applications probe (*skill*) by May 15, 2024 (*by when*).<br><br>* Parentheses added to indicate parts of a goal. | Alex will improve his reading (no method of measurement of criterion). |
| By the winter benchmarking period, at least 65 percent of students in the sixth grade will score at or above benchmark on the DIBELS composite score. | By spring benchmark, at least 80 percent of students will score at the proficient range (*who* is unclear). |

**Figure 2.9: Examples and nonexamples of goals.**

To set goals, we offer a few considerations. The expected performance or benchmark criterion can typically be used to establish the goal. If the problem exists because of the gap between the observed and expected performance, then it stands to reason to set a goal based on the closing of that gap. For example, if you're driving fifteen miles per hour over the sixty-five miles per hour speed limit, setting a goal of sixty-five (zero over the speed limit) makes sense. If only 70 percent of students scored at proficiency when at least 80 percent should, then setting a goal at 80 percent makes sense. When setting goals schoolwide for Tier 1 concerns, 5–15 percent improvement is a reasonable expectation from one benchmark period to the next, whereas 5–30 percent is a reasonable expectation for the year. In general, younger grade levels (that is, K–2) can expect more growth relative to older grade levels (that is, intermediate elementary and up; Burns et al., 2005; Greenwood et al., 2008; Hyson, Kovaleski, Silberglitt, & Pedersen, 2020; McIntosh & Goodman, 2016).

For individual student goals, historically, educators often set the target for the end of the year when using benchmark criteria (for example, spring benchmark). However, students may experience rapid growth at the beginning of the year that levels off or slows down later in the year (AIMSweb, 2012; Van Norman, 2021). Therefore, when interpreting their growth early in the school year, educators may conclude the intervention worked and fade support before the student's skills are solidified. Thus, caution is warranted when interpreting such goals, so it may be more suitable to set goals for the next benchmark period rather than an end-of-year benchmark (for example, in the fall, set the goal for the winter benchmark; in winter, set it to spring; Van Norman, 2021). Sometimes the gap between the expected performance and observed performance of a student may be too large; therefore, setting a goal at the benchmark criterion would be unrealistic (Bailey & Weingarten, 2019; Parker et al., 2018; Van Norman, Nelson, & Parker, 2018). In such cases, it may make sense to set the goal based on national norms and the average rates of growth for a given content area, particularly for students who are well below benchmark (Van Norman et al., 2018). In such cases, educators can set the goal based on the weeks of instruction, content area, and grade level of the student, while also considering a goal that will catch the student up to the desired standard or criterion.

To calculate a goal using average or normative growth rates, determine the number of weeks a student will receive intervention and multiply that number by the average rate for that student's content and grade level. Further, multiply that number by 1.5 and add it to their baseline performance (multiplying by 1.5 ensures an ambitious goal is set that will catch students up to their peers or to the expected performance). For example, a fifth-grade student who reads fifty words per minute will receive an intervention for ten weeks, and let's say the average weekly growth rate on an Oral Reading Fluency probe in the fifth grade is 1.2 words. The resulting goal would be:

*50 words read correct per minute + [(1.2 average growth of words read correct per week × 1.5 multiplier) × 10 weeks of intervention] = 68 words read correct per minute*

For goals, use this formula:

**Baseline or Observed Performance + [(Average Growth Rate × 1.5 Multiplier) × Number of Weeks] = Goal**

Generally speaking, we recommend using the expected criterion or benchmarks to set goals (that is, the criterion used in step 1 of the problem-solving model), particularly for students receiving Tier 2 supports. If that benchmark is too ambitious, we then suggest using average rates of growth, particularly for students receiving Tier 3 supports (we share average growth rates in chapter 6, page 185, when discussing goals for students receiving Tier 3 supports). It may be tempting to not multiply by 1.5 for some students for fear of setting too high a goal, but setting goals without that multiplier will lead to weak goals that would keep the students behind; if they're progressing at an average rate and are below performing, setting a goal with only average rates creates a goal inadvertently set to keep them behind. Use the 1.5 multiplier to allow for a goal that supports students catching up to their desired performance in a reasonable amount of time. We offer pros and cons for setting goals based on benchmarks or growth rates in figure 2.10.

| Method | Pros | Cons |
| --- | --- | --- |
| Benchmark or Expected Performance | • Clear-cut method<br>• Represents a level of mastery<br>• Can compare against winter and spring benchmarks when judging growth | • May be too ambitious, leading to inadvertent changes to support |
| Average Growth Rates | • Offers an average or realistic rate of growth | • May lead to a goal that isn't set to catch the student up (particularly if the growth rate isn't multiplied by 1.5)<br>• Have to consider student's starting point for accurate judgment of growth |

**Figure 2.10: Pros and cons of various goal-setting approaches for students.**

### Progress Monitoring

Having written a goal, the next step is to determine how best to measure the goal. Typically, educators can write goals that operationally define their own measurement. For example, in figure 2.8 (page 57), the goal indicates that the individual student will score a certain number on a mathematics probe. One way to measure goals is to use the same assessment in step 1 of the problem-solving model (problem identification). As mentioned, if you noted the problem with that measure, it would logically make sense to use it again to check whether the problem is resolved, similarly to how, if your check engine light turned on to indicate a problem, it would follow that if it turned off, then the problem is resolved.

However, educators may find that a different measure may be more sensitive to the growth or impact of the plan compared to the screening assessment used. Certainly as the team conducts problem analysis, it may discover that the screening assessment may not be targeted enough to measure the problem (sometimes that check engine light is too general an indicator to know if a particular problem is resolved). For example, team members may decide that although Oral Reading

Fluency indicated a schoolwide need in this reading skill for students (for example, 35 percent of students scored below grade-level criterion), the plan was centered on phonics development. As such, the team may want to use accuracy of text while reading or accuracy with nonsense words as a more sensitive measure for the goal. We recommend choosing the most efficient and sensitive measure of growth as the outcome measure for tracking a plan.

### Measurement of Plan Fidelity

In addition to a progress-monitoring tool, educators also need a fidelity measure for the plan. *Fidelity*, which refers to the extent to which a plan is implemented as intended (Roach, Lawton, & Elliott, 2014), plays an important role because it allows educators to determine the extent to which a plan was implemented, thus enabling them to then evaluate the plan's impact. This logic is critical, as educators may judge a student's growth or the impact of a plan without checking that the student even received the intervention or plan (Collins & Harlacher, 2023; Harlacher et al., 2013). In such cases, they may attribute failure of a plan to its design, but in reality, it wasn't even implemented. (Similarly, imagine blaming your medication for not making you feel better when you didn't take it as prescribed or thinking your exercise routine didn't work when you didn't follow it.) We'll discuss using fidelity and outcome data in the next step, plan evaluation, but for this step, educators will select a fidelity tool to measure the extent to which a plan was implemented as intended. Because there may be several areas to measure for a plan, educators should aim for efficient and quick measures of fidelity.

When thinking about how to measure fidelity, educators can think about direct and indirect measures of fidelity (Harlacher & Rodriguez, 2018; Roach et al., 2014). *Direct fidelity measures* are ones where educators directly observe the plan in action, such as using a checklist and observing each item of the plan that's implemented. *Indirect fidelity measures* are ones where educators assess fidelity by examining the results or impact of the intervention, such as completed worksheets, lesson plans, or attendance records. Direct and indirect measures each have their pros and cons. Direct measures are more time consuming, but they provide a purer or clearer measure of fidelity. Indirect measures, on the other hand, are more efficient and educators can use a variety of data to assess fidelity this way. However, some of the information may be limited (for example, using attendance as a fidelity measure is efficient, but it doesn't speak to the quality of implementation; Harlacher & Rodriguez, 2017).

Fidelity consists of several dimensions that educators can measure to assess overall implementation (National Center on Intensive Intervention, n.d.a; Roach et al., 2014; Watkins & Hornak, 2022). We outline these factors in figure 2.11 (page 62), but keep in mind that it's not necessary to measure all these dimensions to measure fidelity. Rather, educators should pick the dimension that makes the most sense for their given plan.

| Dimension | Description | Examples of Direct Measure | Examples of Indirect Measure |
|---|---|---|---|
| Adherence | The extent to which the plan was delivered as intended | Using a checklist of steps of an intervention (observation or self-report) | Examining elements within lesson plans |
| Exposure and Dose | The actual time or exposure to a plan | Recording the number of minutes of actual instruction compared to intended minutes | Measuring attendance |
| Quality of Delivery | How well the plan is delivered or the use of effective practices within the plan | Rating on a scale of 1–5 for how well an instructional strategy was used | Evaluating the quality of the work completed |
| Student Engagement | The level of students' engagement and attention with the plan | Rating on a scale of how engaged students were during a lesson  Observing the percentage of time students are on-task | Calculating the percent of completed assignments or work |

**Figure 2.11: Fidelity dimensions and examples of ways to measure them.**

### Measurement of Assessment Fidelity

It's important that any data gathered are objective and valid, so educators will want to ensure those gathering the data are well trained to administer the assessment. Improper training can lead to inaccurate data collection, which can lead to inaccurate or invalid data, which then lead to inaccurate decisions. When teachers administer a screening assessment, they should not only be trained in the tool, but they should also understand why the tool is used to assess the student's risk level (Bailey et al., 2020).

For example, Jason was working with a student as a school psychologist many years ago in his office when he overheard a teacher administering a Phoneme Segmentation Fluency probe through the walls. To properly administer that assessment, educators ask students to tell them the sounds they hear in a word (for example, "Tell me the sounds in *cat*." In this example, the student would say "k/ah/t"). In this situation, the teacher was elongating the words and exaggerating the sounds. The teacher would say "Tell me the sounds in ccccaaaaatttt" and "Now tell me the sounds in pppppiiiiiiigggggg." Though well intentioned, the teacher was tipping off the student as to the right answer, which invalidated the student's responses. Even if teachers want students to do well on the screening assessment, they could artificially inflate the students' answers and make it seem like they had mastered a skill that they actually hadn't. Valid data start with valid administration of the tool, so proper training and coaching are essential. By ensuring teachers know how to administer a tool and why it's important, then schools can ensure their data are valid.

To have proper administration of assessments, we recommend that leadership teams periodically gather fidelity data on the administration of those assessments. The team can conduct fidelity checks by quickly observing educators administering the assessment, asking teachers to complete a self-checklist after they administer it, or both. The observation or self-checklist is simply an outline of the steps; if educators follow the step, they mark *yes*, and if they don't, they mark *no*. As seen in figures 2.12 and 2.13 (page 64), the data can be tallied to determine a percentage of steps followed, thus providing a fidelity datapoint. We recommend gathering fidelity data on a quarterly basis and having fidelity of 95–100 percent for accuracy of administration. We also suggest reviews and reminders of administration for assessments prior to every benchmark period as another method to ensure fidelity.

| Step for Administration | | |
|---|---|---|
| 1. Did you record the student's name? | Yes | No |
| 2. Did you read the standardized directions? | Yes | No |
| 3. Did you time the student for one minute for each reading passage? | Yes | No |
| 4. Did you mark a bracket to indicate where the student read to? | Yes | No |
| 5. Did you mark a slash for each word read incorrectly? | Yes | No |
| 6. Did you give all three reading probes? | Yes | No |
| **TOTALS** | ____/6 | ____/6 |

**Figure 2.12: Example of a fidelity tool for oral reading fluency administration.**

### *Plan Evaluation*

Following the implementation of the plan, the final step of the problem-solving model is evaluation. Educators examine both the fidelity and outcome data to determine the extent to which the plan was implemented as intended and then if it was successful. Determining whether the plan worked or not is simple enough: just compare the outcome data or result to the identified goal. However, educators will first want to check that the plan was implemented with fidelity, as it's difficult to evaluate whether the plan was effective without knowing if it was even implemented

| Steps for Administration | | |
|---|---|---|
| 1. Did you (or the administrator) say the following to students?<br><br>"We're going to take an eight-minute mathematics test.<br><br>"Read the problems carefully and work each problem in the order presented, starting at the first problem on the page and working across the page from left to right. Do not skip around.<br><br>"If you do not understand how to do a problem, mark it with an X and move on. Once you have tried all of the problems in order, you may go back to the beginning of the worksheet and try to complete the problems you marked.<br><br>"Although you may show your work and use scratch paper if that is helpful for you, you may not use calculators or any other aids. Keep working until you have completed all the problems or until I tell you to stop. Do you have any questions?" | Yes | No |
| 2. Did you (or the administrator) answer any questions students had? | Yes | No |
| 3. Did you (or the administrator) say the following to the students?<br><br>"Here are your tests. Write your name, your teacher's name, and the date on the first page only in the space provided. Do not start working until I tell you to begin." | Yes | No |
| 4. Did you (or the administrator) allow time for students to write their information? | Yes | No |
| 5. Did you (or the administrator) say "Begin" and allow the appropriate time for the test? (For example, eight minutes) | Yes | No |
| 6. Did you (or the administrator) walk around the room to make sure that the students were working the problems in order? | Yes | No |
| 7. Did you (or the administrator) use the following prompts when needed?<br><br>If you notice that a student is skipping ahead without attempting each problem, say: "Try to work each problem. Do not skip ahead unless you do not know how to work a problem."<br><br>If a student asks a question or requests clarification, say: "I can't help you. Work the problem as best you can. If you don't understand the problem, you may move on to the next problem." | Yes | No |
| 8. Did you (or the administrator) say when the time was up (after eight minutes), "Stop and put down your pencil"? | Yes | No |
| 9. Did you (or the administrator) then remind students to make sure they had their name, the teacher's name, and the date written on their probe in the correct place? | Yes | No |
| TOTALS | ____/9 | ____/9 |

Note: Administrator refers to the person administrating the assessment.

**Figure 2.13: Example of a fidelity tool for administration of a mathematics computation probe.**

in the first place. Consequently, educators should start by looking at their fidelity data and determining whether the plan was implemented to a sufficient degree.

When examining fidelity data, a fair question is, How strong should fidelity be? We suggest fidelity around 90–95 percent, though some view 81 percent and above as strong fidelity (Roach et al., 2014). We argue for 90 percent because studies that show an intervention or practice being effective typically have around 90 percent fidelity (Hawken et al., 2021; Simmons et al., 2007; Vaughn et al., 2003). Bear in mind this is our general guideline and that educators should consider their context and the specific strategies they used when evaluating their fidelity data.

Given the suggested criterion, fidelity and outcome data intersect to create four possible results (Collins & Harlacher, 2023; IRIS Center, 2021).

1. Fidelity data are high (plan implemented as intended) and the outcome data are high (plan was effective). In this situation, we can conclude that the plan was implemented as intended and that it was successful. Therefore, educators can consider fading the plan while ensuring students maintain the skills they learned.

2. Fidelity data are high and the outcome data are low (plan was not effective). Educators can go back to the drawing board and problem solve why the plan didn't work. Here they can start a new cycle of problem solving and return to problem analysis.

3. Fidelity data are low (the plan wasn't implemented) and outcome data are high. In this situation, frankly, educators got lucky. The situation resolved itself, but it's unclear what happened or how the plan was related to the resolution. It's akin to going to the doctor because of a body ache and then suddenly the pain subsides without any treatment (or lack of following a treatment). Educators would want to investigate what happened to understand how the problem resolved itself.

4. Fidelity data are low and the outcome data are low. This would be an expected result because the plan wasn't implemented. Educators will want to examine why fidelity was low (for example, Do the staff need more training to implement the plan? Was the plan not feasible? Was the student absent frequently?) and then make adjustments to improve fidelity. They can then continue with the plan, knowing that fidelity will be better.

Understanding the relationship between fidelity and outcome data is critical, as educators will want to make sure they attribute success appropriately to a plan when it's warranted (Collins & Harlacher, 2023; Harlacher et al., 2013). It would be pseudoscientific and harmful to students to attribute positive outcomes to situations where the plan wasn't implemented well. Educators could walk away thinking they used a practice that was effective when, in fact, it was not. Remember the discussion in the introduction (page 1) about biases. Educators will want to be accurate and truthful when evaluating data, so they should always have both fidelity data and outcome data (Harlacher et al., 2013; 2015). In chapters 3 (page 73), 4 (page 113), 5 (page 151), and 6 (page 185), we'll discuss plan evaluation specifically for the different tiers, but in figure 2.14, we summarize the four general conclusions educators can make during plan evaluation.

|  |  | Outcome Data | |
|---|---|---|---|
|  |  | High | Low |
| **Fidelity Data** | High | Plan was effective; consider fading plan. | Plan was ineffective; conduct problem analysis and revise plan. |
|  | Low | Plan was not implemented, but unclear what led to positive results. Consider problem analysis to see why the problem resolved. | Plan was not implemented, so it's expected there were no positive results. Improve fidelity and implement plan again. |

**Figure 2.14: Four conclusions during plan evaluation: Intersection of fidelity and outcome data.**

Two considerations when going through step 4 of the problem-solving model are how to judge student growth and the use of data warehouse.

### Judgment of Student Growth

How do you analyze progress-monitoring graphs for students? We wish there was a universal answer for this, but it simply depends on the grade level, the content you're measuring, length of the intervention, and the amount of variability or "bounce" within the data (VanDerHeyden & Burns, 2019; Van Norman, 2021; Van Norman & Christ, 2016). When examining a student's graph, typically the more datapoints and the longer the intervention, the more reliable the decision can be. In particular, accuracy of decisions improves when ten to twelve weeks of weekly data are gathered (Van Norman, 2021). We recommend gathering six to nine datapoints across at least ten to twelve weeks of intervention (Christ & Silberglitt, 2007; Van Norman, 2021). This certainly poses some logistic issues, as you may gather data twice per month, resulting in only four datapoints after eight weeks. We suggest that data collection be flexible and that educators gather more progress-monitoring points when the data seem variable. For example, if a student's scores are highly discrepant from the goal line, we recommend gathering more data to improve the accuracy of the decision (Van Norman, 2021). Further, if educators are able to administer three progress-monitoring probes at each data collection point rather than one probe (and use the median score as the datapoint), this can increase the accuracy of the of data (Christ, Zopluoglu, Monaghen, & Van Norman, 2013).

When judging growth, educators have three commonly used options. One is to use a *datapoint rule*, such as if the last four or five datapoints are below the goal line, then a change is needed (Van Norman, 2021). There's also *trendline analysis*, in which a student's trendline is compared to the goal line (for example, if the trendline is below the goal line, then a change is needed; Van Norman & Christ, 2016). Finally, a *median rule* can be applied in which the last three datapoints are reviewed and if the median of those datapoints is below the goal line, then a change is needed (Van Norman, 2021). Because of the high error measurement and sensitivity of progress-monitoring probes, it's recommended that educators use either the median or trendline rule. These decision rules aren't as influenced by outliers as the datapoint rule (Parker et al., 2018; Van Norman, 2021) and are relatively more accurate compared to the datapoint rule (Hintze, Wells, Marcotte, & Solomon, 2018; Van Norman et al., 2018).

We offer the following recommended guidelines when making decisions about your progress-monitoring schedule and judging student growth (Ardoin, Christ, Morena, Cormier, & Klingbeil, 2013; Van Norman, 2021; Van Norman et al., 2018).

- Provide the intervention for eight to twelve weeks before judging growth or making definitive conclusions.

- Have at least seven to ten datapoints before judging student growth and, if possible, gather weekly data.

- Use the median or trendline rule over the datapoint rule.

- When in doubt of the accuracy of the data, gather more. More data improves the estimate of the student's growth. So if you're unsure of the student's progress or if you don't have enough data to make a decision, you'll need more.

### Data Warehouses

Once you've gathered the data, they need to be entered into a data warehouse for easy analysis. Many assessments have their own data warehouses for storage and analysis, but educators can also use their own electronic spreadsheet or handwritten worksheets when making data-based decisions. Each of these approaches comes with its pros and cons, which we outline in figure 2.15 (page 68).

|  | Pro | Con |
|---|---|---|
| Electronic Spreadsheet | Easy to access; compatible across software and hardware<br><br>Can customize as needed | Takes technical skill to build and develop, particularly if an issue arises with its function |
| Publisher Warehouse | Already created and easy to access<br><br>Usually designed to color code those results for ease of analysis | Likely a cost to use<br><br>May require some training or time to learn its features |
| Handwritten Worksheets | Quick and easy; low technology; no training needed | Cumbersome; takes more time to use; not easily editable |

**Figure 2.15: Pros and cons of possible data warehouses.**

Regardless of the data warehouse selected, there are a few factors to keep in mind. One, the data should be easily accessible by staff. When educators get together to analyze data, they should be able to access the data quickly and easily. Being unable to do so prevents them from having a data-focused meeting. Two, the data need to be displayed visually within a graph, particularly when analyzing growth over time (that is, progress monitoring). When educators are looking for trends or want to quickly identify who is at or above a threshold, a line graph or bar graph can quickly illustrate the needed information. However, listing data in a table does not allow for this quick analysis. For example, look at figure 2.16. It would take you a minute or two to determine the student's growth. When these same data are displayed visually in figure 2.17, it makes it much easier to analyze growth (you can quickly see the student's scores are increasing over time). When possible, have data displayed visually for making decisions. Third, we recommend that student data are kept private and confidential to the greatest extent possible. Using initials or code numbers can help with this, and many data warehouses may have this as a key feature.

| Date of Assessment | Score |
|---|---|
| March 2 | 35 |
| March 4 | 32 |
| March 9 | 40 |
| March 11 | 44 |
| March 16 | 55 |
| March 18 | 49 |

**Figure 2.16: Example of data for progress monitoring that hinders ease of interpretation.**

To create their own data warehouses, educators can access Microsoft Excel or Google Sheets rather easily. Some websites offer templates, such as Intervention Central

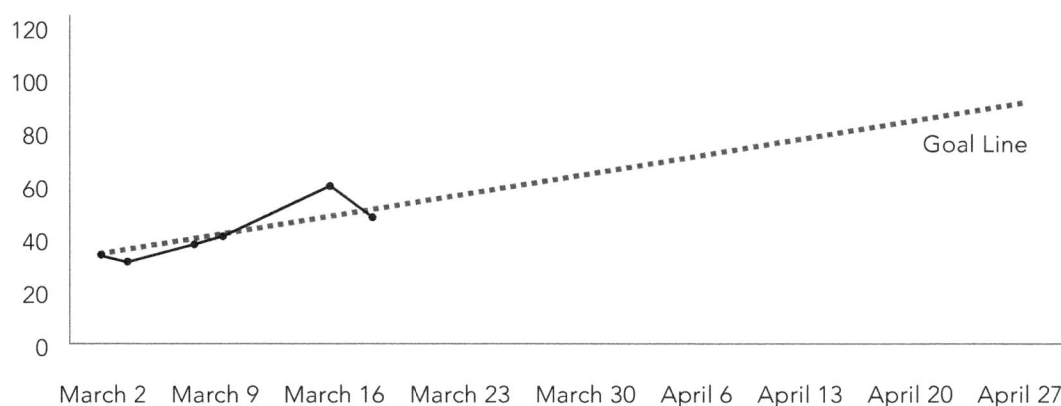

**Figure 2.17: Example of well-displayed data for progress monitoring.**

(see https://bit.ly/3pJsWlJ) and the National Center for Intensive Intervention (https://bit.ly/3NQMoF7).

## Summary

One of the strengths of the problem-solving model is its applicability to various levels of decision making within schools, including decisions for individual students, groups of students, and entire school systems (Harlacher et al., 2015; McIntosh & Goodman, 2016). Because of that, the model provides a perfect heuristic for making data-based decisions across the tiers within MTSS. MTSS provides the backdrop within which the model can be used. Because one of the components of MTSS is data-based decision making, we view the problem-solving model as a natural and logical fit for use within MTSS. In figure 2.18 (page 70), we outline key questions to ask when using the model within MTSS. Although there are more nuanced questions within each step beyond those listed, we have included the main questions for brevity. In the remaining chapters of this book, we dig into each of these questions and illustrate how educators and teams can use them to make data-based decisions. We'll start with applying the model to Tier 1, the schoolwide level, in the next chapter.

| Step | Action | Schoolwide | Tier 1 (Core) | Tier 2 | Tier 3 |
|---|---|---|---|---|---|
| 1 | Problem Identification | Are at least 80 percent of students at each *grade level* successful with core supports alone? Are at least 80 percent of students in each *student group* successful with core supports alone? | Are at least 80 percent of students at a given grade level successful with core supports alone? | Which students are at risk? | Which students are most at risk? Which students are not making sufficient growth? |
| 2 | Problem Analysis | Is there a common instructional need across the school or identified group of students in need? Are teachers across grade levels consistently implementing standards of practice around instruction, curriculum, and environment? | What is the most common instructional need within the grade level? | What is each student's instructional need? | What is the student's instructional need? Why is the student not making adequate growth? |
| 3 | Plan Identification and Implementation | What adjustments to schoolwide instruction, curriculum, and environmental supports can be made to target identified common instructional needs? What supports do staff need to address the identified common instructional needs (for example, training, coaching, time, materials, and so on)? | What adjustments to grade-level core support (that is, instruction, curriculum, and environment) can be made to target identified common instructional needs? | What intervention addresses that need? | What adjustments to instruction, curriculum, and environment can improve the student's skills? |
| 4 | Plan Evaluation | Did the adjustments improve the health of the schoolwide core? | Did the adjustments improve the health of the grade-level core? | Is the fidelity at least 90 percent? Is the intervention effective overall? Which students is the intervention working for? Which students is it not working for? | What is the fidelity of the plan? Is the plan working for the student? |

**Figure 2.18: Problem-solving model within MTSS.**

# PART 2

# Data-Based Decision Making
# at the Systems Level

# CHAPTER 3

# Data-Based Decision Making at the Schoolwide Level

Of all the tiers in a multitiered system, a strong Tier 1 is the most vital. A healthy Tier 1 system of instruction and supports ensures that Tier 2 and Tier 3 are not overwhelmed by students in need of additional layers of support (Harlacher et al., 2015; McIntosh & Goodman, 2016). Schools should strive toward building a Tier 1 that is accessible to all students, sufficient for most students, and harmful to no students. It should be clearly defined, so that all relevant groups have a clear understanding of what the school means when it says all students receive Tier 1 support. This includes staff, families, and the broader school community.

In this chapter, we discuss how school leaders can use the problem-solving model to determine the effectiveness of their schoolwide Tier 1 system. We summarize each step of the model in figure 3.1 (page 74), including questions that guide each step. Additionally, we provide reproducible worksheets (page 102) to accompany teams as they complete the steps. Chapter 4 (page 113) will go deeper in how to do this at the grade level.

## Problem Identification

In step 1, the team examines schoolwide screening data to determine overall effectiveness of Tier 1 supports across the school. The goal is to determine whether your Tier 1 system is meeting the needs of the majority of your students. If you find that Tier 1 is not meeting the needs of most students, you would determine that there is a Tier 1 problem. Recall that we define a problem as a gap between observed performance and expected performance, with a larger gap indicating a

| Step | Action | Key Questions | Tasks |
|------|--------|---------------|-------|
| 1 | Problem Identification | • Are at least 80 percent of students at each grade level successful with core supports alone?<br><br>• Are at least 80 percent of students in each student group successful with core supports alone? | • Review and analyze current and previous schoolwide screening data by grade level.<br><br>• Review and analyze current and previous schoolwide screening data by student group.<br><br>• Ensure fidelity of screening data. |
| 2 | Problem Analysis | • Is there a common instructional need across the school or the identified group of students in need?<br><br>• Are your teachers across grade levels consistently implementing standards of practice around instruction, curriculum, and environment? | • Determine if there is a common area of need across the school.<br><br>• Review available implementation data around instruction, curriculum, and environment.<br><br>• Examine if there is disproportionality in student access to high-quality instruction and supports. |
| 3 | Plan Identification and Implementation | • What adjustments to schoolwide instruction, curriculum, and environmental supports can staff make to target identified common instructional needs?<br><br>• What supports do staff need to address the identified common instructional needs (for example, training, coaching, time, materials, and so on)? | • Develop a schoolwide plan for addressing identified needs.<br><br>• Develop a tool for monitoring the plan.<br><br>• Select a goal for the following year. |
| 4 | Plan Evaluation | • Did the adjustments improve the health of the schoolwide core? | At next screening, ask:<br><br>• "Is fidelity at least 90 percent?"<br><br>• "Is the schoolwide plan effective?" |

**Figure 3.1: Key questions for schoolwide use of the problem-solving model.**

larger problem. Within an MTSS framework, we know that a healthy Tier 1 would have approximately 80 percent of students identified as on track, low risk, or at or above benchmark (Harlacher et al., 2015; McIntosh & Goodman, 2016). This will be your expected performance: 80 percent of students on track. You can then identify the magnitude of your problem by comparing that expected performance of 80 percent to the actual percentage of your students who are currently on track (that is, observed performance). The larger the gap between your observed performance and the expected performance of 80 percent, the larger your problem is, and the more substantial your plan will need to be in order to address it.

To better understand the impact of your schoolwide Tier 1 supports, you should review and analyze current and previous schoolwide screening data by both grade level and student group. This will help identify areas of strength and areas of need in your Tier 1 supports, leading to a more effective plan. In addition, you should also ensure that your screening data are accurate by checking fidelity.

### Review and Analyze Current and Previous Schoolwide Screening Data by Grade Level

Start by examining your screening data by grade level to determine whether there is a systemic need, or whether there is only a need at some grade levels. This will help determine your next steps. To do this, you will want to examine the current percentage of students proficient at each grade level, as well as the growth over the course of the year. To determine which grade levels may need more support, you should look for two patterns in the data. First, look for grade levels that have significantly less than 80 percent of students identified as proficient. Second, look for grade levels that have made little to no growth over the course of the year.

Consider the two sample schools in figure 3.2. Each school examines its schoolwide reading screening data and finds that approximately 60 percent of students are at low risk for reading difficulties in the spring. Given that only six out of ten

| Grade Level | Percentage of Students Proficient at School A | | | Percentage of Students Proficient at School B | | |
|---|---|---|---|---|---|---|
| | Fall | Winter | Spring | Fall | Winter | Spring |
| Kindergarten | 48 | 69 | 81 | 56 | 68 | 65* |
| Grade 1 | 65 | 72 | 80 | 56 | 63 | 56** |
| Grade 2 | 60 | 73 | 76* | 65 | 72 | 64* |
| Grade 3 | 50 | 62 | 71* | 56 | 52 | 55** |
| Grade 4 | 46 | 50 | 44** | 58 | 62 | 58** |
| Grade 5 | 46 | 49 | 40** | 46 | 49 | 55** |
| All Grade Levels | 53 | 60 | 62* | 56 | 61 | 60* |

Note: * is moderate need (60–79 percent); ** is high need (less than 60 percent)

☐ 80 percent and above     ▨ 60–79 percent     ■ 60 percent and below

**Figure 3.2: Sample schoolwide reading data for two schools.**

students are on track to become proficient readers, the school leadership teams at both schools determine that they need to make some changes to the school-wide reading system. But before we recommend any schoolwide changes, such as adopting an entirely new reading curriculum or making wholesale changes to the instructional strategies and routines, let's first take a closer look at the grade-level data for each of these schools.

While both schools have approximately the same percentage of students who are proficient in reading (62 versus 60 percent), the pattern of grade-level data is actually quite different. In school A, we see that reading instruction in the early grades (K–3) is fairly effective at ensuring 70–80 percent of students develop the necessary early literacy skills. Significant student growth from fall to spring is evident across each of these grade levels as well. But reading instruction in the intermediate grades (4–5) needs significant improvement, as students are not growing across the grade level, leaving the majority of students not proficient. For this school, a schoolwide plan may not be needed. The leadership team may choose to focus on improving grades 4 and 5 through using the Tier 1 grade-level problem-solving process described in chapter 4 (page 113). In school B, a different pattern emerges. The data are actually quite consistent across grade levels with most grade levels significantly below 80 percent of students being proficient and showing little to no growth across the year. This school should use the schoolwide problem-solving process described in this chapter to address the systemic issues of reading instruction. In figure 3.3, we provide a template for examining your schoolwide screening data by grade level. The reproducible "Schoolwide Tier 1 Worksheets for Problem-Solving Model" on page 102 also includes this template.

| Grade Level | Percentage of Students Proficient | | |
| --- | --- | --- | --- |
| | Fall | Winter | Spring |
| Kindergarten | | | |
| Grade 1 | | | |
| Grade 2 | | | |
| Grade 3 | | | |
| Grade 4 | | | |
| Grade 5 | | | |
| All Grade Levels | | | |

Figure 3.3: Template for schoolwide screening data.

### *Review and Analyze Current and Previous Schoolwide Screening Data by Student Group*

In addition to examining your schoolwide data by grade level, disaggregate the data across your school to examine the differential impact of your instruction and supports for your different student groups, which should include students who share similar racial or ethnic backgrounds, students experiencing poverty, students with disabilities, English learners, or other school-assigned classifications. By disaggregating your schoolwide data by student group, you can answer the question, *Who* are our Tier 1 supports working for and *who* are they not working for? A healthy and truly equitable Tier 1 system should ensure that 80 percent of all student groups are successful.

Consider the following example. In examining their schoolwide behavior screening data, a school found that 90 percent of students at their school have one or fewer office discipline referrals. Staff initially celebrate the fact that their Tier 1 behavior supports seem to be working for most students and believe that currently they need no changes. However, when they disaggregated their data, they found some significant disproportionality in who receives referrals. In particular, they found that 95 percent of White students across the school received one or fewer office discipline referrals, but only 65 percent of Black students received one or fewer office disciplines. Black students were being referred at a significantly higher rate than White students. What's even more concerning was that they actually saw a decline in the percentage of Black students with one or fewer referrals over the course of several years of data. In this scenario, the Tier 1 behavior support system is working for White students, but it is not working for Black students. Their system is creating and widening the disparities between different student groups. After disaggregating their data, they found an urgent need to make changes to the Tier 1 behavior supports at their school.

In an educational system with limited resources, disaggregating data can help you target your Tier 1 problem solving toward the areas where it is needed the most. Failing to examine your screening data in this way can lead to inequitable practices that maintain or increase disproportionality. It can also lead to predicable results that tend to look the same year after year, with little to no improvement. Refining your Tier 1 supports in ways that benefit your most marginalized populations of students is one of the most effective ways to improve overall results for your school.

Disaggregating data by student group at the schoolwide level also has the benefit of allowing you to see patterns that you may not otherwise see at the grade level or the intervention group level. If your school has a relatively small number of students from historically marginalized groups, it may be easy for grade levels to attribute their lack of success to individual student factors.

To illustrate this point, we offer the following example. Out of a total of sixty first graders currently enrolled in your school, you find that only four are identified as economically disadvantaged. Of those four students, you find that only one is currently meeting the benchmark in reading, and three are well below the benchmark.

In a grade-level discussion, it might be easy to attribute the lack of reading success for those three economically disadvantaged students to individual factors. However, if you were to find that same pattern at each grade level, it then becomes harder to attribute that lack of reading success to individual student factors. If three of the four economically disadvantaged students in your grade were well below the reading benchmark, you might attribute that to some sort of individual learner issues for those three students. But if eighteen out of twenty-four economically disadvantaged students in your school were well below the reading benchmark, it would be much easier to see that your Tier 1 reading system is not meeting the needs of that student population. In both of these scenarios, 75 percent of the students identified as economically disadvantaged are currently unsuccessful. But having a larger group of students to examine helps us to avoid the fundamental attribution error, which we discussed in chapter 1 (page 15), making it easier to see the flaws in your system, instead of attributing the lack of success to perceived flaws in your students.

Even if you find that most or all of your grade levels have 80 percent of student identified as proficient, we still recommend disaggregating your screening data by student group. Just because your Tier 1 supports are meeting the needs of 80 percent of students across your grade levels, it does not necessarily mean that your Tier 1 supports are equitably meeting the needs of all student groups. Use the template in figure 3.4 to analyze your schoolwide data by student group. The reproducible "Schoolwide Tier 1 Worksheets for Problem-Solving Model" on page 102 also includes this template with extra blank rows to help customize for your school's needs.

| Student Group | Percentage of Students Proficient | | |
|---|---|---|---|
| | Fall | Winter | Spring |
| All Students | | | |
| Black Students | | | |
| Indigenous Students | | | |
| Latino/a Students | | | |
| White Students | | | |
| Economically Disadvantaged Students | | | |
| English Learners | | | |
| Students With Disabilities | | | |
| Other Student Groups | | | |

Figure 3.4: Template for disaggregated schoolwide screening data.

### Ensure Fidelity of Screening Data

Recall that in chapter 2 (page 41), we describe the need for risk verification, the process of corroborating your data with other data sources to ensure its accuracy. At Tier 1, conducting risk verification with all students would take a significant amount of time and resources. For this reason, we suggest some alternative ways to ensure that your screening data are accurate. First, ensure that you are using a high-quality screener that is reliable, valid, and appropriate for your student population. For more information on selecting an appropriate screener, you can visit the National Center on Intensive Interventions' Screening Tools Chart (https://bit .ly/43n7NeU). But having a reliable, valid screening tool is not enough. You must also ensure that you have collected your screening data with fidelity. In figure 3.5, we share four ways you can verify your screening data and increase your confidence that you have collected the data with accuracy.

| | |
|---|---|
| **Conduct spot checks for fidelity.** | Choose a small number of screening sessions across grade levels to check fidelity of test administration. Many available screeners have fidelity checklists already available to ensure standardized administration. These fidelity checklists provide reminders on standardized administration, including when to prompt students, what to do when a student gets stuck, timing and scoring rules, and a variety of other important components of the testing session. You could also choose to *double-score* some students. To do this, you would have a second tester score along with the primary tester, and then compare scores to ensure that both testers are scoring in a similar way. |
| **Take a closer look at patterns in your data.** | Although not a direct measure of fidelity, a closer examination of patterns in your data can sometimes suggest inconsistencies in test administration. For example, vastly different results, depending on who the tester was, when or where the students were tested, or other discrepancies, might suggest a lack of fidelity. Consider the following example. A school has been screening its K–3 students using mathematics computation probes for several years and then decides to add grades 4–5 to the screening routine. In the first year of administering the data, they find that 86 percent of fourth graders scored at low risk on the fall mathematics screening. However, when they looked at the performance of that same cohort of students in the spring of third grade, they found that only 54 percent of students scored at low risk. It is highly unlikely that over the summer there was such a significant increase (+32 percent) in the percentage of students at low risk in mathematics. The more likely explanation is that there were some inconsistencies in how they collected screening data between grades 3 and 4, and they may want to follow up by directly checking fidelity. |
| **Compare results to other available data sources.** | If there are other schoolwide or gradewide data sources available, you can use them to confirm your screening results. For example, your core reading curriculum may have built-in formative or summative assessments you can administer to all students. Comparing the results of these assessments to your screening data can help verify that the screening data are accurate. However, even if your screening data do not match your classroom data, you should have high confidence in your screening data if (1) you are using a reliable, valid screener that is appropriate for your student population, and (2) you have ensured that it is administered with fidelity. Differences between screening data and classroom data in this scenario may be due to biases or lack of standardization in your classroom data, rather than problems with your screener. |
| **Ensure accurate data entry.** | One easy fidelity check is to ensure that all data were entered correctly, particularly if there was any manual data entry. It's easy to make mistakes when inputting data, so double checking or spot-checking data entry can be a quick and easy fix for questions around data accuracy. |

**Figure 3.5: Ways to verify fidelity of screening data.**

After you have analyzed your schoolwide data at step 1, you have some options for next steps. Figure 3.6 provides guidance on what those next steps might be, depending on the patterns you find in your schoolwide data.

| If most grade levels are . . . | And most student groups are . . . | Then your recommended next steps are . . . |
|---|---|---|
| Around or above 80 percent | Around or above 80 percent | • Use the grade-level process in chapter 4 (page 113) to problem solve for the individual grade levels below 80 percent.<br>• Consider continuing the schoolwide process to problem solve for student groups below 80 percent. |
| Around or above 80 percent | Below 80 percent | • Use the grade-level process in chapter 4 (page 113) to problem solve for the individual grade levels below 80 percent.<br>• Continue the schoolwide process to problem solve for student groups below 80 percent. |
| Below 80 percent | Below 80 percent | • Continue the schoolwide process to improve schoolwide supports to better meet the needs of all grade levels and student groups. |

**Figure 3.6: Next steps depending on your problem identification.**

## Problem Analysis

In step 2, the team examines multiple data sources to answer the question, *Why are less than 80 percent of our students successful across most of our grade levels or student groups?* This includes a deeper dive into the screening data to determine any common areas of need, as well as looking at implementation data related to the instruction, curriculum, and environment. It also means looking at whether there is disproportionate access among students to high-quality instruction and supports. By examining these data sources, the team can develop an informed hypothesis about why the student success data look the way that they do. This includes identifying which important skills are missing for many or most students in your school, as well as potential barriers to student success. Targeting these priority skills and removing barriers to student success will be the focus of your schoolwide Tier 1 plan.

### Determine Whether There Is a Common Area of Need Across the School

Recall that in step 1 (problem identification), your team looked at an overall risk indicator score to determine the percentage of students who are at low risk. During step 2 (problem analysis), you need a deeper dive into the data to better understand your areas of strength and areas of need across grade levels and student groups. There are several ways to do this, depending on your screener. If you use a curriculum-based measure as your screener, you can examine the percentages of students identified as above benchmark on each of the subtests, or subskills, to determine your areas of strength and areas of need. Screeners that assess multiple skills in a single measure, such as SpringMath (VanDerHeyden et al., 2012) or the Strengths and Difficulties Questionnaire (Goodman, 1997), often include diagnostic reports that allow you to view student strengths and areas of need. If you collect office discipline referral data as your behavior screener, then you can take a deeper look at which problem behaviors and locations seem to be more prevalent and in need of attention. Regardless of the type of screener you are using, most will have some method of examining areas of strength and areas of need across students. Chapter 4 (page 113) provides a more detailed list of the subskills often measured by screeners in the different content areas.

When digging deeper in the screening data, it's important to remember that although learning doesn't always occur in the same step-by-step sequence for every student, certain fundamental skills are sometimes necessary to master higher-order skills. For example, students will not be able to fully comprehend what they read if they lack the ability to accurately read the words on the page with automaticity. In mathematics, students who lack basic number sense will not be able to efficiently engage in advanced problem solving. When identifying the priority skill to target at Tier 1, we recommend that you start with the most foundational skill that is impeding student success and work your way up the hierarchy of skills until you find an area of need for many or most students. Some content areas have a clear sequence of skills to learn before they can master higher-order skills, such as reading or mathematics (for example, learning to multiply single digits before multiplying double digits). Other areas, such as behavior or social-emotional learning, do not necessarily have a prescribed sequence (for example, expectations of responsibility, safety, and respect are not necessarily sequential). Thus, schools will need to prioritize based on their context and data. The example in figure 3.7 (page 82) demonstrates what this might look like in reading, and a general template is available at the end of the chapter on page 103.

At this particular school, educators have established that most grade levels are well below 80 percent proficient, as indicated by the composite score. This indicates a need to problem solve at the schoolwide level. The next step is to analyze the problem by looking at the most basic foundational skills to determine whether there is a widespread student need in phonemic awareness and decoding. It appears that most students have sufficient phonemic awareness skills, as indicated by kindergarten and first-grade Phoneme Segmentation Fluency data. Working their way up the hierarchy of skills in reading, educators next look at phonics, or decoding, skills. Looking at the Nonsense Word Fluency measure, they see that most students are

| Example: Identifying the Priority Skill for Many or Most Students (Schoolwide) | | | | | | | |
|---|---|---|---|---|---|---|---|
| Reading Skill | Phonemic Awareness | Phonics | | | Fluency | Vocabulary and Oral Language | Comprehension | Overall Proficiency |
| Acadience Screening Subtest | Phoneme Segmentation Fluency | Nonsense Word Fluency–Correct Letter Sounds | Nonsense Word Fluency–Whole Words Read | Oral Reading Fluency–Accuracy | Oral Reading Fluency–Words Correct | N/A | Maze | Composite |
| Percentage of Students at or Above Benchmark | | | | | | | | |
| Kindergarten | 94 | 86 | 80 | N/A | N/A | N/A | N/A | 88 |
| Grade 1 | 95 | 78* | 79* | 65* | 67* | N/A | N/A | 70* |
| Grade 2 | N/A | N/A | N/A | 55** | 60 | N/A | N/A | 58** |
| Grade 3 | N/A | N/A | N/A | 44** | 48** | N/A | 50** | 48** |
| Grade 4 | N/A | N/A | N/A | 48** | 46** | N/A | 44** | 46** |
| Grade 5 | N/A | N/A | N/A | 54** | 62** | N/A | 48** | 54** |

Note: * is moderate need (60–79 percent);
** is high need (less than 60 percent)aa

☐ 80 percent and above    ▨ 60–79 percent    ■ 60 percent and below

**Figure 3.7: Sample schoolwide data indicating a schoolwide instructional need.**

able to identify individual letter sounds, as indicated by the Correct Letter Sounds data. The Whole Words Read data also tell them that most students are able to decode short simple words. Students who have not mastered these foundational skills should receive additional Tier 2 or 3 interventions. Next, educators look at whether their students accurately and fluently read connected text on the Oral Reading Fluency measure. Here is where they start to see some Tier 1 concerns.

When examining accuracy of oral reading, educators find a range of performance across the grade levels but none that are at or above 80 percent for this skill, indicating a Tier 1 need across the school. Further up the hierarchy, they see similarly low numbers for Oral Reading Fluency–Words Correct and reading comprehension (Maze). Given the relationship between automaticity of text reading and reading comprehension, their hypothesis is that many or most of their students don't understand what they are reading due to their insufficient word-reading skills. If their students are struggling to decode words while they read, their reading will be choppy and disfluent, making it difficult to understand what they are reading. This lack of fluent reading skills will also impact their ability and desire to independently read a wide range of text, limiting their exposure to rich vocabulary and content knowledge. This is known as the *Matthew effect*, a phenomenon in which good readers read more often, leading to increased content knowledge and vocabulary, which further enhances their reading abilities (Stanovich, 1986). Poor readers tend to read less, depriving them of rich content knowledge and vocabulary, which continues to limit their reading skills.

Given the hypothesis that lack of accurate and fluent text reading is limiting their students' reading comprehension, educators decide to target decoding skills across their school as the priority skill. Their Tier 1 program seems insufficient to support their students becoming accurate and fluent readers. Educators would need to improve in this area as a major step toward developing more proficient readers at their school. In this particular example, they have identified a clear area of need across the school. But it should be noted that this will not always be the case. If a clear schoolwide instructional need does not exist, educators may choose to focus on problem solving at the individual grade levels, as described in chapter 4 (page 113).

### Review Available Implementation Data Around Instruction, Curriculum, and Environment

In addition to identifying whether a common area of need, or priority skill, exists across your school, you will want to take a reflective look at the standards of practice for Tier 1 (that is, the instructional practices, curriculum materials, and environmental supports you're implementing). The outcomes you see in your school are a direct reflection of the level of support your system provides your students. By purposely examining the instruction, curriculum, and environment, you can identify both areas of strength to leverage and areas of need to improve.

Your team can use the following three questions to guide this problem analysis of Tier 1 instruction and supports across your school. A more detailed description of how to address each question follows.

1. Does your school have standards of practice in instruction, curriculum, and environment?

2. Are they implemented consistently?

3. Where do they need to be improved or supplemented to increase student success?

### Does Your School Have Standards of Practice in Instruction, Curriculum, and Environment?

When analyzing your schoolwide practices and supports, a good place to start is by asking if your school or district has common agreements for Tier 1 instruction and supports. In other words, has your school or district clearly identified what will be taught at Tier 1 (curriculum), how it will be taught (instruction), and the learning supports that will enable student learning (environment)? We refer to these agreements as Tier 1 *standards of practice*, and they form the basis of a consistent instructional system for all students. They do not need to be a comprehensive detailing of how every minute should be spent in the classroom but should provide enough information to allow for a clear understanding of the non-negotiables at Tier 1, ensuring consistency across classrooms. Think of your Tier 1 standards of practice as the foundation of what you expect to see across all classrooms. Individual teachers build on that foundation, using a wide variety of instructional and environmental supports, to respond to the needs of their individual students. But your Tier 1 standards of practice should be first built on a foundation of high-quality, evidence-based strategies, materials, and routines. Figure 3.8 provides some guidance on the general features that your Tier 1 standards of practice should reflect. For a specific example of what Tier 1 standards of practice might look like in the area of reading instruction, see the reproducible "Sample Tier 1 Reading Standards of Practice" on page 109.

If your school or district does not have high-quality Tier 1 standards of practice that adequately address instruction, curriculum, and environment, we can hypothesize that this may be a contributing factor to your problem identified at step 1. The lack of consistent guidelines for Tier 1 core instruction and supports is probably impeding your school's ability to adequately serve all students. Without these guidelines, instructional supports may look very different from classroom to classroom, creating an inconsistent educational experience for students.

### Are Your Tier 1 Standards of Practice Implemented Consistently?

Developing your standards of practice is the first step in ensuring consistent Tier 1 instruction and supports. Your next step should be determining how consistently your school implements those agreements. The process of checking fidelity at Tier 1 requires that you observe your classrooms and have conversations with teaching staff to get a full picture of what implementation looks like across your school. The purpose of this process is not to catch teachers by surprise and find them doing something wrong. Rather, we should provide clear guidance for teachers on expectations for their classrooms, so they can focus on what's important. This process may include a checklist of the specific look-fors in your Tier 1 standards of practice that allow you to determine how many classrooms demonstrate these agreements. Figure 3.9 (page 86) provides a sample standards of practice fidelity form.

| Instruction |
|---|
| ☐ Explicit and systematic instruction in skills and strategies |
| ☐ Consistent instructional routines are taught and used |
| ☐ Frequent student opportunities to respond |
| ☐ Affirmative and corrective feedback provided to students |
| ☐ Whole-group instructional activities to engage all learners |
| ☐ Small-group instruction for students who need it |
| ☐ Building of students' background knowledge |
| ☐ Development of oral language through student discourse |

| Curriculum |
|---|
| ☐ High-quality and evidence-based materials |
| ☐ Scope and sequence that address the needs of your learners |
| ☐ Culturally relevant materials for your student population |
| ☐ Grade-level content provided to all students |
| ☐ Supplemental materials to enhance areas of need in core materials |

| Environment |
|---|
| ☐ Classroom rules and expectations are explicitly taught |
| ☐ Physical learning space is conducive to learning (for example, comfortable temperature) |
| ☐ Classroom rules and expectations are consistently reinforced |
| ☐ A schoolwide discipline structure is in place for responding to instances of unwanted behavior |
| ☐ A variety of methods are used to build relationships with and among students |
| ☐ Classrooms are physically set up in a way that is conducive to learning |
| ☐ Agreed-on schedule for instructional minutes |
| ☐ A variety of active engagement strategies for students |

**Figure 3.8: General features of Tier 1 standards of practice.**

*Visit **MarzanoResources.com/reproducibles** for a free reproducible version of this figure.*

| | Number of Classrooms Implementing | ÷ | Number of Total Classrooms | = | Percentage Implementing |
|---|---|---|---|---|---|
| **Time (120 minutes)** | | | | | |
| **Whole Group** | | | | | |
| Twenty to thirty minutes foundational skills (phonemic awareness, phonics, fluency) instruction | | ÷ | | = | |
| Twenty to thirty minutes oral language, vocabulary, and comprehension instruction | | ÷ | | = | |
| Thirty minutes writing instruction | | ÷ | | = | |
| **Small Group** | | | | | |
| Thirty to forty minutes skills-based small groups | | ÷ | | = | |
| **Curriculum Materials** | | | | | |
| Main selection | | ÷ | | = | |
| Decodables | | ÷ | | = | |
| Sound spelling cards | | ÷ | | = | |
| Fluency passages | | ÷ | | = | |
| **Instructional Strategies** | | | | | |
| Explicit instruction provided (I do, we do, you do) | | ÷ | | = | |
| Precision partnering routine used | | ÷ | | = | |
| Elicit frequent student responses | | ÷ | | = | |
| Corrective feedback routine used | | ÷ | | = | |
| **Environmental Supports** | | | | | |
| All students included in whole-group instruction | | ÷ | | = | |
| Behavior expectations reinforced during the reading block | | ÷ | | = | |
| Room setup includes a space for whole-group and small-group instruction | | ÷ | | = | |
| Overall Fidelity | | | | | |

**Figure 3.9: Sample standards of practice fidelity form (reading and writing instruction).**

*Visit **MarzanoResources.com/reproducibles** for a free reproducible version of this figure.*

## Who Should Develop Your Tier 1 Standards of Practice?

Ideally, these common agreements around Tier 1 should be developed at the district level. This is preferable to individual school-based standards of practice for several reasons. First, your agreements around instruction, curriculum, and environment aim to ensure a consistent educational experience for all students. When schools within a district all develop unique standards of practice, the educational experience can vary widely from school to school. For example, if each of your schools uses different core reading instructional materials or different expectations for behavior, a student who transferred within your district would have a very disjointed educational experience. Additionally, having consistent standards of practice allows the district to effectively provide training across the district, allocate resources such as staff, materials, and funding, and maintain a clear focus and vision across all schools. It is extremely difficult for a district to provide high-quality professional learning and coaching if each school is using its own unique programs.

However, while these standards of practice should be relatively standardized across the district, schools should still be encouraged to customize these agreements to meet the needs of their specific student populations. For example, a district might adopt a high-quality Tier 1 reading curriculum for all schools to use during core reading instruction, but some schools in the district with higher populations of English learners may need to identify supplemental oral language materials to help support daily language acquisition. In the area of behavior, individual schools may take the district agreements on behavior expectations and tailor the teaching of these expectations to the specific locations in their school.

If you find that your school has Tier 1 standards of practice yet it is not implementing them consistently across the majority of classrooms, your problem analysis should include an examination of your system capacity and infrastructure. It is not enough simply to provide teachers with your standards of practice and expect them to implement those at a consistently high level. A checklist of what to do is not a road map for how to do it. You must consider how well your system enables your teachers to do this work. Figure 3.10 (page 88) provides a rubric that examines how well your system is supporting the effective implementation of your Tier 1 standards of practice. If you find that implementation is not consistent, reviewing the questions in figure 3.10 can help identify issues that may be contributing to a lack of consistent implementation.

### How Can You Update Your Tier 1 Standards of Practice to Improve Student Success?

Your Tier 1 standards of practice serve as a starting place for analyzing why less than 80 percent of your students may be at low risk. Well-implemented Tier 1 agreements that rely on high-quality materials, strategies, and supports should result in most of your students being successful. However, even the most well-designed and

| How well does your school or district leadership team support consistent implementation of Tier 1 standards of practice through the following actions? | Not Yet Initiated | In Progress | Fully Implemented |
|---|---|---|---|
| Is there a formal process for developing Tier 1 standards of practice that includes a review of evidence-based practices and programs? | | | |
| Is there a formal process for developing Tier 1 standards of practice with a diverse team of decision makers including teachers, family, and community members? | | | |
| Did you clearly communicate Tier 1 standards of practice to staff? | | | |
| Did you provide initial training for staff? | | | |
| Do you provide ongoing training and coaching support for staff? | | | |
| Do you allocate needed resources (time, materials, people, or funding) for implementation? | | | |
| Do you identify and remove possible barriers to implementation? | | | |
| Do you conduct ongoing monitoring of implementation? | | | |
| Is there a process for refining Tier 1 standards of practice that includes student-outcomes data, implementation-fidelity data, and staff feedback? | | | |

**Figure 3.10: Examining your system capacity and infrastructure to support implementation.**

*Visit **MarzanoResources.com/reproducibles** for a free reproducible version of this figure.*

well-implemented Tier 1 standards of practice will most likely need some fine-tuning and customization to meet the ongoing needs of your students. When your data indicate that (1) your standards of practice are consistently implemented across classrooms and (2) many or most students are still lacking one or more important priority skills, it generally means that your standards of practice do not adequately address that need and must be refined.

Consider the following example. A school allocates ninety minutes of time to daily reading instruction, utilizing a mix of small-group and whole-group instruction. This includes a mix of instructional activities targeting the foundational skills of reading, including phonemic awareness, phonics, and oral reading fluency, as well as activities to build oral language and reading comprehension. Figure 3.11 describes how to allocate time to the different instructional activities according to the Tier 1 standards of practice for this particular school.

| Time Allocated (Will vary by grade level) | Whole Group or Small Group | Activity |
|---|---|---|
| Twenty to thirty minutes | Whole group | Phonemic awareness: segmenting and blending<br>Phonics: letter sounds, word work, and spelling<br>Fluency: reading connected text |
| Twenty to thirty minutes | Whole group | Oral language and vocabulary<br>Reading comprehension |
| Thirty to forty-five minutes | Small group | Skill-based small reading groups |

**Figure 3.11: Tier 1 standards of practice for time spent in core reading instruction.**

After reviewing the screening data, the leadership team identifies that reading fluency is a priority skill for many or most students across the grade levels. Screening data indicate that explicit phonics instruction is a relative strength at this school, giving students the foundation for decoding words accurately. However, students do not get enough opportunities to practice their oral reading and develop automaticity in connected text. Fluency instruction generally occurs at the end of the twenty- to thirty-minute whole-group phonics lesson, and is sometimes left off due to word work activities running long. As a result of the Tier 1 problem analysis, the school team then develops a hypothesis that more students would be proficient readers if teachers dedicated more time to oral reading fluency instruction. The team then chooses to supplement the Tier 1 standards of practice to address the added need for oral reading fluency instruction. During the next step, plan identification and implementation, the team will specifically plan what this will look like.

### Examine Whether There Is Disproportionality in Student Access to High-Quality Instruction and Supports

In addition to ensuring that you are implementing high-quality, evidence-based instructional strategies, curriculum materials, and environmental supports, you may need to take a step further to examine whether all student groups have access to those agreements. Disproportionality in student outcomes is often the result of disproportionality in the instruction and support that you are providing. If there are large gaps in the outcomes of different student groups, there may be unseen barriers in your school that prevent certain student groups from benefiting from your system. Developing a plan to improve the general instructional quality may not lead to improved student outcomes if you are not purposeful about ensuring all students have access to those improvements. The following list includes some examples of how effective practices may be inequitably distributed in a school.

- An explicit instructional routine with frequent opportunities to respond and corrective feedback is consistently used throughout the reading block. But during this time, some student groups are disproportionately being sent to the office for minor behavior infractions that should be addressed in the classroom. As a result of being removed from the classroom, those students are not able to benefit from the explicit instruction and frequent opportunities to respond that other students receive.

- The teacher leads students through a read-aloud activity to build oral language and reading comprehension for twenty to thirty minutes each day during the reading block. However, students who need additional reading interventions are removed from this activity and sent to receive a Tier 2 intervention during this time. Instead of supplementing their core instruction, this intervention effectively supplants it, depriving them of receiving grade-level content, oral language, vocabulary, and reading comprehension instruction.

- During the morning meeting each day (the first twenty minutes of school), the teacher provides a social-emotional learning lesson and builds the classroom community through a variety of inclusive activities. However, some students are frequently tardy due to various reasons, including the need to help get their siblings ready for school, a lack of reliable transportation, or parents' work schedule. These students frequently miss this opportunity to participate in the morning meeting, and thus feel left out from their classroom community.

- During mathematics instruction, the teacher leads a counting activity providing frequent opportunities for students to respond. However, instead of ensuring all students are responding through choral responses or partner responses, the teacher consistently calls on the same few students who raise their hands to answer questions. While other students also occasionally raise their hands to participate, the teacher tends to focus on a few students who she knows will provide the correct answer.

## Plan Identification and Implementation

At step 3, your team develops a plan based on the information collected during your problem analysis. This plan should be well aligned with the hypothesis your team developed around why less than 80 percent of students across most grade levels or student groups are successful. When creating a plan at the schoolwide level, it is important to consider both what you want the students to do and what you want the adults to do.

The first part of your plan will address the identified area of need with the goal of improving student skills and functioning in that area. For example, if you find that only 40 percent of your students have basic number sense in mathematics, your schoolwide plan should target developing students' number sense. The second part of your plan should address the training, supports, and other resources that your staff will need to better support and teach number sense to the students. Your leadership team should be purposeful about both these parts of your plan, as it is only by changing the behavior and actions of the adults in your school that you will be able to change the outcomes for your students. In the following sections, we discuss developing the plan, monitoring the plan, and selecting a goal for the following year.

### Develop a Schoolwide Plan for Addressing Identified Needs

Based on the information from your problem analysis, you may have identified an area of need for many or most students. This could be a priority skill across several grade levels or disproportionality in outcomes between student groups. It does not necessarily mean that all students at all grade levels have the same need and you will be delivering a one-size-fits-all plan for everyone. For example, you may have determined that basic number sense is a general need across grade levels, but your third- and fifth-grade classes have strong number sense and don't require extra support in this area. As you develop an action plan for addressing your area of need, consider how you will make changes to the instruction, curriculum, and environment, then refer to these three questions that you examined during your problem analysis.

1.  Does your school have standards of practice in instruction, curriculum, and environment?

2.  Are they implemented consistently?

3.  Where do they need to be improved or supplemented to improve student success?

#### What if My School or District Does Not Have Tier 1 Standards of Practice?

If you do not have Tier 1 standards of practice, build your action plan around developing those agreements, with a particular focus on addressing the priority skill need at your school. For example, if you find that many or most of your students are consistently unable to decode words accurately and fluently, it makes sense to develop agreements that target improvement in your phonics instruction. This may include actions such as adopting a new phonics program or supplementing your existing program (curriculum), training and supporting teachers to implement explicit phonics instructional routines (instruction), or setting up a reading block that allows for whole- and small-group activities to provide additional phonics instruction (environment). Refer to figure 3.8 (page 85) and the sample standards of practice on page 109 to help guide development of those agreements.

### What if My School Has Tier 1 Standards of Practice, but They Are Not Implemented Consistently?

If you do have Tier 1 standards of practice and they are not being implemented consistently across classrooms, you will want to refer to figure 3.10 (page 88) to determine actions your team can take to better support your plan and improve fidelity. This may include providing training to staff, providing ongoing coaching and feedback to refine implementation, securing more instructional materials so staff have what they need, or identifying additional barriers that are preventing staff from implementing the standards of practice at a high level.

### What if My School Has Consistently Implemented Tier 1 Standards of Practice, but They Need to Be Improved or Supplemented?

If you have Tier 1 standards of practice that are consistently implemented across classrooms but they are not meeting the needs of at least 80 percent of your students across grade levels or student groups, you will need to revisit and improve them in the area of need. In developing your plan, consider changes to instruction, curriculum, and environment across your school. If you find that there is significant disproportionality in outcomes between student groups, you should make a plan to increase access to your high-quality instruction, curriculum, and environmental supports for your underserved student groups.

## *Develop a Tool for Monitoring Your Plan*

Once you develop your plan, you also need to include a way to monitor implementation to ensure a high degree of fidelity. If you have existing Tier 1 standards of practice, you should already have a system for monitoring fidelity. Recall the fidelity checklist in figure 3.9 (page 86) used to observe implementation across classrooms. Once you agree on the components of your plan, developing a fidelity checklist will help you ensure that all the components are being implemented across classrooms. In addition to developing a fidelity tool, think about four additional questions to ensure you're collecting fidelity data efficiently.

1. Who will monitor fidelity?

2. When will we monitor fidelity?

3. How will we use the fidelity checklist? Will someone do classroom observations or will teachers fill it out as a self-report?

4. What's the process for responding to and supporting teachers when they have difficulty implementing with fidelity?

## *Select a Goal for the Following Year*

With the plan in place and being monitored, you'll next set a goal for spring of the following year, which is when you will collect your final screening data. Changing the Tier 1 practices across your school requires a coordinated effort that often involves a cycle of professional learning, implementation, monitoring, and adjustments. Setting a goal for one full year from when you develop your plan will allow for this cycle to take place. This means you can implement your plan over the course of the following school year and track its progress using your screening data at subsequent screening periods.

When setting schoolwide goals, it's important to recognize that schoolwide improvement is different from the improvement we can expect from individual students or even individual grade levels. Effective, targeted instruction for individual students or small groups of students can impact significant growth in a relatively short amount of time. It's not necessarily uncommon to see students move from high risk to low risk in a given content area within a few months if the instruction and support are powerful enough. However, that type of rapid schoolwide growth in a school that has significant areas of need would be less common. For example, moving from 40 percent of students at your school identified as proficient readers to 80 percent within a few months would be an extremely short timeline and most likely unrealistic. A school that has only 40 percent of its students currently reading proficiently would need to make some significant changes to schoolwide practices, including evaluating curriculum materials, changing widespread instructional strategies, and possibly undergoing some cultural shifts in what it means to teach reading. Simply put, schoolwide change takes time. Consider this when setting schoolwide goals. A more appropriate schoolwide goal might be to increase the percentage of students who are on track by 5–15 percent over the course of the year. You may also choose to set a targeted goal aimed at increasing proficiency in particular grade levels or student groups that were identified at an increased level of need during step one: problem identification. We provide an example template for developing a schoolwide plan in figure 3.12. The reproducible "Schoolwide Tier 1 Worksheets for Problem-Solving Model" on page 102 also includes this template.

| Priority Skills: *Phonics* |
| --- |
| **Do you have disproportionate outcomes by student group?** |
| If **No** ➡ Develop a plan to improve general instruction, curriculum, and environmental supports across your school. |
| If **Yes** ➡ Which student groups will you address in this plan? |
| *Our plan will improve phonics skills for all students, with particular attention to English learners and Latino/a students.* |

**Figure 3.12: Example of a schoolwide plan.**

continued ▶

| What changes will you make to the instruction? | Who is responsible? | When will it occur? |
|---|---|---|
| Implement a systematic phonics routine that includes review, teacher modeling, guided practice, and independent practice.<br><br>Sections of the daily phonics lesson include:<br><br>1. Phonemic awareness warm-up<br><br>2. Letter-sound or grapheme activity<br><br>3. Blending and reading words<br><br>• Word lists for automatic word recognition<br><br>• Decodable books or other connected text to build fluency<br><br>• Spelling or writing | All grade-level teachers | Twenty to thirty minutes during whole-group instruction in the reading block |
| **What changes will you make to the curriculum?** | **Who is responsible?** | **When will it occur?** |
| Supplemental phonics curriculum with new sound-spelling cards, decodable books, and texts for practicing reading fluency | All grade level teachers | Twenty to thirty minutes during whole-group instruction in the reading block |
| **What changes will you make to the environment?** | **Who is responsible?** | **When will it occur?** |
| Teach new phonics routine to students<br><br>Use choral response routines along with partner routines for student responses | All grade level teachers | During the reading block |
| **What will school leadership do to improxve the infrastructure and capacity of staff to implement the plan?** | **Who is responsible?** | **When will it occur?** |
| Adopt and train staff in new supplemental phonics curriculum<br><br>Ongoing coaching and opportunities for peer observation | School leadership team<br><br>Literacy specialist | Adopt program by August, train teachers in September preservice<br><br>Bi-monthly |

## Plan Evaluation

The final step of the Tier 1 schoolwide problem-solving process involves the examination of multiple data sources to determine how well you implemented your plan and how it has impacted student outcomes. The two main data sources you should examine are (1) fidelity data to determine the quality of plan implementation and (2) student outcome data to determine plan effectiveness. Figure 3.13 provides two questions for teams to ask to guide this process of evaluating your plan. The first is checking the fidelity of the plan to determine how well it was implemented. Based on these results, your team can determine whether you need to improve the fidelity of your Tier 1 plan or if you can move on to the second question of whether the plan was effective; that is, you examine whether the plan increases the percentage of students in your school at low risk.

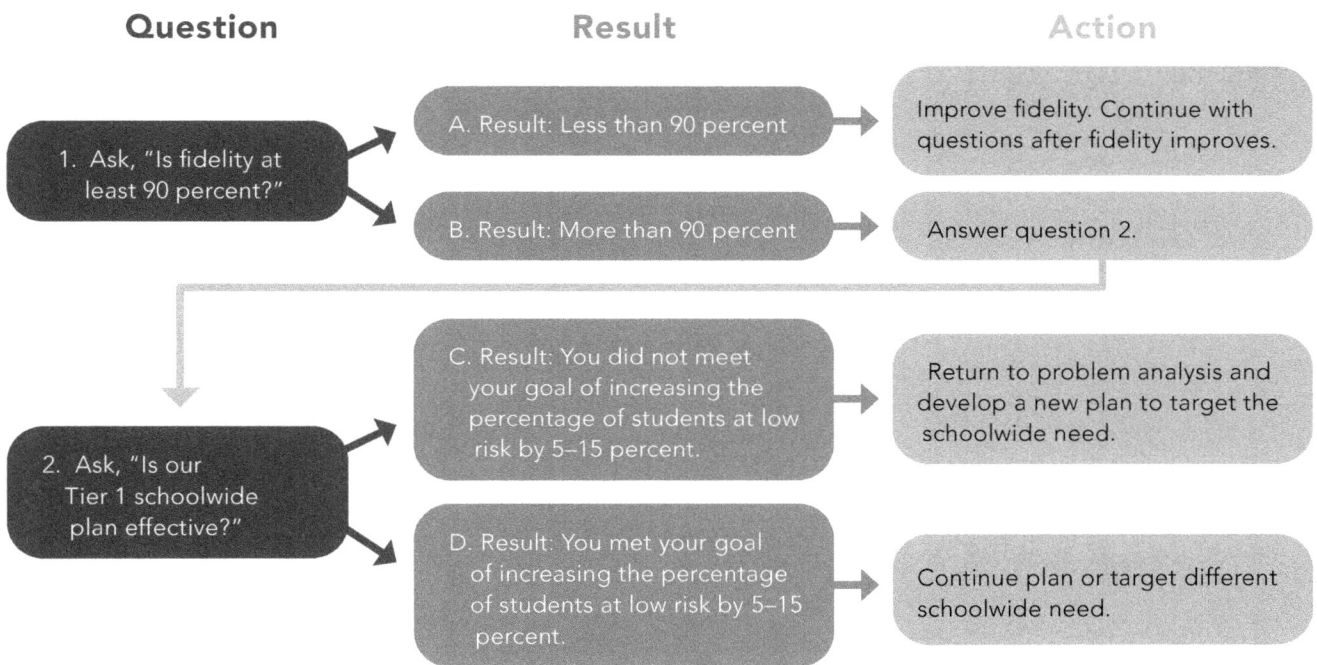

| Question | Result | Action |
| --- | --- | --- |
| 1. Ask, "Is fidelity at least 90 percent?" | A. Result: Less than 90 percent | Improve fidelity. Continue with questions after fidelity improves. |
| | B. Result: More than 90 percent | Answer question 2. |
| 2. Ask, "Is our Tier 1 schoolwide plan effective?" | C. Result: You did not meet your goal of increasing the percentage of students at low risk by 5–15 percent. | Return to problem analysis and develop a new plan to target the schoolwide need. |
| | D. Result: You met your goal of increasing the percentage of students at low risk by 5–15 percent. | Continue plan or target different schoolwide need. |

**Figure 3.13: Plan evaluation for Tier 1 (schoolwide).**

### 1. Ask, "Is Fidelity at Least 90 Percent?"

The first move is examining the overall fidelity of your schoolwide plan to determine the degree to which it was implemented, with the goal being at least 90 percent implementation. Your plan will have multiple components, with some components being implemented across multiple classrooms. For example, let's say your schoolwide plan focused on creating and implementing the standards of practice for reading and writing instruction that we outlined in figure 3.9 (page 86). Figure 3.14 (page 96) provides an example of what a completed fidelity tool might look like for that plan.

| | Number of Classrooms Implementing | ÷ | Number of Total Classrooms | = | Percentage Implementing |
|---|---|---|---|---|---|
| **Time (120 minutes)** | | | | | |
| **Whole Group** | | | | | |
| Twenty to thirty minutes foundational skills (phoneme awareness, phonics, fluency) instruction | 18 | ÷ | 20 | = | 90 |
| Twenty to thirty minutes oral language, vocabulary, and comprehension instruction | 20 | ÷ | 20 | = | 100 |
| Thirty minutes writing instruction | 20 | ÷ | 20 | = | 100 |
| **Small Group** | | | | | |
| Thirty to forty minutes skills-based small groups | 16 | ÷ | 20 | = | 80 |
| **Curriculum Materials** | | | | | |
| Main selection | 20 | ÷ | 20 | = | 100 |
| Decodables | 17 | ÷ | 20 | = | 85 |
| Sound spelling cards | 18 | ÷ | 20 | = | 90 |
| Fluency passages | 18 | ÷ | 20 | = | 90 |
| **Instructional Strategies** | | | | | |
| Explicit instruction provided (I do, we do, you do) | 13 | ÷ | 20 | = | 65 |
| Precision partnering routine used | 14 | ÷ | 20 | = | 70 |
| Elicit frequent student responses | 12 | ÷ | 20 | = | 60 |
| Corrective feedback routine used | 13 | ÷ | 20 | = | 65 |
| **Environmental Supports** | | | | | |
| All students included in whole-group instruction | 20 | ÷ | 20 | = | 100 |
| Behavior expectations reinforced during the reading block | 18 | ÷ | 20 | = | 90 |
| Room setup includes a space for whole-group and small-group instruction | 18 | ÷ | 20 | = | 90 |
| Overall Fidelity | 255 | ÷ | 300 | = | 85 |

**Figure 3.14: Sample completed fidelity form for reading and writing standards of practice.**

Given that your Tier 1 schoolwide plan will be implemented across an entire school year, it's often helpful to check in on the fidelity of your plan midyear. This allows you plenty of time to adjust your plan and improve fidelity if you find that some components are not being implemented consistently. The sample data in figure 3.14 indicate that most of the plan is being implemented across classrooms fairly well, with overall fidelity at 85 percent. But the common instructional strategies that make up these standards of practice are not being implemented consistently across classrooms. This information can be helpful in determining where best to provide support for your staff. For example, if follow-up conversations with teachers reveal that they are having trouble implementing the explicit instructional routines, the reading specialist and principal can help provide the training and support that teachers need. If you wait until the end of your plan to check fidelity, you may not have sufficient time to improve it prior to examining student outcome data. You'll have different courses of action depending on whether fidelity is less than or more than 90 percent.

### A. Result: Less Than 90 Percent

If the result is significantly less than 90 percent (A. Result in figure 3.13, page 95), you will want to examine why plan fidelity was not higher. Since you will be reviewing fidelity prior to the end of the year, this will give you an opportunity to identify areas for improvement to ensure a higher level of fidelity before the end of the year. The following list outlines questions to help identify possible reasons why fidelity was low. In general, low plan fidelity is often due to a lack of clear communication, training, and ongoing support to staff. Taking action on these questions will help ensure that staff members have what they need to implement the plan with a high degree of fidelity.

- Have you communicated the plan clearly to all staff?

- Have you provided sufficient training to staff to implement the plan?

- Have you provided ongoing coaching to staff to implement the plan?

- Have you identified and removed possible barriers to the implementation of the plan?

- Have you allocated sufficient resources (time, materials, people, and funding) for implementation?

### B. Result: More Than 90 Percent

If the result is more than 90 percent (B. Result in figure 3.13, page 95), then your team can conclude that the Tier 1 plan is being implemented as intended. You will want to continue supporting and implementing your plan until the end-of-year screening. At that time, you'll want to determine whether your plan was effective in improving the percentage of students at low risk.

## 2. Ask, "Is Our Tier 1 Schoolwide Plan Effective?"

To answer this question, you'll want to determine the percentage of students who you have identified as low risk on the end-of-year screening and compare it to the previous year. This comparison will tell you if you increased the percentage of students at low risk and by how much. As with the first question, your next steps are determined by your answer: you either did not meet the goal or you did meet the goal.

### C. Result: You Did Not Meet Your Goal of Increasing the Percentage of Students at Low Risk by 5–15 Percent

A well-implemented plan matched to the schoolwide need should result in a significant increase in the percentage of students identified at low risk. If you did not meet your goal, you will want to review your plan to determine how you can improve it. If you have already determined that your plan was implemented with high fidelity (that is, more than or equal to 90 percent), then you will want to reanalyze *why* the problem is occurring and develop a new plan. A Tier 1 plan may be unsuccessful for a variety of reasons. See figure 3.15 for a list of possible reasons a well-implemented plan might be unsuccessful and some follow-up questions to ask to better determine why the plan didn't work.

| Possible Reasons Your Plan Was Unsuccessful | Follow-Up Questions to Ask |
|---|---|
| There was difficulty in interpreting the data and an appropriate priority skill was not identified. | • Was there a clear priority skill consistent across grade levels?<br>• Were there several different priority skills across grade levels? |
| The plan did not match the general instructional need across the school. | • Were the strategies and routines chosen as part of the plan evidence based for improving the priority skill? |
| The scale of the plan was not comprehensive enough to address the needs of students across the school. | • Was there some growth in the percentage of students at low risk but not enough to meet your goal?<br>• Were adequate resources given to your plan?<br>• Were there competing initiatives or instructional plans being implemented at the same time? |
| Staff buy-in for the plan was low, resulting in surface implementation. | • Were staff voices included in the development of your plan?<br>• Was there an opportunity for staff to provide feedback on the plan prior to implementation?<br>• Do staff prefer providing interventions to students who need additional support instead of changing core instructional practices? |

**Figure 3.15: Reasons why a plan might be unsuccessful.**

### D. Result: You Met Your Goal of Increasing the Percentage of Students at Low Risk by 5–15 Percent

If you are successful and you meet your goal of improving the percentage of students at low risk, you have an important next step: celebrate! Changing schoolwide outcomes is difficult and requires a sustained focus over time for your entire school staff. Schoolwide success requires collective effort. For next steps, you may choose to continue or intensify your plan if you are not yet at 80 percent of students at low risk. Your plan has had a positive impact on students and continuing with that plan may allow you to see a continued increase in student success. You may also find that a more pressing instructional need requires your attention and shifts your problem-solving focus. Whatever your decision for next steps is, implementation of a successful schoolwide plan should build new skills in your staff members that they can continue to use moving forward, resulting in sustained student success.

## Team Roles

To accomplish this schoolwide work, a functional school leadership team is necessary. This team is charged with supporting MTSS implementation and sustainability by ensuring clear communication with staff, training and supporting evidence-based practices, and monitoring and evaluating implementation. An essential role of the team is examining the schoolwide data and using a problem-solving process to identify strengths and areas of need. Your team should include a number of key partners that are essential to supporting high-quality Tier 1 instruction and supports across the school. Having a team also helps enhance the sustainability of the problem-solving process over time. The more team members who are trained in the process and integral in decision making, the more resilient the process will be even if you have high staff turnover. The following list includes possible school leadership team members and their roles.

- **Building administrators:** Building administrators, such as school principals and assistant principals, serve as instructional leaders, setting the vision for MTSS at their school. They are key decision makers, determining how best to allocate resources (time, money, people, and materials), securing training and support for staff, identifying and removing barriers, and using data to refine the system when needed.

- **Grade-level teachers:** Teachers from a variety of grade levels should be represented on the school leadership team. They have the most insight into what happens each and every day in the classroom and have the most daily contact with students. They are essential in helping the team better understand the impact of its plans on staff and students.

- **Content specialists:** Content specialists including literacy specialists, mathematics specialists, and behavior specialists can help provide expertise when developing schoolwide plans to address student needs in a given area.

- **Special education teachers:** Special education teachers can help ensure that the needs of students with disabilities are incorporated in schoolwide plans. They often also bring expertise in key instructional and support strategies that will benefit all students.

- **Other key partners:** Other key partners may include school psychologists, speech language pathologists, school counselors, students, and family and community members. In addition to the decision makers listed here, you will want to include any other partners who can bring additional insight to the team, especially those who can help speak for often marginalized populations. For example, family and community partners can help ensure student needs are fully understood and create school-home connections that enhance the quality of schoolwide Tier 1 plans.

## Common Roadblocks and Possible Solutions

Here and within chapters 4 to 6, we include common roadblocks and solutions that educators may encounter with the use of data and applying the problem-solving model. For data-based decision making at the systems level, we discuss roadblocks that include a lack of consistent instructional needs, a lack of standards of practice, and difficulty determining the percentage of students successful with core supports alone.

### Lack of a Consistent Instructional Need Across the School

In analyzing your schoolwide data, it's possible that your school leadership team won't find a consistent instructional need across grade levels or student groups. This may be especially true if your school data indicate most students are successful in the content area for which you are problem solving. For example, if you have 70 percent of students identified as low risk for reading difficulties, you will most likely have some student groups or grade levels that are highly successful and don't need significant Tier 1 problem solving. If there is no consistent instructional need across your school, your schoolwide plan may be more targeted at improving outcomes for specific grade levels or student groups. It is not necessary that you distribute your plan equally across different groups. An equitable plan calls for all students to get what they need, which may not necessarily be the same thing for each student.

### Your School District Has No Tier 1 Standards of Practice

Ideally, your school district should have districtwide agreements on Tier 1 that provide a foundation for your school to build on. These agreements should be standardized across all schools in the district. Individual schools then should customize them to meet the specific needs of their students. If your district does not have Tier 1 standards of practice, and does not plan on creating them, your school can create your own agreements. Ensure that your agreements align with existing district initiatives and priorities, such as a district-adopted curriculum used at Tier 1 or any other instructional programs that have been the focus of district training.

### *Difficulty in Determining the Percentage of Students Successful With Core Supports Alone*

When considering whether your Tier 1 supports are effective, your ultimate goal should be for at least 80 percent of your students to be successful *with core supports alone*. This is an important distinction that the following example helps explain. In looking at your schoolwide data, your team finds that 90 percent of your students are at low risk for behavior difficulties. You initially determine that your Tier 1 behavior supports are sufficient and don't plan to make any changes. However, a deeper dive reveals a different story. Though the overall data look good, you find that many of the students identified as low risk are receiving more than core supports. In fact, you find that approximately one out of every three students identified as low risk is also receiving a Tier 2 or Tier 3 behavior intervention. So, the percentage of students who are successful *with core supports alone* is actually closer to 60 percent. This finding indicates a need to problem solve at the Tier 1 level to ensure it is meeting the needs of more students and the system is not over-reliant on Tier 2 and Tier 3. As your team begins the process of problem solving across the tiers, your first step may be to just examine overall percentages of students who are low risk without accounting for students receiving interventions. This can help provide an overall snapshot of your entire system. As you refine your data-management skills, you will want to develop a process for examining your data in a more specific way to determine the percentage of students who are low risk and are also not receiving any additional Tier 2 or Tier 3 intervention support.

## Summary

At the schoolwide level, educators use the problem-solving model and schoolwide screening data to determine whether 80 percent of students at each grade level and within each student group are successful. If they determine that less than 80 percent of students are successful on the screener, they dive deeper into available data to identify any possible barriers at Tier 1 that are preventing students from being successful. This includes identifying priority skills, or common areas of need for many or most students. Schools also examine whether there are existing common agreements or standards of practice around instruction, curriculum, and environmental supports at Tier 1, and whether those agreements are being implemented consistently. Teams then develop a plan to improve Tier 1 supports. This plan targets students' instructional, curricular, and environmental needs  and aims to increase the percentage of students identified as successful on screening measures at each grade level and across student groups. After implementing the schoolwide plan, educators examine fidelity data and screening data at subsequent schoolwide screening periods to determine whether the fidelity of the schoolwide plan is sufficient and whether it's supporting an increase in the percent of students who are successful. In the next chapter, we'll shift from a schoolwide focus to a grade-level focus.

# Schoolwide Tier 1 Worksheets for Problem-Solving Model

**Summary of Schoolwide Problem Solving at Tier 1**

| Step | Action | Key Questions | Tasks |
|---|---|---|---|
| 1 | Problem Identification | • Are at least 80 percent of students at each grade level successful with core supports alone?<br>• Are at least 80 percent of students in each student group successful with core supports alone? | • Review and analyze current and previous schoolwide screening data by grade level.<br>• Review and analyze current and previous schoolwide screening data by student group.<br>• Ensure fidelity of screening data. |
| 2 | Problem Analysis | • Is there a common instructional need across the school or the identified group of students in need?<br>• Are your teachers across grade levels consistently implementing standards of practice around instruction, curriculum, and environment? | • Determine whether there is common area of need across the school.<br>• Review available implementation data around instruction, curriculum, and environment.<br>• Examine whether there is disproportionality in student access to high-quality instruction and supports. |
| 3 | Plan Identification and Implementation | • What adjustments to schoolwide instruction, curriculum, environmental supports can we make to target identified common instructional needs?<br>• What supports do staff need to address the identified common instructional needs (for example, training, coaching, time, materials, and so on)? | • Develop a schoolwide plan for addressing identified needs.<br>• Develop a tool for monitoring your plan.<br>• Select a goal for the following year. |
| 4 | Plan Evaluation | • Did the adjustments improve the health of our schoolwide core? | At next screening:<br>• Ask: "Is fidelity at least 90 percent?"<br>• Ask: "Is our schoolwide plan effective?" |

## Step 1: Problem Identification

1. Review and analyze current and previous schoolwide screening data by grade level. Use the following worksheets to determine whether core is currently sufficient (more than 80 percent proficient) at each grade level, and if there has been growth over time.

2. Review and analyze current and previous schoolwide screening data by student group. Use the following worksheets to determine whether core is currently sufficient (more than 80 percent proficient) for all student groups, and whether there has been growth over time.

3. Ensure you have collected your screening data with fidelity.

### Current and Previous Schoolwide Screening Data (by Grade Level)

| Grade Level | Percentage of Students Proficient | | |
|---|---|---|---|
| | Fall | Winter | Spring |
| | | | |
| | | | |
| | | | |
| | | | |
| | | | |
| | | | |
| All Grade Levels | | | |

*Note: Write in the grade levels that you examine in the first column.*

**Screening Data Disaggregated by Student Group**

| Student Group | Percentage of Students Proficient | | |
|---|---|---|---|
| | Fall | Winter | Spring |
| All Students | | | |
| Black Students | | | |
| Indigenous Students | | | |
| Latino/a Students | | | |
| White Students | | | |
| Economically Disadvantaged Students | | | |
| English Learners | | | |
| Students With Disabilities | | | |
| Other Student Groups: | | | |
| | | | |
| | | | |
| | | | |

**Step 2: Problem Analysis**

4. Determine whether there is a common priority skill area of need across the school by examining screening subtest or component data.

5. Review available implementation data around instruction, curriculum, and environment to determine whether there are areas that can be improved across the school.

6. Examine whether there is disproportionality in student access to high-quality instruction and supports.

## Priority Skill Hierarchy

**Directions:** Select the skill area you are problem solving for, then list the component skills that make up that skill area. For example, in reading you would list the five components of reading (phonemic awareness, phonics, fluency, vocabulary, and reading comprehension). Then list the specific screening subtests that measure each skill and the percentage of students who were above the benchmark on the subtest at each grade level.

| Skill Area (select one): ☐ Reading ☐ Mathematics ☐ Behavior ☐ Social-Emotional Learning ☐ Other: _____ | | | | |
|---|---|---|---|---|
| Component Skills | | | | |
| Assessment | | | | |
| Grade Level: | | | | |
| | | | | |
| | | | | |
| | | | | |
| | | | | |
| | | | | |

*Note: Write in the grade levels that you examine in the first column.*

| Is there a common priority skill need for many or most students across grade levels? If so, what is it? |
|---|
| |
| Review available implementation data around instruction, curriculum, and environment. |
| |
| Does your school have standards of practice in instruction, curriculum, and environment? Are they implemented consistently? Where do they need to be improved or supplemented to improve student success? |
| |

## Step 3: Plan Identification and Implementation

7. Develop a schoolwide plan for addressing the priority skill need. Ensure your plan adequately addresses changes to the instruction, curriculum, and environment in addition to supporting the capacity of staff to implement the plan. See the following Schoolwide Plan worksheet to help guide this process.

8. Determine how you will monitor your grade level plan.

9. Set a goal for the percentage of students you expect to see at low risk next year as a result of your plan.

### Schoolwide Plan

| Priority Skills: | | |
|---|---|---|
| **Do you have disproportionate outcomes by student group?** | | |
| If **No** ➡ Develop a plan to improve general instruction, curriculum, and environmental supports across your school. | | |
| If **Yes** ➡ Which student groups will you address in this plan? | | |
| | | |
| **What changes will you make to the instruction?** | **Who is responsible?** | **When will it occur?** |
| | | |

| What changes will you make to the curriculum? | Who is responsible? | When will it occur? |
|---|---|---|
| | | |

| What changes will you make to the environment? | Who is responsible? | When will it occur? |
|---|---|---|
| | | |

| What will school leadership do to improve the infrastructure and capacity of staff to implement the plan? | Who is responsible? | When will it occur? |
|---|---|---|
| | | |

**Step 4: Plan Evaluation**

10. Evaluate your Tier 1 schoolwide plan using the questions in the following table.

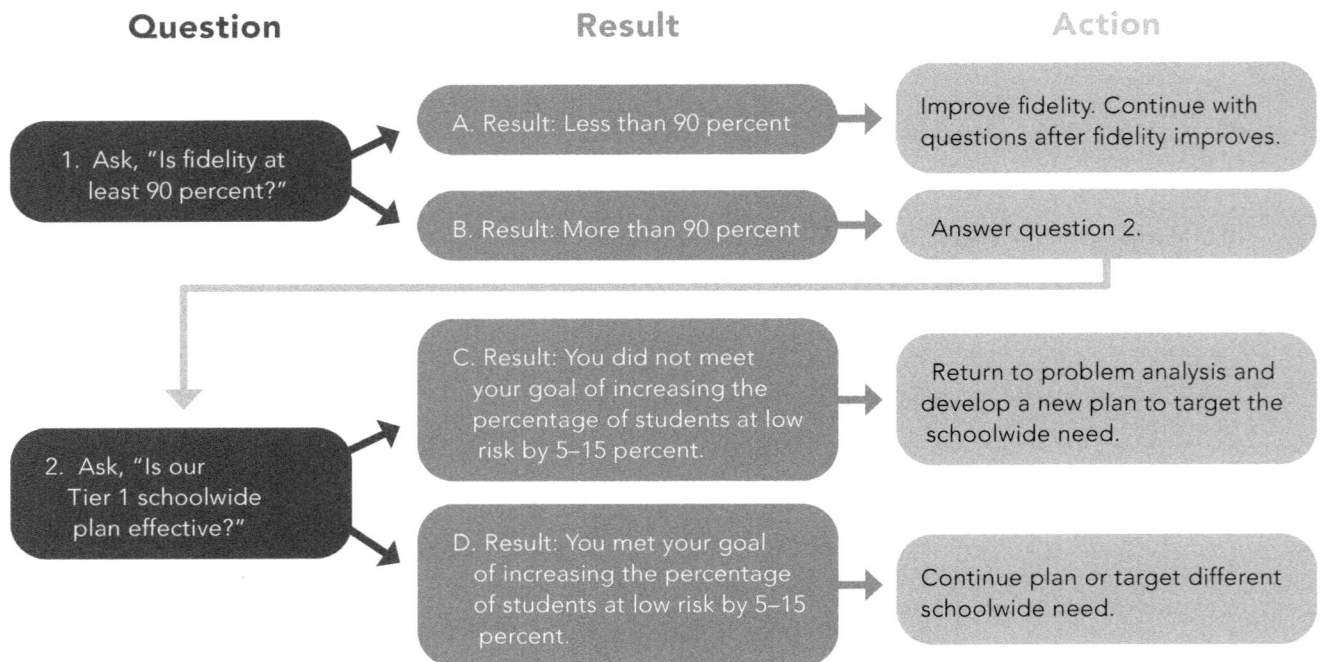

| Question | Result | Action |
|---|---|---|
| 1. Ask, "Is fidelity at least 90 percent?" | A. Result: Less than 90 percent | Improve fidelity. Continue with questions after fidelity improves. |
| | B. Result: More than 90 percent | Answer question 2. |
| 2. Ask, "Is our Tier 1 schoolwide plan effective?" | C. Result: You did not meet your goal of increasing the percentage of students at low risk by 5–15 percent. | Return to problem analysis and develop a new plan to target the schoolwide need. |
| | D. Result: You met your goal of increasing the percentage of students at low risk by 5–15 percent. | Continue plan or target different schoolwide need. |

**Untangling Data-Based Decision Making** © 2024 Marzano Resources • MarzanoResources.com
Visit **MarzanoResources.com/reproducibles** to download this free reproducible.

# Sample Tier 1 Reading Standards of Practice

| General Elementary Structured Literacy Agreements | | |
| --- | --- | --- |
| **Time** | **Materials** | **Instruction** |
| Ninety minutes: includes whole- and small-group instruction (See page 85 for descriptions of whole- and small-group agreements.) | • District-approved core program, including supplements<br><br>• Use teacher's guide as designed or adapted by district<br><br>• Grade-level student materials, which all students can access and use | • Explicit and systematic instruction<br><br>• Active engagement<br><br>• Instructional routines<br><br>• Differentiated instruction<br><br>• Scaffolded instruction<br><br>• Ample practice opportunities with corrective feedback |

| Whole-Group Instruction<br>Time: Sixty minutes daily | | |
|---|---|---|
| **Component** | **Materials** | **Instruction** |
| Foundational Skills<br>(Phonemic Awareness, Phonics, and Fluency) | • Sound-spelling cards posted (grades K–2 and 3, per program, grades 4 and 5, as available)<br>• Decodables (K–2 and 3, per program)<br>• Fluency passages | • Word work (including manipulatives and whiteboards)<br>• Sound spelling cards taught (grades K–2 and 3, per program, grades 4 and 5, as available)<br>• Decoding and encoding routines<br>• Fluency routines |
| Oral Language | • Daily oral language<br>• Common texts | • Strategic partners in structured discussions<br>• Sentence frames using academic language and story vocabulary |
| Vocabulary | • Vocabulary cards (posted) | • Explicit vocabulary routine<br>  • Including reading, writing, and speaking<br>  • Precision partners<br>• Vocabulary strategies<br>• Independent vocabulary learning strategies |
| Grammar | • Core program grammar materials | • Brief, explicit, and systematic<br>• Reviewed as part of sentence-level comprehension of text |
| Reading Comprehension | • Main selection<br>• Paired selection<br>• Supplemental texts as indicated by district team | • Read aloud<br>• Precision partners<br>• Teach students to apply comprehension skills and strategies<br>• Sentence-level comprehension<br>• Writing in response to reading |

| Small Group Instruction on Targeted Skills | | |
|---|---|---|
| • Teacher led<br>• Matched to instructional need based on district agreed-on diagnostic reading data<br>• Flexible grouping | | |
| **Time** | **Materials** | **Instruction** |
| • Thirty to forty-five minutes daily<br>  • Kindergarten: ten to fifteen minutes per group<br>  • Grades 1–5: fifteen to twenty minutes per group<br>• Teacher does not see every student on all five days; frequency based on intensity of need | • Core program materials<br>  • Decodables<br>  • Leveled readers (used to target specific reading skills)<br>  • Fluency passages<br>  • Word work<br>  • Sound spelling cards<br>  • Vocabulary cards<br>• Approved supplemental programs (for example, Enhanced Core Reading Instruction [ECRI], Heggerty, or Florida Center for Reading Research [FCRR] materials)<br>• Manipulatives<br>• Whiteboards | • Intensity of explicit and systematic instruction depends on group needs<br>• Explicit modeling of skills<br>• Frequent student opportunities to respond<br>• Frequent affirmative and corrective feedback |

*Source: © Oregon Response to Instruction and Intervention. (n.d.c). Sample elementary reading standards of practice. Accessed at https://docs.google.com/document/d/13yax3gmmafiP6uif6F8GPecERI9qS7HtZ9Q3y5Ey6SM/edit?usp=share_link on July 13, 2023. Adapted with permission.*

# CHAPTER 4

# Data-Based Decision Making at Tier 1

In the previous chapter, we discussed how school leadership teams can use the problem-solving process to examine the effectiveness of schoolwide Tier 1 supports. In this chapter, we shift our focus to address the role of teacher-driven grade-level teams in the Tier 1 problem-solving process. We discuss how to use data to determine the effectiveness of your Tier 1 support at individual grade levels, which is sometimes referred to as the *core review process*. We present each step of this process, as illustrated in figure 4.1 (page 114), including questions that guide each step and information to accompany teams as they complete the core review process. Then we examine common roadblocks and possible solutions to ensure effective grade-level problem solving at Tier 1. We end the chapter with reproducible worksheets for the problem-solving model (page 142) to help walk teams through the entire process.

## Problem Identification

In step 1, the grade-level team examines gradewide screening data to determine whether Tier 1 support is sufficient for most students at the grade level. Response to intervention experts Amanda M. VanDerHeyden and Matthew K. Burns (2010) indicated that a Tier 1 classwide need exists when student difficulties are the result of potential issues in your system rather than low student capabilities (see also VanDerHeyden & Witt, 2014). As you would in your schoolwide Tier 1 problem-solving process, define a problem with the Tier 1 support at your grade level as the difference between the observed performance (percentage of grade-level students at low risk) and the expected performance (approximately 80 percent of grade-level students at low risk). Tier 1 problem solving at the grade level should occur, at a minimum, following each schoolwide screening. Typically, this means meeting three times each year, in the fall, winter, and spring. Meetings should take approximately sixty to ninety minutes, depending on your team's familiarity with the

| Step | Action | Key Questions | Tasks |
|------|--------|---------------|-------|
| 1 | Problem Identification | • Are at least 80 percent of students at your grade level successful with core supports alone? | • Review and analyze current and previous screening data.<br>• Review student progress between screening periods.<br>• Disaggregate screening data to determine equitable impact of core supports. |
| 2 | Problem Analysis | • What is the most common instructional need within the grade level? | • Identify priority skills needed by many or most students |
| 3 | Plan Identification and Implementation | What adjustments to grade-level core support (such as instruction, curriculum, or environment) can we make to target identified common instructional needs? | • Develop gradewide plan for addressing priority skill need.<br>• Determine how you will support and monitor your plan.<br>• Select a goal for next screening. |
| 4 | Plan Evaluation | Did the adjustments improve the health of our grade-level core? | At next screening:<br>• Ask, "Is fidelity at least 90 percent?"<br>• Ask, "Is our Tier 1 grade level plan effective?" |

**Figure 4.1: Key questions for use of the problem-solving model at Tier 1.**

problem-solving process. To better understand the impact of your grade-level Tier 1 supports, you should review and analyze current and previous screening data, review student progress between screening periods, and disaggregate screening data to determine equitable impact of core supports.

### Review and Analyze Current and Previous Screening Data

Start the grade-level Tier 1 problem-solving process by examining your current screening data to determine what percentage of students at your grade level are at low risk. During this first step, teachers may have an inclination to examine the screening data for their own individual classrooms. While this makes intuitive sense, we recommend aggregating screening data across the entire grade level, rather than looking at individual class data. Teachers should most certainly examine their own classroom data, but the core review meeting is focused on collaboration across the grade-level team. These meetings bring teachers and support staff together to develop a common gradewide plan and not a set of separate individual classroom plans. Class-level reports should be available for teachers to examine at another time.

Once you have identified the percentage of grade-level students who are at low risk using your composite score or overall risk-indicator score, you will want to look at previous data to determine whether your Tier 1 supports are effective at increasing the percentage of students who are at low risk. For example, in the winter, you can compare current data to fall data. In the spring, you can look at how students have progressed from fall to winter to spring. These comparisons can help determine how effective your grade-level Tier 1 supports are and help guide next steps. As an example, look at the second-grade data from two schools in figure 4.2.

| Percentage of Second Graders at Low Risk at School A | | Percentage of Second Graders at Low Risk at School B | |
|---|---|---|---|
| Fall | Winter | Fall | Winter |
| 35 | 55 | 53 | 55 |

Figure 4.2: Second-grade screening data from two schools.

Both of these schools have the same percentage of second-grade students who are identified at low risk for reading difficulties in the winter (55 percent). As a result, both schools appear to need some significant improvement in their Tier 1 supports at second grade. This may include substantial changes to their current instructional practices. However, when comparing their progress from winter to fall, two different stories emerge. At school A, there was significant improvement in the percentage of second-grade students who were at low risk in the fall (35 percent) as compared to the winter (55 percent). This significant progress would be a cause for celebration and may not necessarily call for a wholesale change in instructional practices. Instead, school A may want to focus its energy on building on their current practices to accelerate growth for more students. Alternatively, at school B, there is relatively little growth from fall (53 percent) to winter (55 percent). This sparks concern that current practices are ineffective or insufficient. This school may want to consider making more significant changes to Tier 1 supports at second grade.

### Review Student Progress Between Screening Periods

In addition to examining the overall percentage of students who are at low risk, you can also explore the effectiveness of core supports by examining students' progress from one screening period to the next. One way to do this is to examine the movement of students between risk categories. In an effective MTSS, you should observe the following two patterns when examining changes in student screening scores across the year.

1. Students who begin the year at low risk in the fall should remain low risk throughout the year.

2. Students who begin the year at some risk or high risk should reduce their level of risk throughout the year.

While the second point refers more to the effectiveness of your Tier 2 and Tier 3 intervention systems, the first point is a key indicator of the health of your Tier 1 systems. If your Tier 1 core supports are effective, approximately 95 percent or more of your students who start the year at low risk should remain at low risk throughout the year (Michigan MTSS Technical Assistance Center, 2021). To stay at low risk, students need to continue to grow their skills to meet the increasing benchmarks throughout the year. If less than 95 percent of students who begin the year at low risk remain at low risk throughout the year, this is another indication of an unhealthy core that requires improvement. The example data in figure 4.3 outline what this might look like.

| Movement From Fall to Winter | | | |
|---|---|---|---|
| Number of students who were low risk in the fall | Of the students who were low risk in fall, how many were . . . | | Percentage |
| 115 | Low risk in winter? | 96 | 83 |
| | Some risk in winter? | 17 | 15 |
| | High risk in winter? | 2 | 2 |

**Figure 4.3: Example data on movement from fall to winter.**

In the fall, this particular grade level had 115 students who were identified as low risk on the screener. When examining how those same 115 students performed on the winter screener, we see that ninety-six of them were still at low risk, seventeen were at some risk, and two were now at high risk. This results in 83 percent of students who started the year at low risk still being at low risk in the winter. These results indicate that core supports are not sufficient because less than 95 percent of students who started at low risk in the fall remained at low risk in the winter. What's most concerning is that two students who started the year at low risk are now at the highest level of risk in the winter. This grade-level team needs to develop a plan to improve Tier 1 core instruction to ensure more students make the appropriate growth across the year.

### Disaggregate Screening Data to Determine Equitable Impact of Core Supports

Examining the overall screening data can give you a general picture of how well the Tier 1 core instruction is working for all students. But this doesn't necessarily give you the full picture and can sometimes be misleading. Disaggregating screening data at the grade level can help identify more specifically who the Tier 1 grade-level instruction is working for and who it is not. This can help identify inequities across your grade level. In chapter 3 (page 73), we discuss the process of disaggregating data at the schoolwide level to identify patterns across your school. Depending on the size of your grade levels, it may be more appropriate to disaggregate at the school level versus the grade level.

## Problem Analysis

In step 2, take a deeper look at screening data to answer the question, Why are less than 80 percent of students at our grade level successful with core supports alone? To do this, examine the common instructional needs of your students to determine the priority skills that many or most students at the grade level lack. By identifying which missing skills are most prevalent among your students, you are building a hypothesis that if you can better develop these skills, your students will be more successful. This allows you to match your gradewide supports to a prevalent instructional need.

Recall that in step 1 (problem identification), your team looked at an overall risk indicator score (for example, a composite score) to determine the percentage of students who are on track or off track. During problem analysis, a deeper dive into the data can help you better understand which particular skills are strengths and which missing skills are areas of need for many or most students at the grade level. In chapter 3 (page 73), we discuss the process of identifying a common area of need using your screening data. This involves examining subskills, or areas of focus within a content area, to determine a priority skill on which to focus. The particular subskills that you examine will be determined by the screener that you use. Figure 4.4 (page 118) describes some possible areas that your screener might assess.

### What Other Data Can I Use?

In addition to gradewide screening data, you may choose to use other data sources to help identify a priority skill need at step 2 (problem analysis). For example, you could use common formative assessments, mastery tests, unit tests, or other in-curriculum assessments. When using these additional assessments, first verify that all teachers are administering them to all students at the grade level and scoring in a consistent way. This allows you to compare student scores across the grade level. You will also need commonly agreed-on criteria for success on any additional assessments used. For example, if you choose to use a gradewide vocabulary assessment, you might determine that students who score 90 percent or above are proficient. This allows you to identify what percentage of students need additional support on the skills measured by your additional assessments. This can help you further target a priority skill need in addition to your screening data.

Please note that not all screeners will assess all these relevant subskills. You will need to determine whether your screener gives you the relevant data to determine a priority skill focus for Tier 1 problem solving and supplement when needed. As an example of how to determine a priority skill to focus on, consider the first-grade reading screening data in figure 4.5 (page 118).

In this example, the first-grade team is examining its winter Acadience Reading screening data. During this screening period, students receive a combination of

| Content Area | Skills or Subskills | |
|---|---|---|
| Reading | Phonemic awareness<br>Phonics<br>Fluency | Vocabulary<br>Comprehension |
| Mathematics | Number sense<br>Mathematics facts<br>Computation (addition, subtraction, multiplication, and division) | Concepts (time, money, and graphs)<br>Problem solving |
| Writing | Spelling<br>Writing mechanics and structure | Writing fluency |
| Behavior | Social<br>Academic<br>Emotional<br>Internalizing | Externalizing<br>Adaptive skills<br>Executive functioning skills |

**Figure 4.4: Possible subskills assessed by your screener.**

| Reading Skill | Phonemic Awareness | Phonics | | | Fluency | Vocabulary and Oral Language | Comprehension |
|---|---|---|---|---|---|---|---|
| Acadience Screening Subtest | Phoneme Segmentation Fluency | Nonsense Word Fluency–Correct Letter Sounds | Nonsense Word Fluency–Whole Words Read | Oral Reading Fluency–Accuracy | Oral Reading Fluency–Words Correct | Not applicable | Maze (multiple-choice Cloze reading assessment) |
| Percentage of Students Proficient | Not applicable | 78 | 60 | 54 | 56 | Not applicable | Not applicable |

**Figure 4.5: Example data for identifying the priority skill for many or most students in winter of first grade.**

measures that primarily assess phonics and oral reading fluency. When examining these data, team members start with the most foundational skills and work their way up the hierarchy to determine where they may target some additional Tier 1 instructional support. These data indicate that most of their students (78 percent) have a firm grasp on their letter sounds, as measured by Nonsense Word Fluency–Correct Letter Sounds. They then decide that their Tier 1 support in letter-sound identification is sufficient and will continue to implement their existing Tier 1 instruction in this area. Students who still have a need in this area will receive Tier 2 or Tier 3 interventions *in addition to Tier 1 support*. Looking further up the hierarchy of skills, it appears that only 60 percent of students are proficient in blending letter sounds together to make words, as measured by Nonsense Word Fluency–Whole Words Read. Looking even further, we also notice that only 54 percent of students are reading accurately (Oral Reading Fluency–Accuracy) and 56 percent of students are reading fluently (Oral Reading Fluency–Words Correct) when reading connected text. These data indicate that, rather than the team focusing its efforts on increasing fluency, many or most of the students may be having difficulty with oral reading fluency due to their insufficient decoding skills. Attempts to increase reading fluency without adequately addressing missing decoding skills would most likely result in students reading quickly with a large number of errors. This type of speed reading is not ideal and typically results in severely compromised reading comprehension. As a result of these screening data, the first-grade team creates a Tier 1 plan targeting some additional support in phonics.

As you can see in this example, you will want to start by examining the most foundational skills and work your way up until you find a skill that seems to be creating a bottleneck for success for many or most students. Recall that in step 1, we used 80 percent as a guideline for the percentage of students who should be at low risk in a healthy system. When examining your subtest or component area data, you can use this same guideline to determine which skills to focus on. Figure 4.6 provides additional guidance to help you determine which areas to focus on.

| Percentage of Students Proficient | Guidelines for Tier 1 Planning |
| --- | --- |
| More than 80 percent | • Tier 1 support in this area is sufficient for most students.<br>　• Consider additional small-group instruction for students who need more support in this area.<br>• Provide additional Tier 2 and Tier 3 interventions to those students who need more support in this area. |
| 60–80 percent | • Tier 1 support in this area should be enhanced.<br>　• Consider modifications to small- and whole-group instruction.<br>• Provide additional Tier 2 and Tier 3 interventions to the 20 percent of students with the highest level of need. |
| Less than 60 percent | • Tier 1 support in this area is insufficient.<br>　• Focus on improving whole-group instruction in this area.<br>　• Provide additional small-group instruction to students who need it.<br>• Provide additional Tier 2 and Tier 3 interventions to the 20 percent of students with the highest level of need. |

**Figure 4.6: Guidance for analyzing screening subtest data.**

Use a template like the one in figure 4.7 to identify the subskills assessed by your screener and identify the particular priority skill to focus on for additional Tier 1 support planning.

---

**Directions:** Select the skill area you are problem solving for, then list the component skills that make up that skill area. For example, in reading, you would list the five components of reading: (1) phonemic awareness, (2) phonics, (3) fluency, (4) vocabulary, and (5) reading comprehension. Then list the specific screening subtests that measure each skill and the percentage of students who were above the benchmark on the subtest.

**Grade Level:** _Second grade_

**Skill Area (select one):**

☑ Reading     ☐ Mathematics     ☐ Behavior     ☐ Social-Emotional Learning     ☐ Other: _____

| Component Skills | Phonemic awareness | Phonics | Fluency | Vocabulary | Reading comprehension |
|---|---|---|---|---|---|
| Assessment | n/a | Passage Reading Fluency—Accuracy | Passage Reading Fluency—Words Correct | n/a | Maze |
| Percentage Above Benchmark | | 43 percent | 37 percent | | 40 percent |

What is the priority skill need for many or most students?

_Phonics—Accurate decoding_

---

**Figure 4.7: Priority skill hierarchy template.**

Visit *MarzanoResources.com/reproducibles* for a free reproducible version of this figure.

## Plan Identification and Implementation

In step 3, after educators have analyzed all the data and identified a common priority skill need for many or most students, they can develop a Tier 1 plan. It's important to note that the creation of a grade-level Tier 1 plan does not supersede the consistent implementation of the school's agreed-on, existing Tier 1 structures. Rather, the Tier 1 plan is a way to *adapt* and *enhance* the core program to meet the needs of the current students. For example, if you find many or most of your students lack phonemic awareness skills, you don't simply stop teaching the other parts of your reading curriculum to teach ninety minutes of phonemic awareness. Rather, you should find ways to strengthen your phonemic awareness instruction as part of your comprehensive core program. This might include the following.

- Being more explicit in your teaching of phonemic awareness during whole-group instruction

- Spending some additional time (five to ten minutes) on phonemic awareness in whole-group instruction

- Adding or lengthening phonemic awareness activities in small-group instruction for those students who need it

- Adding brief phonemic awareness practices during other times of the day (for example, morning meeting, transition times, and other content-area classes where appropriate)

- Integrating phonemic awareness instruction and practice during other parts of the reading block (for example, decoding and encoding)

In creating this Tier 1 plan, it's important to recognize that students need to gain a deep reservoir of broad knowledge and weave together a variety of skills to be successful. Literacy is much more than phonics. Mathematics is much more than computation. Prosocial behavior is much more than being respectful. Rather than using your Tier 1 plan to overfocus on isolated skills, your plan should provide students with more modeling and practice on needed skills while supporting them in how to integrate those skills into a much broader set of skills and knowledge. As a useful analogy, think about the importance of a healthy, well-balanced diet containing multiple food groups. If your doctor tells you that your diet needs to incorporate more fruits and vegetables, you don't simply replace other healthy foods with fruits and vegetables. Instead, you add more fruits and vegetables into your diet or select more healthy fruits and vegetables to eat while still eating a wide variety of healthy foods from the other food groups. In fact, you might find that although eating more fruits and veggies is a priority, there are other areas of your diet that require improvement as well.

In the following sections, we'll discuss how to develop a gradewide plan for addressing the priority skill need, determine how you will support and monitor your plan, and select a goal for the next screening.

### *Develop a Gradewide Plan for Addressing Priority Skill Need*

Your gradewide plan should consider multiple ways to address priority skills with a focus on changing the alterable variables that you can control. This involves examining and addressing the instructional, curricular, and environmental needs of your students. The questions in figure 4.8 (page 122) can be helpful in guiding these conversations and developing a plan.

| Instruction | • What common instructional routine or strategy can you use to target the priority skill?<br>• What common active engagement strategy can you use to support instruction in the priority skill? |
|---|---|
| Curriculum | • What core materials can you use to target the priority skill?<br>• What supplemental materials might you need? |
| Environment | • What common behavior or classroom management strategy will you use to support instruction of the priority skill? |

**Figure 4.8: Questions to consider during plan development.**

As you develop your plan by answering these questions, it can often be helpful to use checklists or inventories of evidence-based strategies and routines to help guide decision making. These tools can help teams select from strategies that have been proven effective and make it easier to develop plans that have a higher likelihood of success. They can also help teachers identify strategies that they may not have otherwise considered. Recall the availability heuristic, in which we tend to make choices based on what we *know* best, instead of what will *work* best. Figure 4.9 shows a strategy and routine checklist for use during Tier 1 problem solving. When using a tool like this to help develop your plan, try to choose one or two strategies or routines from each domain (instruction, curriculum, and environment) for your grade-level team to implement. These strategies or routines should be well matched to the particular priority skills you will be focusing on. For example, using decodable books would be a good tool for improving phonics skills but would be less useful when focusing on reading comprehension. It may also help to use a checklist like the examples in figures 4.9, 4.10 (page 124), and 4.11 (page 124) specific to the content area that is the focus of your problem solving (for example, reading, mathematics, behavior, or social-emotional support).

Here are a few additional tips to help you structure the plan development step of the Tier 1 problem-solving process.

- **Make sure it's a match:** Ensure the strategies or routines that your teams select are a good fit to target the identified priority skills. For example, a partner reading routine would be an effective strategy to provide additional oral reading fluency support. Alternatively, if the data indicate that most of your students have a more basic need for more explicit instruction in phonemic awareness, a partner reading routine would be a less desirable primary instructional strategy.

- **Clarify why your plan should work:** The strategies or routines you choose, as well as the priority skills to target, should be congruent with what you know about how students learn. Having your team discuss *why* the chosen strategy should work can help to ensure your plan is aligned

| Instruction |
| --- |
| What common instructional routine or strategy will you use to target the priority skill?<br><br><br>What common active engagement strategy will you use to support instruction in the priority skill? |

☐ Build and prime background knowledge.

☐ Increase modeling of skills.

☐ Simplify teacher language.

    ☐ Use visuals to help explain concepts.

    ☐ Use teacher think-alouds with concise, clear language.

☐ Increase student opportunities to respond through the use of:

    ☐ Opportunities to respond after each step of instruction

    ☐ Distributed practice over time

    ☐ Retrieval practice

    ☐ Choral responses

    ☐ Partner responses (for example, think-pair-share)

    ☐ Team responses

    ☐ Response cards, whiteboards, clickers, hand signals, and so on

☐ Visuals and manipulatives

☐ Scaffold student responses through the use of:

    ☐ Sentence frames

    ☐ Graphic organizers

☐ Other scaffolds (describe):

☐ Increase feedback through the use of:

    ☐ Corrective feedback immediately following student errors

    ☐ Frequent affirmative feedback when students are correct

**Figure 4.9: Possible instructional evidence-based strategies and routines to incorporate into Tier 1 gradewide plans.**

*Visit **MarzanoResources.com/reproducibles** for a free reproducible version of this figure.*

| Curriculum |
| --- |
| What core materials can you use to target the priority skill?<br><br>What supplemental materials might you need? |
| ☐ Decodable books<br>☐ Sound-spelling cards<br>☐ Content-rich texts<br>☐ Culturally relevant texts<br>☐ Manipulatives<br>☐ Scripted lesson plans<br>☐ Other materials (describe): _____ |

**Figure 4.10: Possible curriculum evidence-based strategies and routines to incorporate into Tier 1 gradewide plans.**

*Visit **MarzanoResources.com/reproducibles** for a free reproducible version of this figure.*

| Environment |
| --- |
| What common behavior and classroom management strategy will you use to support instruction of the priority skill? |
| ☐ Teach or reteach behavior expectations.<br>☐ Teach or reteach instructional routines.<br>☐ Use active supervision.<br>☐ Provide 5:1 ratio of positive to corrective feedback.<br>☐ Build or enhance positive relationships among students and with students.<br>☐ Reinforce positive behavior (for example, praise, contingent reinforcers, and so on).<br>☐ Consistently use a graduated range of consequences for negative behavior.<br>☐ Limit or reduce transition times.<br>    ☐ Develop and teach routines for transitions.<br>    ☐ Reinforce efficient transitions.<br>☐ Other management strategies (describe): _____ |

**Figure 4.11: Possible environmental evidence-based strategies and routines to incorporate into Tier 1 gradewide plans.**

*Visit **MarzanoResources.com/reproducibles** for a free reproducible version of this figure.*

with scientific evidence and has a high likelihood of success. For example, if your data indicate that your students need more support in decoding multisyllabic words, you would want a routine that makes sense given what we know about how the brain learns to read. This might include teaching students a routine for identifying the different parts of the words, paying attention to morphology, and putting those different parts together to decode multisyllabic words. Alternatively, having students use flash cards to simply memorize multisyllabic words would not be in line with the science of reading.

- **Sweat the details:** While teachers have a wide repertoire of teaching skills, it's important to clearly define and describe what the chosen common strategies will look like in the classroom. There are several different ways to implement a given routine and many different logistic details that help make a strategy or routine more straightforward. Predetermining details such as what the routine looks like, when it will be implemented, and what materials are needed to implement it will help take the burden off teachers figuring that out for themselves. Sharing videos of the routine or implementation checklists of the steps in the routine can help teachers and ensure clarity for those on your team.

- **Choose common routines implemented by all:** It is important that all classrooms in the grade level implement the routines and strategies the team selects consistently. Consistent instructional routines have several benefits. For students, a consistent routine allows them to focus their attention on the content of learning and not the way in which they will learn. They won't have to learn significantly different routines and strategies in each classroom they encounter, allowing their cognitive energy to focus on the content. Common routines also benefit the teachers. Once they have taught the routines, teachers can simply reinforce them, saving instructional time. Teachers can spend more time responding to the students' needs in the classroom rather than using the time continually planning and teaching new routines and strategies. It also allows teaching teams to learn and grow together as they work on implementing and refining new strategies. This *does not* mean that each and every teacher needs to teach in exactly the same way, removing all autonomy, professional judgment, and uniqueness in teaching styles. Rather, your team agrees to implement some common strategies, targeted at a common instructional need, which creates consistency for students and teachers.

### Determine How You Will Support and Monitor Your Plan

In addition to creating common agreements around instruction, curriculum, and environment, your plan should also include a support plan and a monitoring component. When making your support and monitoring plan, consider these points.

- **Display common agreements publicly:** Posting your common agreements in a prominent location in the school (for example, staff room or main office) helps demonstrate that they are a priority. An important and necessary feature of Tier 1 problem solving is the alignment of practices across grade-level teachers and staff. Having a public display of all the grade-level plans often reveals commonalities across grade levels (for example, multiple grade levels focused on improved phonics instruction using explicit instructional strategies) and encourages cross-grade collaboration. Figure 4.12 shows an example of what this might look like.

- **Provide ongoing coaching to examine and support classroom implementation:** Public practice is a key component of an effective instructional system. If there is no follow-up on your plan, the implicit message is that it is not important. Ongoing coaching and support help ensure that teachers fully understand the plan and have the training and skills to implement it well. Even despite best intentions, implementation of a new plan is often uneven at first. Teachers will need opportunities to implement, receive feedback, and use that feedback to improve. Providing a structure for teachers to receive that feedback can help ensure the effective implementation of your plans.

- **Conduct regular interim meetings (for example, collaborative team meetings in a PLC) to revisit and refine the plan:** While you will use the screening data to drive the creation of the Tier 1 plan, fall, winter, and spring screening times should not be the only times that teams meet to develop and review Tier 1 plans. Weekly or monthly meetings can help teams revisit their plan, discuss any implementation issues they are experiencing, and determine if the plan needs any modifications prior to the next screening time. Teams can also examine any ongoing student data collected as part of the plan at these interim meetings.

- **Ensure teacher voice is at the forefront of plan creation:** While specialists and administrators should provide coaching and support in the development of the Tier 1 plan, teacher voice should be at the forefront of selecting which common practices they will implement. Specialists can help ensure that the chosen strategies or routines are evidence based and a good match for supporting the identified priority skill. Administrators can ensure that teachers have the resources they need to implement the plan. But ultimately, it is the teachers who will implement it. Ensuring teachers are the primary drivers of creating the plan increases ownership and the likelihood that they will implement the plan consistently and with high quality.

In addition to providing implementation support, the grade-level team should develop a monitoring component to ensure the plan is implemented as intended

| Grade | Screening Data | | | Action Plan | | | | |
| | Percentage of Students Proficient | | | Curriculum | Instruction | Environment | Professional Development Needs |
| | Previous | Current | Goal | Priority Skill and Focus Area | Common Instructional Strategy | Common Engagement or Behavior Strategy | |
| K | 50 | 67 | 80 | Phonemic awareness—Blending | Increase teacher modeling of blending using a consistent hand signal | Teach positive behavior and use classwide behavior reinforcement chart | Coaching on classroom management |
| 1 | 60 | 62 | 75 | Phonics—Simple consonant-vowel-consonant words | Provide additional opportunities to respond using decodable texts | Limit transitions to increase instructional time | Additional training and modeling from coaches on explicit phonics routines from core curriculum, including a routine for using decodables |
| 2 | 52 | 60 | 72 | Phonics—Vowel teams and r-controlled vowels | Increase opportunities to respond using choral and partner responses | 5:1 positive to corrective feedback | Coaching on classroom management and providing frequent opportunities to respond |

**Figure 4.12: Public display of data template.**

continued ▼

| Grade | Screening Data — Percentage of Students Proficient | | Action Plan | | | |
| | Previous | Current | Goal | Curriculum — Priority Skill and Focus Area | Instruction — Common Instructional Strategy | Environment — Common Engagement or Behavior Strategy | Professional Development Needs |
|---|---|---|---|---|---|---|---|
| 3 | 62 percent | 71 | 80 | Fluency | Use partner reading routine | Explicitly teach and reinforce partner routine, including sentence stems for providing feedback to partners | None requested |
| 4 | 36 | 52 | 65 | Fluency | Use partner reading routine | Carefully assign partners to ensure engagement and on-task behavior | Seeing the partner reading routine as implemented by third-grade teachers |
| 5 | 49 | 51 | 60 | Fluency | Partner reading routine using social studies and science passages | Increase inclusivity of classroom by structuring activity for students to share parts of their home culture | Training on before, during, and after reading strategies to ensure comprehension |

*Visit MarzanoResources.com/reproducibles for a free reproducible version of this figure.*

(for example, with fidelity). Core review plans have multiple components implemented across multiple classrooms by multiple educators. Despite your best-laid plans, initial implementation of any plan is often rocky and in need of ongoing refinement. By monitoring your implementation, you can work out the kinks and improve implementation to improve student success. One way to monitor implementation is with an implementation checklist that lists the essential components of the plan. A coach, fellow grade-level teacher, or administrator could use the checklist during an observation to determine what areas of the plan are going well and what areas need refinement. Teachers can also use checklists to self-report their implementation of the plan, providing teachers with a consistent reminder of all the components of the plan. See an example implementation checklist for a Tier 1 plan in figure 4.13.

Grade Level: _____    Observers: _____
Priority Skill:

**Directions:** Observe each classroom and determine if the agreement was:
0 (Not implemented)   1 (Partially implemented)   2 (Fully implemented)

| | Common Agreements | Classrooms | | | | Total |
| --- | --- | --- | --- | --- | --- | --- |
| | | A | B | C | D | |
| Our common instructional strategy was: | | 0  1  2 | 0  1  2 | 0  1  2 | 0  1  2 | __/8 |
| Our common engagement strategy was: | | 0  1  2 | 0  1  2 | 0  1  2 | 0  1  2 | __/8 |
| Our common curriculum materials used were: | | 0  1  2 | 0  1  2 | 0  1  2 | 0  1  2 | __/8 |
| Our common environmental support was: | | 0  1  2 | 0  1  2 | 0  1  2 | 0  1  2 | __/8 |
| **Total:** | | __/8 | __/8 | __/8 | __/8 | __/32 |
| General notes: | | | | | | |

**Figure 4.13: Example of an implementation checklist for Tier 1 plan.**

*Visit **MarzanoResources.com/reproducibles** for a free reproducible version of this figure.*

### *Select a Goal for Next Screening*

After developing your plan, select a goal that clearly outlines the percentage of students you expect to see at low risk at the next screening period. There are no hard rules on how much progress you can expect to see in your grade level, as several contextual factors will impact student growth from one screening period to the next. In reading, for example, observations of screening measures often indicate more growth in the earlier grade levels (K–2) as compared to intermediate grade levels (3–5) and secondary settings. In general, more growth is possible when starting from a lower level of initial student success (for example, 20 percent of students identified as on track) compared to a higher level of initial student success (70 percent of students identified as on track). As a general guideline, teams should set goals that aim to increase the percentage of students meeting the benchmark by 5–30 percent from one screening period to the next (Burns et al., 2005; Greenwood et al., 2008; Jimerson et al., 2007).

Setting a goal can sometimes be a difficult conversation. Teams should do their best to set a goal that is achievable but that will take considerable effort to achieve. With limited time for Tier 1 problem solving, teams should not spend more than a few minutes determining an appropriate goal. Most of your time should be spent on analyzing data and developing a plan.

We also recommend that these goals are not a part of your teacher evaluation process or included in any high-stakes decision making, such as decisions about teacher retention. Screening measures are not high-stakes assessments. They are intended to generally inform and guide instruction. Linking your core review goals to high-stakes decisions can lead to undesirable outcomes such as less ambitious goals, artificial inflation of student screening scores, and an overall decrease in teacher buy-in to the Tier 1 problem-solving process. For these reasons, we highly discourage linking this process to teacher evaluation.

Use the template in figure 4.14 to capture your plan information. The reproducible "Grade-Level Tier 1 Worksheets for Problem-Solving Model" on page 142 also includes this template.

## Plan Evaluation

At step 4, come back together after collecting the next round of screening data and evaluate how well the core review plan worked. This process involves determining how well the plan was implemented (that is, fidelity) and what the impact of the plan was on student growth at the grade level (that is, outcomes). Figure 4.15 (page 132) provides two questions for teams to ask to guide this process of evaluating their plan. You will first want to check the fidelity of your plan to determine how well it was implemented. Based on the results, your team can determine if you need to improve fidelity of your Tier 1 plan or if you can move on to the second question and examine whether the plan increases the percentage of students in your school at low risk, ideally by 5–30 percent.

| Instruction |
| --- |

What common instructional routine and strategy will we use to target the priority skill?

A repeated partner reading routine will include the following steps.

- Pair students. Ensure each student has a chance to read. Partner 1 starts.
- Time partner 1 in a two-minute first read, followed by self-graphing of words correct and errors.
- Time partner 1 in a two-minute second read, followed by self-graphing of words correct and errors.
- Compare first and second read, noting difference in words correct and errors.
- Students earn points toward classwide reward when words correct increase and errors decrease.
- Repeat the process with partner 2.

What common active engagement strategy will we use to support instruction in the priority skill?

Repeated reading routine will be done in partners to enhance engagement. Teachers will teach and model the partner routine for students. Teachers will assign partners to ensure that no pairs of students have disproportionately large differences in fluency skills. Students will receive sentence stems and scripts to help them provide feedback using positive language. Teachers will guide discussions about passage content following the fluency activity to enhance comprehension and discourage speed reading.

| Curriculum |
| --- |

What core materials can we use to target the priority skill?

Teachers will use passages from the science and social studies curriculum for the partner reading activity to enhance knowledge building during the partner reading activities.

What supplemental materials (if any) might we need?

Teachers will use additional passages as needed.

| Environment |
| --- |

What common behavior and management strategy will we use to support instruction of the priority skill?

Teachers will provide verbal reinforcement to students when they use the partner reading routine appropriately. Teachers will move through the classroom listening to the different pairs of students and provide feedback as needed. Teachers will use the points system for increases in words correct and decreases in errors to provide increased motivation.

**Figure 4.14: Gradewide plan template.**

continued ▶

| Goal for Next Screening | | |
|---|---|---|
| | **Current Screening Data** | **Goal for Next Screening** |
| **Percent Low Risk** | 56 percent | 70 percent |
| **Percent Some Risk** | 24 percent | 15 percent |
| **Percent High Risk** | 20 percent | 15 percent |

| Monitoring and Support Plan | Who Is Responsible? | How Often? |
|---|---|---|
| Instructional coach will walk through each classroom to provide support and ensure teachers are able to implement the routine consistently. The coach will use a checklist of the steps of the routine to ensure teachers are implementing all steps. | Instructional coach | Walkthroughs at least monthly |

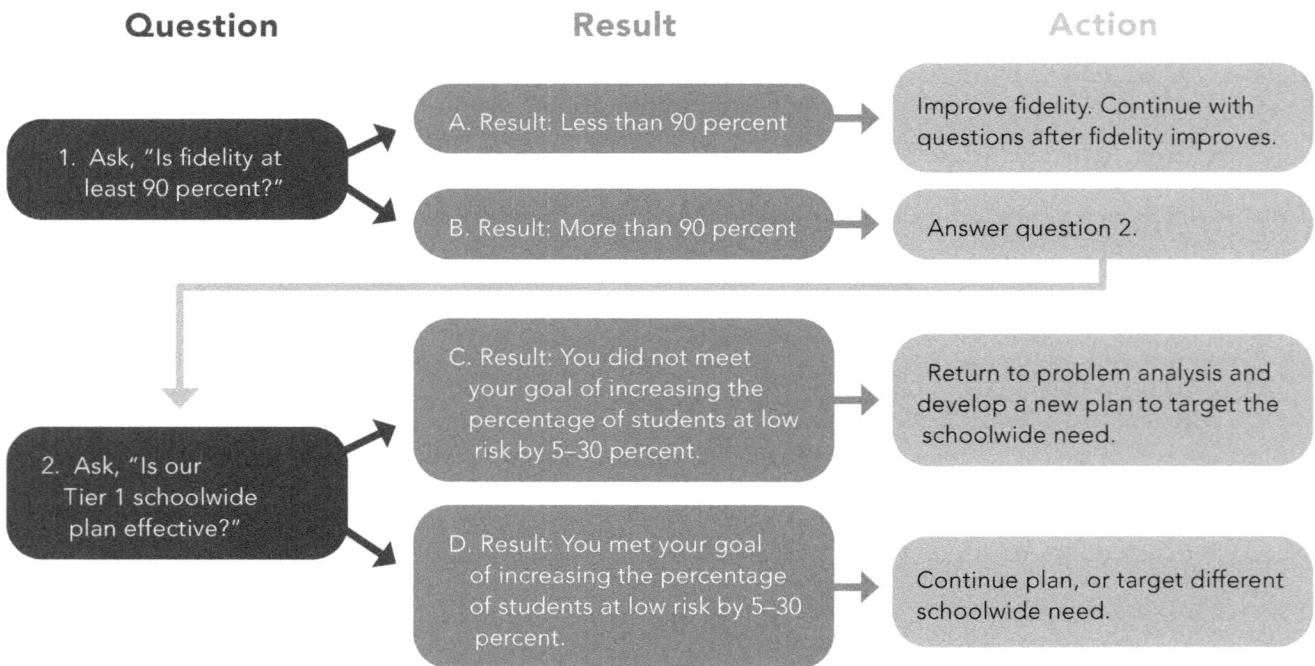

**Question**

**Result**

**Action**

1. Ask, "Is fidelity at least 90 percent?"

A. Result: Less than 90 percent → Improve fidelity. Continue with questions after fidelity improves.

B. Result: More than 90 percent → Answer question 2.

2. Ask, "Is our Tier 1 schoolwide plan effective?"

C. Result: You did not meet your goal of increasing the percentage of students at low risk by 5–30 percent. → Return to problem analysis and develop a new plan to target the schoolwide need.

D. Result: You met your goal of increasing the percentage of students at low risk by 5–30 percent. → Continue plan, or target different schoolwide need.

**Figure 4.15: Plan evaluation for Tier 1 (grade level).**

### 1. Ask, "Is Fidelity at Least 90 Percent?"

To know what impact your plan had on student growth, your team must have a clear understanding of how well the plan was implemented. The first action is examining the overall fidelity of your grade-level plan, with the goal being at least 90 percent implementation. Your plan will have multiple components that all grade-level teachers and possibly support staff are implementing. See figure 4.16 to see what fidelity data from a sample plan might look like.

Grade Level: _Fourth Grade_    Observers: _Mrs. Peterson_

Priority Skill: _Oral reading fluency_

**Directions:** Observe each classroom and determine if the agreement was:
0 (Not implemented)   1 (Partially implemented)   2 (Fully implemented)

| | Common Agreements | Classrooms | | | | Total |
|---|---|---|---|---|---|---|
| | | A | B | C | D | |
| Our common instructional strategy was: | Increased opportunities to respond and corrective feedback with the use of a partner reading activity | 2 | 1 | 2 | 2 | 7/8 |
| Our common engagement strategy was: | Precision partnering routine | 2 | 2 | 2 | 2 | 8/8 |
| Our common curriculum materials used were: | Fluency passages from the weekly reader | 2 | 2 | 2 | 2 | 8/8 |
| Our common environmental support was: | Teaching and reinforcing routine for before, during, and after fluency partner activity | 2 | 1 | 1 | 2 | 6/8 |
| **Total components observed in place:** | | 8/8 | 6/8 | 7/8 | 8/8 | 29/32 |
| **Percentage of components observed** | | 100 | 75 | 88 | 100 | 91 |
| General notes: Most components are in place. We'll need to review the routine for managing the partnering activity with teachers, as two out of four teachers had difficulty teaching that to their students. | | | | | | |

**Figure 4.16: A sample plan for Tier 1.**

*Visit **MarzanoResources.com/reproducibles** for a free reproducible version of this figure.*

It's often helpful to check in on the fidelity of your plan prior to the next screening period. This allows you plenty of time to adjust your plan and improve fidelity if you find that some components are not being implemented consistently. For example, if your plan contains a specific instructional routine, you will be able to provide additional professional learning and coaching opportunities to improve fidelity prior to the next round of collecting and analyzing screening data. One of the primary purposes of collecting fidelity data is to determine whether additional support is needed to improve implementation. If you wait until the end of your plan to check fidelity, you may not have sufficient time to improve fidelity prior to examining student outcome data. You'll have different courses of action depending on whether the result is less than or more than 90 percent.

### A. Result: Less Than 90 Percent

If data indicate that your plan is not being implemented with a high degree of fidelity (A. Result in figure 4.15, page 132), you will want to dig deeper and figure out why fidelity was not higher. Since you will be reviewing fidelity prior to the next screening period, this will give you an opportunity to identify areas for improvement to ensure a higher level of fidelity before you examine the outcome data. The following list outlines questions that your team can ask to help identify possible reasons why fidelity was low. These questions should look familiar, as they are the same questions from chapter 3 (page 73) that your team would have asked if the fidelity of your schoolwide plan was low. Taking action on these questions will help ensure that staff members have what they need to implement the plan with a high degree of fidelity.

- Have you communicated the plan clearly to grade-level staff?
- Have you provided sufficient training to grade-level staff to implement the plan?
- Have you provided ongoing coaching to grade-level staff to implement the plan?
- Have you identified and removed possible barriers to implementation of the plan?
- Have you allocated sufficient resources (time, materials, people, and funding) for implementation?

### B. Result: More Than 90 Percent

If fidelity is high (B. Result in figure 4.15, page 132), then your team can conclude that the Tier 1 plan is being implemented as intended. You will want to continue supporting and implementing your plan until the next screening period. At that time, you'll want to determine whether your plan was effective in improving the percentage of students at low risk.

## 2. Ask, "Is Our Tier 1 Grade-Level Plan Effective?"

To answer this question, you'll want to determine the percentage of students identified at low risk on the next screening period and compare it to the previous screening period. This comparison will tell you if you increased the percentage of students at low risk and by how much. As with the first question, your answer determines your next steps: you either did not meet the goal or you did meet the goal.

### C. Result: You Did Not Meet Your Goal of Increasing the Percentage of Students at Low Risk by 5–30 Percent

A well-implemented plan matched to the grade-level need should result in a significant increase in the percentage of students identified as low risk. If you did not meet your goal, you will want to review your plan to determine how you could improve it. If you have already determined that your plan was implemented with high fidelity (that is, more than 90 percent), then you will want to re-analyze *why* the problem is occurring and develop a new plan. A grade-level plan may be unsuccessful for a variety of reasons. See figure 4.17 for a list of possible reasons that a well-implemented grade-level plan might be unsuccessful and some follow-up questions to better determine why the plan didn't work.

| Possible Reasons Your Plan Was Unsuccessful | Follow-Up Questions to Ask |
|---|---|
| There was difficulty in interpreting the data, and an appropriate priority skill was not identified. | • Does someone on your team have expertise in analyzing the screening data?<br>• Does your screening data have subtests or multiple components that assess different skills? |
| The plan did not match the general instructional need at the grade level. | • Were the strategies and routines chosen as part of the plan evidence based for improving the priority skill?<br>• Did you develop a hypothesis that clearly explained how the plan would address the instructional need? |
| The scale of your plan was not comprehensive enough to address the needs of students across the grade level. | • Was there some growth in the percentage of students at low risk, but not enough to meet your goal?<br>• Did you give adequate resources to your plan?<br>• Were you implementing competing initiatives or instructional plans at the same time? |
| Staff buy-in for the plan was low, resulting in surface implementation. | • Were all grade-level teachers included in developing the plan?<br>• Was there an opportunity for staff to provide feedback on the plan prior to implementation?<br>• Were staff given enough resources and training to be successful?<br>• Do grade-level teachers believe that most students (for example, 80 percent) can be successful given the right Tier 1 supports? |

**Figure 4.17: Why might your plan be unsuccessful?**

While your aim is always to have successful plans resulting in improved student outcomes, you should not fail to take advantage of the learning opportunity that an unsuccessful plan presents. Looking back on *why* your plan did not work can help your team grow as educators. A better understanding of where your plan went wrong will help you be better prepared when developing your next plan in a continuous problem-solving cycle.

### D. Result: You Met Your Goal of Increasing the Percentage of Students at Low Risk by 5–30 Percent

If you are successful and you meet your goal of improving the percentage of students at low risk, you have an important next step: celebrate! Improving outcomes for your grade-level students takes collective work from your entire grade-level team. For next steps, you may choose to continue or intensify your plan if you are not yet at 80 percent of students at low risk. Your plan has had a positive impact on students, and continuing with that plan may allow you to see a continued increase in student success. You may also find that a more pressing instructional need requires your attention and shift your problem-solving focus. For example, you may have significantly improved phonics skills across your grade level, with 80 percent (or more) of students proficient in that skill. But their oral language skills and vocabulary are in need of additional attention. Whatever your next steps are, implementation of a successful schoolwide plan should build new skills in your staff that they can continue to use moving forward, resulting in sustained student success. You shouldn't stop implementing the highly effective strategies that resulted in an increase in student success. Rather, you should build your repertoire of valuable instructional tools through this grade-level problem-solving process.

## Tier 1 Team Roles

Our recommendation is that each grade level or department has its own Tier 1 team to evaluate the health of core support for its students. This team is responsible for ensuring that core instruction meets the needs of most students (more than 80 percent) at the grade level and making any necessary instructional changes when it is insufficient. Although grade-level and content-area teachers often form the core of this team, there are several other staff members who directly support this work, including administrators and specialists. It's important to note that student performance may look very different between classrooms at a grade level. However, the primary job of the Tier 1 team is to come together to evaluate core instruction across the entire grade level and build collective teacher efficacy (Donohoo, 2017). This involves engaging in the following tasks.

- Review screening data to identify the percentage of students at the grade level who are on track.

- Use data to identify the most common priority skill need for students at the grade level.

- Develop a common plan for addressing the common priority skill needs.

- Work together to implement the common plan and ensure consistency across classrooms.

- Check in regularly with grade-level colleagues to ensure everyone has the resources and support to implement the plan.

- Modify the plan when data indicates a need to do so.

### *Members*

Your Tier 1 grade-level team for the problem-solving process should include a number of the following key partners who are essential to implementing high-quality Tier 1 instruction and supports.

- **Grade-level teachers:** Grade-level teachers are most responsible for providing Tier 1 instruction directly to students and will often have the most knowledge of the Tier 1 curriculum and instruction at their grade level. They should be the primary decision makers in developing data-based plans, as they will be the primary ones to deliver the plan.

- **Building administrators:** Building administrators, such as school principals and assistant principals, should take an active role in Tier 1 grade-level teams. They should serve as instructional leaders, helping to set the vision for Tier 1, and are necessary to have at the table when instructional decisions are being made. They directly support the Tier 1 plans by allocating necessary resources (time, money, people, and materials), securing training for staff, and continuing to follow up with teams to help them implement and refine the plans.

- **Content specialists:** Content specialists, including literacy specialists, mathematics specialists, and behavior specialists, often serve as your building-level experts in a given content area. Their expertise and knowledge are essential in ensuring plans are based on evidence and have a high likelihood of success.

- **Special education teachers:** To ensure that Tier 1 is accessible to students with disabilities, it is important to include special education teachers in Tier 1 problem solving. Their expertise in serving students with the most intensive needs can help develop plans that will not only be accessible to students with disabilities but will also benefit all students.

- **Other key partners:** Other key partners can become part of this team depending on their level of knowledge and expertise, as well as the content area that is the focus of the problem solving. Some examples of other team members could include school psychologists to assist in the interpretation and use of data, paraprofessionals to support behavior-management strategies during recess, and school counselors to help develop Tier 1 behavior or social-emotional plans. Instructional assistants may also become part of this team if they play a role in delivering Tier 1 instruction and supports.

## *Meetings*

Each meeting generally follows the same problem-solving steps previously described. Figure 4.18 provides guidelines for conducting these meetings. There are also some additional considerations depending on what time of year the team is meeting: fall, winter, or spring.

---

Before Meetings

- Gather the necessary data for the meeting, including screening data and fidelity data (if available).
- Ensure current and previous data are clearly summarized for the team on your problem-solving form.

During Meetings

- Follow the steps of the problem-solving model.
- Clearly document the plan and ensure all team members have a clear understanding of the steps to implement the plan.
- Allow all team members the opportunity to ask questions and discuss what support they will need to implement the plan

After Meetings

- Follow up regularly to ensure all team members are able to implement the plan with fidelity.
- Provide follow-up coaching and support to improve fidelity as needed.

---

**Figure 4.18: Guidelines for before, during, and after Tier 1 meetings.**

### Fall

In the fall, grade-level teams are starting with a new group of students for whom they have not yet provided instruction. While there may be some general familiarity with the needs of their new students due to collaboration with teams from earlier grades, there is a heavy reliance on the screening data to guide decision making. Team members may examine plans from previous years prior to this meeting to better familiarize themselves with what instructional supports have been provided in the past and with what level of success.

### Winter

In the winter, grade-level teams should review the previously implemented plan based on the fall data. Start by answering the questions from step 4 of the Tier 1 problem-solving process.

1.  Did you implement the plan as intended?

2.  What impact did the plan have on student growth (from fall to winter)?

Answer these questions by examining any fidelity data collected as part of the implementation (for example, walkthroughs and observations) and comparing winter screening data to the grade-level goal set by the team in the fall. Reviewing the effectiveness of the fall plan often helps to inform the winter plan.

### Spring

Because this meeting occurs at the end of the school year, grade-level teams typically will not develop a plan for their current students in the spring. However, you should take this opportunity to review the effectiveness of your fall and winter plans and hopefully gain a better understanding of what worked and what didn't work. While this Tier 1 problem-solving process focuses primarily on improving student outcomes, a secondary benefit is using this process to provide job-embedded professional learning as teams develop, implement, and evaluate student-focused plans. Even when plans are not effective in improving student outcomes, teachers should gain a better understanding of how best to support current and future students.

The spring meeting is also a great opportunity for grade-level teams to ensure a smooth transition for students to the next grade level. We recommend having each grade-level team meet with the team at the next grade level. For example, kindergarten teams would meet with first-grade teams, first-grade teams would meet with second-grade teams, and so on. This allows for teachers to gain a better understanding of the students they will have next year by seeing what skills the students have, what strengths and needs they bring, and what instructional supports have been more and less effective in improving their outcomes. It also prevents grade-level teams from trying strategies that the previous grade-level team already tried with little success.

## Common Roadblocks and Possible Solutions

Next, we discuss common roadblocks related to Tier 1 and data-based decision making. These roadblocks include too much focus on individual students instead of systems, a core review process dominated by a few voices without input from the whole team, difficulty agreeing on common routines, and lack of alignment between gradewide and schoolwide Tier 1 plans.

### *Too Much Focus on Individual Students Instead of Tier 1 Systems*

Tier 1 problem solving can sometimes get derailed by conversations about individual students because those conversations tend to be easier for teachers who often have deep knowledge of their students. Talking about individual students and responding to their needs makes the conversations feel more personal and student centered. Alternatively, conversations about classwide needs require a deeper focus on prevention and increased reliance on the data, making them seem less personal and student centered. While there is a time and place for problem solving for individual students (for example, Tier 2 and 3 problem solving), any effective system needs to reserve time for addressing more systemic concerns in Tier 1. A system that over-relies on problem solving student by student is inefficient and prone to over-attributing problems to the students and their individual circumstances rather than inefficiencies and areas for improvement in instructional systems. Tier 1 problem solving keeps the focus on solving the problems in the systems.

To help keep the focus on Tier 1 problem solving, ensure that a robust system of Tier 2 and Tier 3 interventions is available to support students in need of support beyond Tier 1. Creating a separate time to problem solve for individual students will allow the team to fully focus on gradewide data during Tier 1 problem solving. Using data reports and graphs that do not contain student names or other identifying information will also help keep the focus on gradewide changes. Set meeting norms that keep the focus on gradewide data and what teachers are doing to support students in instruction, curriculum, and environment; this can also be helpful in keeping the meetings on track.

### Core Review Process Dominated by a Few Voices Without Input From the Whole Team

Engaging in the core review process requires that team members have a general familiarity with the screening data, a wide variety of evidence based practices, and the problem-solving process. As teams begin engaging in this process, some teachers may be less active as participants in the meeting. This may be due to a variety of factors, including a lack of knowledge, being a newer member of the grade-level team, or not seeing the value of this teaming process at Tier 1. It is important that all team members actively participate in the meeting. The success or failure of the plan depends on the success or failure of the whole team. Improving Tier 1 is not something that can be done by a few individuals.

To ensure all team members participate, remember that it can help to designate a facilitator whose job it is to ensure everyone provides input on the plan. You can also designate specific tasks or sections of the conversation for each team member to lead or participate in. In general, you will want to make sure each and every team member gives input in developing the plan or feedback once the plan is developed.

### Difficulty Agreeing on Common Routines Due to Significant Differences in Student Needs Between Classes

When coming together as a gradewide team, there may be significant variability between classes within the same grade level. This may be due to how students are assigned to the different classes within a grade, differences in teaching styles across the grade level, or different types of classes within a grade level. For example, you may have classes taught in two separate languages at the same grade level, with different priority skill needs in the two different languages.

To address this, you can share with your team the importance of continuity in instructional routines for students. Students learning instructional routines that they can use across classrooms frees up their cognitive energy to focus on the content of the learning and not on how they will learn it. Having common routines saves teachers time and helps students learn more efficiently. If you have biliteracy programs, in which classes at the same grade level are taught in different languages, consider sharing some common routines and strategies that can be applied in both languages. For example, a Spanish language classroom and an English language classroom may have different priority skills to focus on, but they can still use similar instructional routines to teach those skills.

### Lack of Alignment Between Gradewide and Schoolwide Tier 1 Plans

There are many similarities between the Tier 1 problem-solving process at the grade level and at the school level. Because these processes are so similar, they should naturally complement each other quite well. In general, grade-level plans should inform the schoolwide plans. For example, if most of your Tier 1 reading plans at the individual grade levels are focused on improving phonics instruction, your schoolwide plan should include a way to support this grade-level work. But what if you have a grade level that doesn't need to focus their current plan on phonics instruction? Perhaps your data indicate that at some grade levels phonics is a strength and there are other skill areas, such as oral language or fluency, that need more attention.

It's important to note that not all grade-level plans need to directly align with the school-level plan. The school-level plan will be more holistic and focus on changing systems across the school, while grade-level plans will be more targeted to the individual needs of the grade level. You will want to ensure that school administrators attend all grade-level meetings and determine how best to support those plans, even if they don't align with the school-level plan. For example, the grade level may need separate professional learning opportunities or high-quality materials that are different from what the rest of the school is receiving.

## Summary

For Tier 1 at the grade level, grade-level teams use the problem-solving model and schoolwide screening data to determine whether 80 percent of students are successful. If they determine that less than 80 percent of students are successful on the screener, they dive deeper into the screening data to identify any priority skills or common areas of need for many or most students at the grade level. Using this information, teams then develop a plan to improve Tier 1 grade-level supports. This includes identifying common instructional strategies, curriculum materials, and environmental supports that can be leveraged to increase the percentage of students identified as successful on the screening measures.

The team should also develop a plan for monitoring and supporting the plan to ensure fidelity. After the grade level plan is implemented, educators examine fidelity data and subsequent screening data during the next screening period to determine whether the fidelity of the grade-level plan is sufficient and whether it's supporting an increase in the percentage of students being successful. In the next chapter, we'll discuss applying the problem-solving model to Tier 2.

# Grade-Level Tier 1 Worksheets for Problem-Solving Model

## Summary of Problem Solving at Tier 1

| Step | Action | Key Questions | Tasks |
|------|--------|---------------|-------|
| 1 | Problem Identification | • Are at least 80 percent of students at your grade level successful with core supports alone? | • Review and analyze current and previous screening data.<br>• Review student progress between screening periods.<br>• Disaggregate screening data to determine equitable impact of core supports. |
| 2 | Problem Analysis | • What is the most common instructional need within the grade level? | • Identify priority skills needed by many or most students |
| 3 | Plan Identification and Implementation | • What adjustments to grade-level core support (such as instruction, curriculum, or environment) can we make to target identified common instructional needs? | • Develop gradewide plan for addressing priority skill need.<br>• Determine how you will support and monitor your plan.<br>• Select a goal for next screening. |
| 4 | Plan Evaluation | • Did the adjustments improve the health of our grade-level core? | At next screening:<br>• Ask, "Is fidelity at least 90 percent?"<br>• Ask, "Is our Tier 1 grade level plan effective?" |

**Step 1: Problem Identification**

1. Review and analyze current and previous screening data. Use the following worksheets to determine whether the core is currently sufficient for most (more than 80 percent) of students at the grade level and whether there has been an increase since the previous screening.

2. Disaggregate your screening data to examine the equitable impact of core supports across different student groups.

**Current and Previous Screening Data**

|  | Fall | Winter | Spring |
|---|---|---|---|
| Percentage Low Risk |  |  |  |
| Percentage Some Risk |  |  |  |
| Percentage High Risk |  |  |  |

**Summary of Student Progress Between Screening Periods**

| Percentage of students at low risk at previous screening | Of students who were low risk at previous screening, how many are currently . . . | | What percentage of previously identified students at low risk are now . . . |
|---|---|---|---|
|  | Low risk? |  |  |
|  | Some risk? |  |  |
|  | High risk? |  |  |

**Disaggregated Screening Data**

| Student Group | Percentage Low Risk in Fall | Percentage Low Risk in Winter | Percentage Low Risk in Spring |
|---|---|---|---|
|  |  |  |  |
|  |  |  |  |
|  |  |  |  |
|  |  |  |  |
|  |  |  |  |
|  |  |  |  |

## Step 2: Problem Analysis

3. Use the screening data subtest to identify a priority skill (or skills) needed by many or most students.

### Priority Skill Hierarchy

**Directions:** Select the skill area you are problem solving for, then list the component skills that make up that skill area. For example, in reading, you would list the five components of reading (phonemic awareness, phonics, fluency, vocabulary, and reading comprehension). Then list the specific screening subtests that measure each skill and the percentage of students who were above the benchmark on the subtest.

| Skill Area (select one):<br>☐ Reading    ☐ Mathematics    ☐ Behavior    ☐ Social-Emotional Learning    ☐ Other: _____ | | | | | |
|---|---|---|---|---|---|
| Component Skills | | | | | |
| Assessment | | | | | |
| Percentage Above Benchmark | | | | | |
| What is the priority skill need for many or most students? | | | | | |

**Step 3: Plan Identification and Implementation**

4. Develop a grade-level plan for addressing the priority skill need. See the following worksheet to help guide this process.

5. Determine how you will monitor your grade-level plan.

6. Set a goal for the percentage of students you expect to see at low risk at the next screening as a result of your plan.

## Grade-Level Plan

| Instruction |
|---|
| What common instructional routine and strategy will we use to target the priority skill? |
| What common active engagement strategy will we use to support instruction in the priority skill? |

| Curriculum |
|---|
| What core materials can we use to target the priority skill? |
| What supplemental materials (if any) might we need? |

| Environment |
|---|
| What common behavior and management strategy will we use to support instruction of the priority skill? |

| Goal for Next Screening | | |
|---|---|---|
| | **Current Screening Data** | **Goal for Next Screening** |
| Percent Low Risk | | |
| Percent Some Risk | | |
| Percent High Risk | | |

| **Monitoring and Support Plan** | **Who Is Responsible?** | **How Often?** |
|---|---|---|
| | | |

**Step 4: Plan Evaluation**

7. Evaluate your Tier 1 grade-level plan using the questions in the following table.

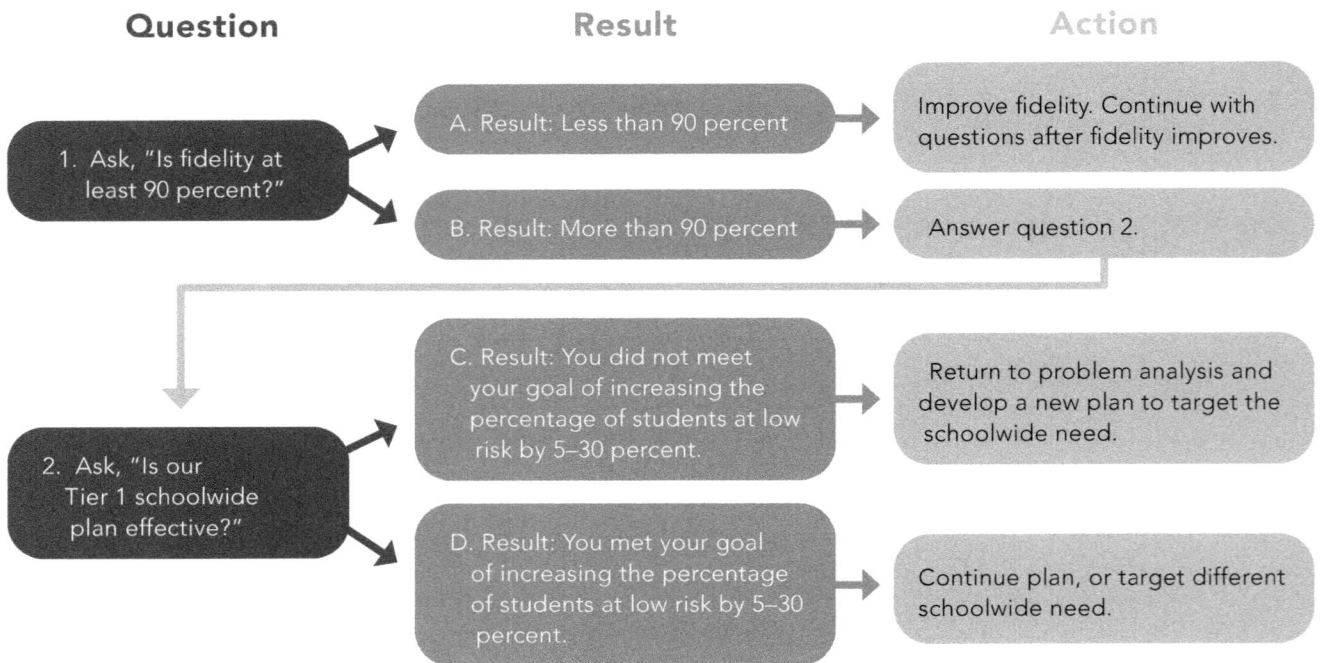

| Question | Result | Action |
|---|---|---|
| 1. Ask, "Is fidelity at least 90 percent?" | A. Result: Less than 90 percent | Improve fidelity. Continue with questions after fidelity improves. |
| | B. Result: More than 90 percent | Answer question 2. |
| 2. Ask, "Is our Tier 1 schoolwide plan effective?" | C. Result: You did not meet your goal of increasing the percentage of students at low risk by 5–30 percent. | Return to problem analysis and develop a new plan to target the schoolwide need. |
| | D. Result: You met your goal of increasing the percentage of students at low risk by 5–30 percent. | Continue plan, or target different schoolwide need. |

**Untangling Data-Based Decision Making** © 2024 Marzano Resources • MarzanoResources.com
Visit **MarzanoResources.com/reproducibles** to download this free reproducible.

# PART 3

# Data-Based Decision Making at the Student Level

# CHAPTER 5

# Data-Based Decision Making at Tier 2 for Groups of Students

As discussed in chapter 2 (page 41), Tier 2 is supplemental or targeted support provided to groups of students who need additional intervention. Schools provide Tier 2 support to students who are slightly at risk for poor learning outcomes, which is often indicated when they score just below benchmark or grade-level standards. They are students with acute needs, so providing a standard intervention now can prevent the problem from becoming chronic or engrained (Harlacher & Whitcomb, 2022; McIntosh & Goodman, 2016).

Tier 2 supports are highlighted by a few features, including the following.

- Additional time beyond the time allotted for core instruction

- More explicit instruction on the skill or skills that the student hasn't mastered yet

- More time to practice the targeted skill or skills and more frequent opportunities to respond

- More frequent feedback on performance of the skill or skills

- A smaller instructional setting (for example, group size of four to eight students)

- Communication with the home setting

- Mechanism or process to fade supports once the student masters the skill or skills (Anderson & Borgmeier, 2010; McIntosh & Goodman, 2016)

In this chapter, we apply the problem-solving model to Tier 2. We discuss each step of the model, including the key questions listed in figure 5.1 and tasks for each step. Following our discussion of the problem-solving model, we then share how to structure a team to use the model for Tier 2. We also include considerations for using the model at Tier 2. The end of the chapter features reproducible worksheets for the problem-solving model (page 180) to accompany educators or teams as they conduct problem solving at the Tier 2 level.

| Step | Action | Key Questions | Tasks |
|---|---|---|---|
| 1 | Problem Identification | • Which students are at risk? | • Identify risk level.<br>• Conduct risk verification for those at risk. |
| 2 | Problem Analysis | • What is each student's instructional need? | • Use the placement protocol to identify key instructional need. |
| 3 | Plan Identification and Implementation | • What intervention addresses that need? | • Confirm placement into the intervention.<br>• Select a goal and progress-monitoring tool.<br>• Select a fidelity tool. |
| 4 | Plan Evaluation | • Is the fidelity at least 90 percent?<br>• Is the intervention effective overall?<br>• Which students is the intervention working for? Which students is it not working for? | • Examine fidelity.<br>• Examine overall effectiveness.<br>• Examine individual student progress. |

**Figure 5.1: Key questions for use of the problem-solving model at Tier 2.**

## Problem Identification

At step 1 of the problem-solving model, educators or teams ask, "Which students are at risk?" or more specifically, "Which students need Tier 2 supports?" To answer this, educators determine who initially scored below the expected criterion and then conduct risk verification to determine who actually needs intervention (Gimpel Peacock et al., 2010; Harlacher & Rodriguez, 2018).

### Identify Risk Level: Who Initially Scored Below the Expected Criterion?

For this task, educators compare each student's score against a criterion or threshold that indicates low risk, some risk, or severe risk. For most screening assessments, the selected data warehouse will provide thresholds and indicate where students scored (in chapter 2, page 41, we list some common thresholds). Students who scored within the *some-risk* range are candidates for Tier 2, whereas students who scored in the *severe-risk* range are candidates for Tier 3 (accordingly, students scoring in the *low risk* range can continue with Tier 1 supports). Educators can use the data warehouse related to the screening assessment they used to make a list of students who scored below criterion, or they can access their own worksheets or spreadsheets to list those whom they identify as at risk. Educators should never make decisions from one datapoint. Rather, they should conduct risk verification to ensure that students who scored below the expected criterion are actually in need of additional support.

### Conduct Risk Verification: Which Students Who Scored Below Criterion Need Tier 2?

*Risk verification* is the process of verifying the accuracy of a student's risk status (Albers & Kettler, 2014; McIntosh & Goodman, 2016). Educators take the initial screening score and then analyze at least two additional data sources to determine whether the student needs additional support. If at least one of the two additional scores fall within the at-risk range, then they can conclude that the student is at risk and needs intervention. If the two additional scores are within normal limits, then the student is not considered at risk and can continue with Tier 1 support alone (Bailey et al., 2020; Center on MTSS, n.d.).

To conduct risk verification, use a chart similar to the example in figure 5.2 (page 154). List the students who scored below the expected criterion in the far left column, along with their initial screening scores (in the example in figure 5.2, it is the score on the Student Risk Screening Scale[SRSS]-Externalizing Scale). Then list two additional screening assessments and indicate their score and risk classification. For those students who have two of the three scores below the expected criterion and within the *some-risk* range, highlight their names (for example, circle, bold, or mark with an asterisk); those students are candidates for Tier 2.

Figure 5.2 lists just a few names of students who scored in the some-risk range on the initial screening tool, but educators will conduct risk verification for all students who scored at risk. Bear in mind that students who are at severe risk on the initial screening score or who have two of three verification scores at severe or high risk are students who may need Tier 3 supports. As seen in figure 5.2, Julian was designated to receive Tier 3 supports because his two verification scores were in the severe-risk category (and his initial score was borderline high and severe risk).

| Name | Initial Screening Score: SRSS-Externalizing Scale | Risk-Verification Measure 1: SRSS-Internalizing Scale | Risk-Verification Measure 2: Major Office Discipline Referrals | Intervention Needed? |
|---|---|---|---|---|
| Demetri | 4* | 1 | 2* | Yes, Tier 2 |
| Liam | 4* | 1 | 5* | Yes, Tier 2 |
| Emma | 7* | 1 | 6** | Yes, Tier 2 |
| Sophia | 5* | 0 | 1 | No |
| Amelia | 4* | 7** | 0 | Yes, Tier 2 |
| Julian | 8* | 5** | 7** | Yes, Tier 3 |

Students who have two of three scores that fall below benchmark are candidates for intervention.
Note: * = some risk, ** = severe risk (see legend)

| Legend | SRSS-Externalizing | SRSS-Internalizing | Major Office Discipline Referrals |
|---|---|---|---|
| Low risk | 0–3 | 0–1 | 0–1 |
| Some risk/Below criterion* | 4–8 | 2–3 | 2–5 |
| High risk/Well below criterion** | 9–21 | 4–15 | More than 6 |

**Figure 5.2: Risk verification for Tier 2.**

Some schools may find it more efficient to conduct problem identification for Tier 2 and Tier 3 at the same time rather than having separate meetings or teams for Tier 2 and Tier 3 determination. We discuss that more in chapter 6 (page 185), but for now, let's focus on Tier 2.

## Problem Analysis

During problem analysis, educators determine the key instructional need for each student who will receive Tier 2 supports. To do so, educators use a placement protocol. We'll examine what a placement protocol is and some examples, and then we'll explain how to create your own.

### *Use of the Placement Protocol: What Is the Key Instructional Need?*

A *placement protocol* is a logic model or flowchart that outlines how the results of the data indicate a student's likely instructional need and offers an intervention to use. We say *likely* because it's a working hypothesis; the student will receive an intervention to address that need, and educators will gather progress-monitoring data to confirm or disconfirm the hypothesis, ultimately leading to fading out of the intervention when the student meets the goal or adjustments or intensification of the intervention if the student doesn't meet the goal. Schools will need to create their own placement protocols, so we discuss how to do that a little later in this section.

Using the placement protocol, educators consider the universal screening data and additional diagnostic data (usually from the risk-verification data) to determine the instructional need of each student. This protocol takes into account the acquisition of the student's skills and the function of the student's behavior, thus enabling educators to sensibly match students to an intervention. This might look like educators examining elementary students' rate of reading and accuracy of text to determine their instructional need for Tier 2 supports (for example, students who read with accuracy but below the expected rate likely need fluency instruction, whereas students who are inaccurate and below rate likely need phonics instruction; Burns, 2021; Parker & Burns, 2014; Szadokierski et al., 2017). From that instructional need, the school can select an intervention to address that need (for example, Read Naturally for fluency [www.readnaturally.com] or Phonics for Reading for phonics [https://bit.ly/3PI42fq]).

Educators typically have a few options at Tier 2, so using the placement protocol ensures a data-based approach to matching a student's instructional need to an effective intervention in a timely manner (Burns et al., 2012; Harlacher & Rodriguez, 2018; Hawken et al., 2021). With a placement protocol, educators examine student data and follow the guidelines outlined within the protocol to determine the instructional need and intervention to use. After presenting examples of placement protocols, we'll discuss how to integrate academics and social, emotional, and behavioral needs into these tools.

#### Examples of Placement Protocols

In the following examples, we offer example placement protocols for reading (figures 5.3, page 156, and 5.4, page 157), behavior (figure 5.5, page 157), and mathematics (figure 5.6, page 158).

As part of the placement protocol, educators also consider the cultural needs of students, such as whether they are proficient in English (as this impacts the intervention selection). For example, a placement protocol could indicate what data to examine to determine the need for a language intervention. When students score low in language arts or reading proficiency, additional data are necessary to determine

| If the Student Scored: | And | And | And | Then the Instructional Need Is: | Provide: |
|---|---|---|---|---|---|
| Below criterion for phonological awareness (Phoneme Segmentation Fluency) | Below criterion in decoding (Oral Reading Fluency–Accuracy) | Below criterion in fluency (Oral Reading Fluency–Rate) | Below criterion in comprehension (Retell, Maze Passages) | Acquisition of phonological awareness | Early Interventions in Reading<br><br>Lindamood Phoneme Sequencing |
| Above criterion for phonological awareness (Phoneme Segmentation Fluency) | Below criterion in decoding (Oral Reading Fluency–Accuracy) | Below criterion in fluency (Oral Reading Fluency–Rate) | Below criterion in comprehension (Retell, Maze Passages) | Acquisition of skills in decoding and phonics | Early Interventions in Reading<br><br>Phonics for Reading (2–5)<br><br>Phonics Boost lessons (2–5)<br><br>Corrective Reading decoding<br><br>REWARDS (3–5) |
| Above criterion for phonological awareness (Phoneme Segmentation Fluency) | Above criterion in decoding (Oral Reading Fluency–Accuracy) | Below criterion in fluency (Oral Reading Fluency–Rate) | Below criterion in comprehension (Retell, Maze Passages) | Fluency | Read Naturally<br><br>Six Minute Solution<br><br>*Examine automaticity with multisyllabic words |
| Above criterion for phonological awareness (Phoneme Segmentation Fluency) | Above criterion in decoding (Oral Reading Fluency–Accuracy) | Above criterion in fluency (Oral Reading Fluency–Rate) | Below criterion in comprehension (Retell, Maze Passages) | Reading comprehension | Read 180<br><br>Achieve3000 |

**Figure 5.3: Example of a placement protocol in reading and intervention selection.**

| If the Student Scored: | And | And | Then the Instructional Need Is: | Provide: |
|---|---|---|---|---|
| Below criterion in Maze Passages | Below criterion in rate of Oral Reading Fluency | Below criterion in accuracy with Oral Reading Fluency | Basic skills instruction in reading | Language! |
| Below criterion in Maze Passages | Below criterion in rate of Oral Reading Fluency | Above criterion in accuracy with Oral Reading Fluency | Fluency instruction in reading | Read Naturally |
| Below criterion in Maze Passages | Above criterion in rate of Oral Reading Fluency | Above criterion in accuracy with Oral Reading Fluency | Reading comprehension strategies<br><br>*Examine grades in content classes and other previous assessments to determine whether vocabulary support is needed with REWARDS Plus | REWARDS Secondary |

**Figure 5.4: Example of a placement protocol for Tier 2 in reading (secondary).**

| If the Student Scored: | And | And | Then the Instructional Need Is: | Gather Additional Detail |
|---|---|---|---|---|
| High risk on Student Risk Screening Scale in externalizing behavior | Office discipline referrals for disruption with academic avoidance or escape | Course grades are C or lower | Provide academic intervention. | Analyze academic data to identify skills needed. |
| High risk on Student Risk Screening Scale in externalizing behavior | Office discipline referrals with motivation of adult attention seeking | Course grades are C or higher | Provide check in–check out. | Examine referrals for nature of behavioral support needed and function of behavior. |
| High risk on Student Risk Screening Scale in externalizing behavior | Office discipline referrals with motivation of peer attention seeking | Course grades are C or higher | Provide check in–check out with modification for peer attention. | Confirm peer or adult attention as motivating factor. |
| High risk on Student Risk Screening Scale in internalizing behavior | Office discipline referrals for avoidance of tasks or others | Consider academic intervention if grades indicate a need. | Provide social and emotional learning instruction. | Analyze items on Student Risk Screening Scale to determine specific social-emotional needs. |

**Figure 5.5: Example of a placement protocol for secondary students and behavioral needs.**

| If the Student Scored: | And | And | Then the Instructional Need Is: | Intervention |
|---|---|---|---|---|
| Below rate on M-COMP | Below 93 percent accuracy on M-COMP | Above or below rate on M-CAP* | Acquisition (number sense, operations, conceptual understanding) | Corrective Mathematics |
| Below rate on M-COMP | Above 93 percent accuracy on M-COMP | Above or below rate on M-CAP* | Proficiency and fluency with operations | Corrective Mathematics |
| Above rate on M-COMP | Below 93 percent accuracy on M-COMP | Above or below rate on M-CAP* | Procedural knowledge with computation | Math 180 |
| Above rate on M-COMP | Above 93 percent accuracy on M-COMP | Below rate on M-CAP* | Applications and procedural knowledge | Essentials for Algebra |

*If below rate on M-CAP, consider a need for applications and procedural knowledge.

M-COMP = Mathematics Computation; M-CAP = Mathematics Concepts and Applications

**Figure 5.6: Example of a placement protocol for Tier 2 in mathematics (elementary).**

whether the instructional need is related to language arts or to a need for second language support (Herrera, Murray, & Cabral, 2019; Rhodes, Hector Ochoa, & Ortiz, 2005). Each state or district has its own tests for language proficiency, so educators will want to consider those data to determine whether a student needs support in literacy, language, or both.

### Integration of Academics With Social, Emotional, and Behavioral Needs in a Placement Protocol

Educators can also consider the integration of academics and behavior when examining student scores (in fact, figure 5.14, page 168, illustrates integration of academics and behavior). If a student scores low in an academic area, it's best to examine behavioral data to determine whether the student needs behavioral support as part of any academic intervention provided (for example, educators can provide emotion-regulation skills to students to manage their frustration during difficult tasks). And if a student has a behavioral need, educators should consider academic data to examine if the student is displaying behavior because of academic difficulties (for example, using defiance or disruption to avoid doing work; McIntosh & Goodman, 2016). In figure 5.7, we illustrate a secondary level example that considers both academic and behavioral data together to determine the instructional needs of a student. As depicted, the example offers the consideration of key academic

| If the Student Scored: | And | And | Then the Instructional Need Is: | Provide: |
|---|---|---|---|---|
| At risk in attendance | At risk in office referrals | At risk in academics (grades, state testing scores) | Content area where academics are at risk | Corrective Reading for language arts<br><br>Corrective Mathematics for mathematics |
| At risk in attendance | At risk in office referrals | At criterion in academics (grades, state testing scores) | Behavioral support for classes where referrals occur | Check in–check out<br><br>*Consider examining referrals for nature of behavioral support needed and function of behavior. |
| At risk in attendance | At criterion for office referrals | At criterion in academics (grades, state testing scores) | School engagement | Adult mentoring if driven by adult attention<br><br>Peer mentoring if driven by peer attention |

**Figure 5.7: Example of a secondary placement protocol that integrates academics and behavior.**

screening information (for example, grades and previous state scores) and behavioral indicators of risk (for example, attendance rate and office discipline referrals).

### *Development of a Placement Protocol*

To create the placement protocol, educators will need a list of assessments used in their school and a list of available interventions (including the skills the intervention targets). Educators will examine their list of assessments and determine cut scores that indicate mastery of a skill (this information can be found in the technical manuals of the assessments or it may be informed by district policy or guidelines). Educators then outline the pattern of scores that indicate an instructional need (such as what's illustrated later in this chapter, in figures 5.11, page 166, 5.12, page 167, 5.14, page 168, and 5.16, page 170).

The selected assessments or data sources should be brief and easy to administer, as the goal is not to engage in extensive assessment; rather, educators need just enough information to inform the general instructional need of students (extensive or time-consuming measures are for use at Tier 3). In figure 5.8 (page 160), we outline several brief assessments that you can use to measure different skills for various content areas at Tier 2. Students who score below criterion on these measures may indicate a need in that area (for example, low score on the Student Risk Screening Scale-Internalizing may indicate a need for an intervention on internalizing behaviors, such as anxiety or depression).

| Content and Skill | Possible Measures or Data Sources |
|---|---|
| **Reading** | |
| Phonological awareness | First Sound Fluency, Phoneme Segmentation Fluency |
| Phonics | Nonsense Word Fluency–Correct Letter Sounds<br>Nonsense Word Fluency–Whole Words Read<br>Oral Reading Fluency–Accuracy |
| Fluency | Oral Reading Fluency–Words Read Correct |
| Vocabulary | Word Use Fluency |
| Reading comprehension | Oral Reading Fluency–Retell<br>Maze reading assessment |
| **Mathematics** | |
| Number sense | Early mathematics probes (for example, number identification fluency, next number fluency, missing number, quantity discrimination)<br>Mathematics Computation probes (M-COMP) |
| Mathematics facts, computation | Single-skill probes<br>Error analysis of M-COMP probes |
| Concepts (time, money, graphs) | Mathematics Concepts and Applications (M-CAP)<br>Single-skill probes |
| **Writing** | |
| Writing mechanics and structure | Curriculum-based measurement (CBM)–Writing (correct writing sequences)<br>Error analysis of CBM–Writing |
| Writing fluency | CBM–Writing (total words written) |
| Spelling | CBM–Writing (words spelled correctly)<br>CBM–Spelling (correct letter sequences) |
| **Social-emotional learning and behavior** | |
| Social-emotional learning and behaviors | Student Risk Screening Scale-Internalizing<br>Student Risk Screening Scale-Externalizing<br>Information on office discipline referrals<br>Peer or teacher nomination<br>Brief interviews with key personnel |
| Function of behavior | Perceived motivation on office discipline referrals<br>Brief functional behavior assessment<br>Functional Assessment Checklist for Teachers and Staff (FACTS) interview<br>Brief interviews with key personnel |

**Figure 5.8: Skills and example assessments used to diagnostically assess students at Tier 2.**

### Intervention Audit

When determining which interventions to include on the placement protocol, educators may want to conduct an intervention audit and follow a process for selecting interventions. An *intervention audit* is the process of taking stock of the current interventions for each grade or content area in a school. Many schools have gathered materials over the years, so it's helpful to check old closets, classrooms, or even the basement to see what's available. For each intervention found, outline if it's evidence based, if there's sufficient materials to use it, if training is available for it, its corresponding grade level, and what skill it targets (Oregon Response to Instruction and Intervention, n.d.b). We offer an intervention audit form in figure 5.9.

| Intervention Name | Is It Evidence Based? | Sufficient Materials to Use? | Training Necessary or Available? | Grade to Use With? | What Skill Does It Target? |
|---|---|---|---|---|---|
| Pirate Math Equation Quest | Yes | No | Yes, instructional coach available | Elementary | Mathematics concepts, word problems |
| | | | | | |
| | | | | | |
| | | | | | |

*Source: © Oregon Response to Instruction and Intervention, n.d.b. Adapted with permission.*

**Figure 5.9: Intervention audit.**

Once educators complete the audit, they then follow a process when making selections about which interventions to include on their placement protocol. Educators will typically want to see if the interventions they have are evidence based, address a need of their students, and can be implemented with fidelity. To evaluate whether the intervention fits within the site's needs, we offer the following four general questions that educators can ask for each intervention (Metz & Louison, 2018).

1.  Does the intervention address a current and relevant need of the student population?

2.  Is there clear evidence that the intervention is effective for that current need?

3.  Does the intervention align with the culture and values of the school?

4.  Does the site have the capacity (for example, training, coaching, time, and resources) to implement the intervention with fidelity?

Schools should answer *yes* to each of these questions to ensure they can effectively use the intervention. If they cannot answer *yes* to each, they can discuss the extent to which the use of the intervention is appropriate and thus whether they can place it on an intervention matrix.

### Placement Protocol Template and Guidelines

Once educators know the interventions that they have access to within their building, they can then match a pattern of scores or data results to indicate *when* to actually use those interventions with a student. For example, a school may have access to an adult mentoring intervention and a peer buddy intervention. However, data indicating a student prefers adult attention would receive the adult mentoring intervention, whereas data indicating a student prefers peer attention would receive the peer mentoring intervention. While constructing the placement protocol, educators will determine which data patterns indicate a certain instructional need, which they then match to one of the interventions available within their school.

We offer a placement protocol template to get started in figure 5.10, but keep in mind that the examples presented throughout this chapter can be modified to fit your context. We suggest choosing one content area to begin with and listing the skills within that content area that you can address under the Then the Instructional Need Is column. Then complete the pattern of scores or data sources to determine the instructional need in the columns to the left (note that you may not use all the And columns). Finally, match the intervention that most directly targets the instructional need in the Intervention column. The reproducible "Tier 2 Worksheets for Problem-Solving Model" on page 180 also includes this template.

| If the Student Scored: | And | And | And | Then the Instructional Need Is: | Provide: |
|---|---|---|---|---|---|
|  |  |  |  |  |  |
|  |  |  |  |  |  |
|  |  |  |  |  |  |
|  |  |  |  |  |  |

**Figure 5.10: Example template for creating a placement protocol.**

Finally, we offer the following guidelines when developing your placement protocol.

- **Keep it simple:** You just need a general idea of the instructional need, so don't make an overly complex placement protocol.

- **Start small:** Identify a small number of interventions to begin and outline a simple data-based process that would indicate whether to use that intervention. Add to the placement protocol over time.

- **Keep the instructional hierarchy in mind:** Think about what data sources indicate if the student is within an acquisition, proficiency, or generalization stage. For example, low scores on accuracy with reading text indicate acquisition, whereas high accuracy and low rate indicate proficiency.

- **Think about efficiency:** Are there screening sources that you can analyze for diagnostic information? For example, the screening assessments for Acadience (acadiencelearning.org) or Measures of Academic Progress (nwea.org/the-map-suite) can provide diagnostic information depending on the scores analyzed.

- **Use the data you have:** Previously gathered data can indicate the instructional need for students if you analyze them differently. For example, you can count the number of office discipline referrals to determine a student's risk status, but can also analyze the type of behavior and perceived motivation on referrals to identify an instructional need for a student.

## Plan Identification and Implementation

If problem analysis is done well, then the next step, plan identification and implementation, is half-done. Because the placement protocol indicates the instructional need, the plan to resolve the student's need is apparent. Selecting the intervention should be quick and easy (just use the placement protocol!), but educators will want to ensure the student is ready and placed appropriately into the intervention. First, educators should confirm placement, then they can select a goal and progress-monitoring tool, and finally they can select a fidelity tool.

### *Confirm Placement Into the Intervention*

Selecting an intervention to use may be as easy as following the placement protocol, but there are logistics to consider. We recommend confirming that the intervention is correct given the results of the problem analysis step and ready to use by communicating and confirming with relevant staff members and family. For example, a staff member should appropriately inform families of the intervention (our rule is that family members shouldn't learn from students that they're receiving an intervention; rather, a staff member should inform them). Further, certain communication will need to occur prior to a student beginning a behavioral intervention, or educators need to administer certain placement tests to ensure appropriate placement into an academic intervention. Here are general considerations when confirming a Tier 2 intervention for a student.

- Are there logistic considerations when providing this intervention, such as scheduling considerations or coordinating across grade levels?

- Who will communicate the intervention to relevant staff, and how should communication take place?

- Who will communicate the intervention to the family and to the student, and how should communication take place?

- Are lesson placement tests needed to ensure the student starts with an appropriate lesson or academic group?

### Select a Goal and Progress-Monitoring Tool

Because this is Tier 2 and students are just below criterion (rather than multiple grades behind), we recommend using your screening assessment from step 1 and setting the goal for the next benchmarking period at the expected criterion or standard for that time period (for example, for fall screening, set the goal to winter standard; for winter screening, set to spring standard). To determine the appropriate goal, educators can examine the expected criterion or the low-risk threshold for their given screening assessment. For example, if students were identified initially with oral reading fluency probes, then your goal for the next benchmark period is based on the benchmark goal for at benchmark (for example, for a third grader identified in the fall, the benchmark goal would be 86 words per minute; Acadience Learning, 2021). Given that the goal is based on oral reading fluency, it's a logical choice to then use oral reading fluency as the progress-monitoring tool. In this situation, the goal and progress-monitoring tool are intertwined—choosing the goal chooses the progress-monitoring tool, so to speak.

In cases where a different progress-monitoring tool is used relative to the screening tool, we still recommend using the expected criterion or next benchmark period for that given tool. For example, perhaps educators screened a group of first graders with oral reading fluency, but the educators want a more targeted progress-monitoring tool and select nonsense word fluency as their progress-monitoring tool. The goal can still be set for the next benchmark period using the expected criterion for that benchmark (for example, fifty-four correct letter sequences and thirteen whole words read in the spring; Acadience Learning, 2021).

### What About Setting Goals for Students Well Below Grade Level?

Tier 2 goals should typically be set for grade level because those students just need a little additional intervention to meet grade-level standards or benchmarks. However, in cases where you may monitor off-grade level (for example, monitoring on third-grade level for a fourth grader), we recommended setting the goal for the off-grade level, but in half a year's time so the goal is set for the student to catch up. When setting goals for below grade level or end of the year, always consider long-term growth and having a clear vision of when you expect the student to reach grade-level benchmarks.

For older students where the curriculum-based measure is not a useful or sensitive enough progress-monitoring tool, the intervention used with the student may have a monitoring system as part of its components. Thus, we encourage readers to follow those guidelines for progress monitoring. In situations where that is not possible (that is, the intervention does not have a monitoring element) or the monitoring system doesn't measure long-term goals, educators can still follow guidelines of progress monitoring. The general guidelines for progress monitoring are to regularly gather data that are reliable, valid, and a sensitive measure of the student's skills or performance. These data can be graphed and analyzed visually and mathematically when needed. For example, perhaps students receive a Tier 2 mentoring intervention because of their risk for school dropout. In this case, daily attendance or direct behavior rating could be used as a progress-monitoring tool (see https://dbr.education.uconn.edu/# and https://bit.ly/46ZkvDR for examples and resources). Although not curriculum-based measure data, these data can be gathered and graphed regularly to provide a measure of student growth and performance.

### Select a Fidelity Tool

At Tier 2, educators will gather fidelity data on a group level, meaning they'll gather information to see if the intervention as a whole was provided versus gathering fidelity data for an individual student. The general question is, Was the intervention provided as intended?

To select a fidelity tool, we recommend using the fidelity assessment that comes with the standard intervention used at Tier 2. For example, interventions such as the *behavior education program* (also known as *check in–check out*) or *corrective reading* offer checklists of critical features that can be observed or self-reported as a measure of fidelity. The checklist outlines the key features of the intervention. Educators can then record their fidelity after each intervention session or on a regular basis by self-reporting the items; alternatively, a colleague could observe the intervention using the checklist. We offer an example for a social-emotional learning lesson in figure 5.11 (page 166). Additional examples are available at RTI Action Network (https://bit.ly/3K7f4Jc).

In situations where a checklist is not possible, we offer an example for measuring fidelity in figure 5.12 (page 167) that allows you to document the total minutes of intervention compared to the intended minutes, as well as whether the targeted skills were taught and the intended strategies or programs were used.

Capture the intervention, goal, and fidelity tool for each student identified for Tier 2 using a template similar to the one in figure 5.13 (page 167). Keep in mind that the goal and fidelity tool can be the same for several students. Most data warehouses have similar templates, so use what is feasible. The reproducible "Tier 2 Worksheets for Problem-Solving Model" on page 180 also includes this template.

| Lesson: Understanding Feelings Lesson Components | Circle One | |
|---|---|---|
| The teacher: 1. Reviews at least one topic from last week's lesson | Yes | No |
| 2. Identifies that the purpose of the lesson is to learn appropriate ways to express feelings | Yes | No |
| 3. Conveys that emotions communicate how people feel | Yes | No |
| 4. Points out different ways to show feelings | Yes | No |
| 5. Identifies two emotions and ways to express them | Yes | No |
| 6. Points out that appropriate expression can be safe and respectful | Yes | No |
| 7. Points out that inappropriate expression can hurt yourself or others | Yes | No |
| 8. Uses handout A | Yes | No |
| 9. Shares at least four examples from the handout | Yes | No |
| 10. Asks students to identify at least one feeling and ways to express those feelings (using handout B) | Yes | No |
| 11. Passes out handout C | Yes | No |
| 12. Asks students to work in small groups on handout C | Yes | No |
| 13. Reviews at least two ideas from the lesson at the end | Yes | No |
| TOTALS | __ /13 | __ /13 |

Figure 5.11: Example of a fidelity checklist for a social-emotional learning lesson.

## Plan Evaluation

After implementing the intervention and gathering data on fidelity and student growth, educators evaluate the extent to which Tier 2 support worked. Educators ask a series of questions that we have outlined in figure 5.14 (page 168), in which you'll see that we start with checking the overall fidelity of the intervention. (That is, Is it at least 90 percent?) Based on the results, educators can determine if they need to improve fidelity or if they can then examine the overall effectiveness of Tier 2 (Is the intervention effective overall?; that is, at least 75 percent should benefit from Tier 2). From there, they can then conduct group analysis or they can examine students' individual performance to either resolve individual issues or fade out the plan for students who are successful. (Which students is the intervention working for? and Which students is it not working for?)

| | Date | Total Minutes of Intervention | Total Intended Minutes | Were All Intended Skills Taught? | Were All Intended Strategies and Programs Used? | If No, Clarify |
|---|---|---|---|---|---|---|
| 1 | | | | ☐ Yes  ☐ No | ☐ Yes  ☐ No | |
| 2 | | | | ☐ Yes  ☐ No | ☐ Yes  ☐ No | |
| 3 | | | | ☐ Yes  ☐ No | ☐ Yes  ☐ No | |
| 4 | | | | ☐ Yes  ☐ No | ☐ Yes  ☐ No | |
| Totals | | Actual minutes | Intended minutes | Number of *yes* answers | Number of *yes* answers | |
| | | | | | | |

Note: Include additional rows as needed.

*Source: © National Center on Intensive Intervention, n.d.d. Adapted with permission.*

**Figure 5.12: Example of a general fidelity checklist.**

*Visit **MarzanoResources.com/reproducibles** for a free reproducible version of this figure.*

| Student | Tier 2 Intervention | Goal | Fidelity Tool |
|---|---|---|---|
| Chad | Check in–check out (CICO) | 80 percent of daily points | Teacher self-report using fidelity checklist of CICO |
| Brooke | CICO | 80 percent of daily points | Teacher self-report using fidelity checklist of CICO |
| Cole | Read Naturally | 75 words read correct per minute | Observation with checklist once per week |
| Greyson | Read Naturally | 75 words read correct per minute | Observation with checklist once per week |

Note: Write each student's name and their intervention, along with the goal and fidelity tool. Add more rows as needed.

**Figure 5.13: Template for instructional plan for students to receive Tier 2.**

| Question | Result | Action |
|----------|--------|--------|
| 1. Ask, "Is fidelity at least 90 percent?" | A. Result: Less than 90 percent | Improve fidelity. Implement plan as intended. Continue with questions after fidelity improves. |
| | B. Result: More than 90 percent | Answer question 2. |
| 2. Ask, "Is the intervention effectiave overall?" | C. Result: Working for less than 75 percent of students | Problem solve at the group level. |
| | D. Result: Working for more than 75 percent of students | Answer question 3. |
| 3. Ask, "Which students is the intervention working for? Which students is it not working for?" | E. Action: Identify students with median datapoint above goal line | Fade out plan. |
| | E. Action: Identify students with median datapoint below goal line | Ensure fidelity for individual students. Adjust supports within ICEL or refer to Tier 3. |

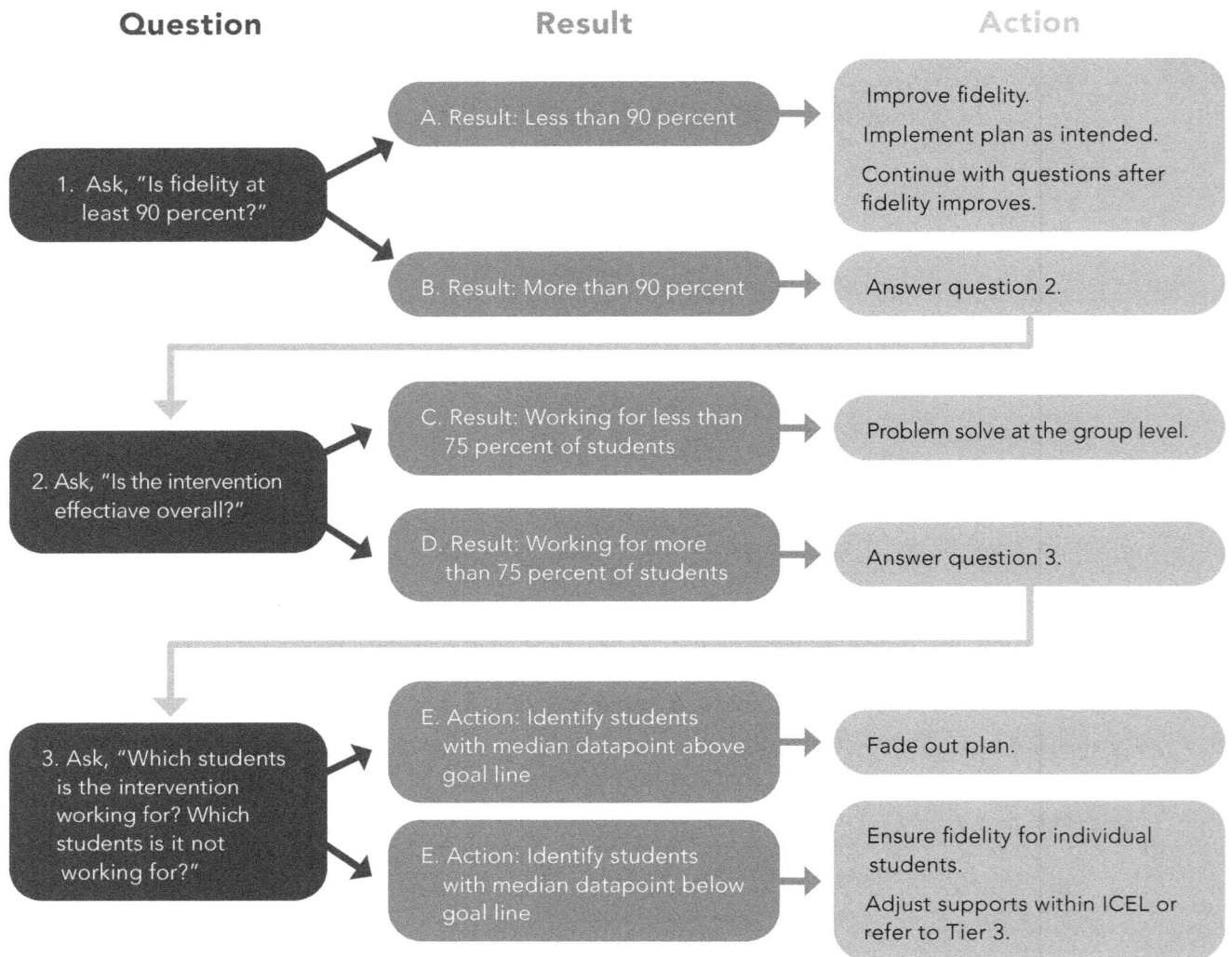

**Figure 5.14: Plan evaluation for Tier 2.**

## 1. Ask, "Is Fidelity at Least 90 Percent?"

To check fidelity, take the gathered fidelity data and calculate a fidelity score for the intervention. Most often, the percentage of components of the intervention implemented is the fidelity score, but it may also be the total points for other variables, such as student engagement. For example, educators can calculate a percentage of components implemented by counting the components implemented and dividing by the total components (for example, seven of ten components would be 70 percent). For ratings of other variables, such as quality of engagement, take the total aggregated ratings out of the total possible. For example, if engagement was rated on a scale of 1 to 3, then three points each intervention session are possible. For twenty-four intervention sessions and three points per session, that's a total of seventy-two possible. A total score of seventy across the interventions would be 97 percent. Once the fidelity score is calculated, judge it against a 90 percent threshold and determine if fidelity is low (less than 90 percent) or high (more than 90 percent).

## A. Result: Less Than 90 Percent

If it is less than 90 percent (A. Result in figure 5.14, page 168), it is best to examine *why* the fidelity score was below 90 percent. Fix the reason why fidelity is low and continue with the intervention. We suggest discussing with the staff why fidelity is low and then developing a plan to improve fidelity. It may be a systems issue related to the staff's ability or preparation to implement. In figure 5.15, we offer some questions that educators can ask related to systems and staff needs when exploring why the intervention isn't being implemented as intended (for example, Does the teacher need support in implementing the intervention? Are students disengaged? Were the total minutes less than intended?).

| Domain | Staff Professional Learning Questions |
|---|---|
| Instruction | Do staff need more training or an adjustment to the training provided? |
| Curriculum | Does the content not align with the staff's philosophy or values? Do staff need more clarification on their roles or expectations? |
| Environment | Are more coaching and feedback needed for staff to implement the plan? |
| Learner | Do supports need to be differentiated between staff? |

**Figure 5.15: Example questions to ask related to low fidelity of Tier 2.**

## B. Result: More Than 90 Percent

If fidelity is more than 90 percent (B. Result in figure 5.14, page 168), then educators can conclude that the intervention is being implemented as intended. Next, we want to determine whether it's beneficial for most students.

## 2. Ask, "Is the Intervention Effective Overall?"

To answer this question, educators calculate the percentage of students who are successful with Tier 2 supports compared to those who are not. This is easily done by visually analyzing progress-monitoring graphs and calculating the percentage of students who are successful with Tier 2 supports versus those who are not.

## C. Result: Working for Less Than 75 Percent

If the intervention is not working for at least 75 percent of students, then educators will want to problem solve at the group level. As an example for when Tier 2 supports are not effective overall, look at figure 5.16 (page 170). In this figure, we display a group of students receiving Tier 2 behavior intervention supports and their average total daily points earned. Students have the same goal to earn at least 80 percent of their total daily points each day, so one can easily see the number of

**Percentage of Daily Points Earned**

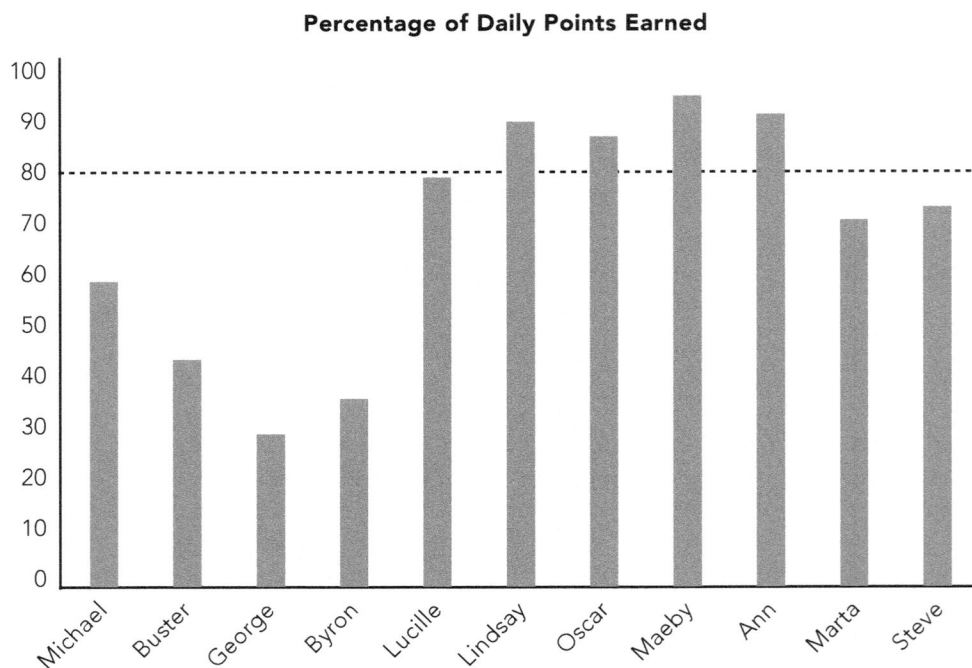

**Figure 5.16: Students receiving a behavior intervention and their daily points earned.**

students who are above the goal line (reached their goal) versus those below the goal line (did not reach their goal). With a little arithmetic, one can calculate that four of eleven students are successful, which is 36 percent of students. This is less than 75 percent (see C. Result in figure 5.14, page 168), so at this point, we know that the intervention is being implemented with fidelity, yet it's not benefiting most students. Educators will want to return to problem analysis and conduct group-level problem solving.

In group-level problem solving, we typically suggest first checking that the focus of instruction matches the needed skills of the students (see figure 5.17). If the intervention does not match the students' needed skills, we recommend modifying the focus of instruction or the curriculum. If the skill being taught *does* match the focus or needs of the learners, then we recommend focusing on the intensity of the instruction. This is general guidance, but we offer more nuanced questions in figure 5.18. Educators are engaging in problem analysis here, searching for a hypothesis as to why the intervention isn't sufficient yet.

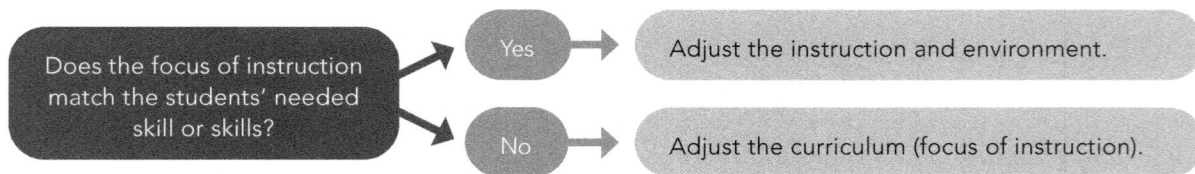

**Figure 5.17: General flowchart for group-level problem solving.**

| Domain | Questions | Ways to Assess |
|---|---|---|
| Instruction | • Was the instruction explicit enough (for example, sufficient modeling, guiding practice, and feedback)? | • Observe aspects of explicit instruction or review lesson plans. |
| | • Was the dosage of instruction strong enough to expect a change? | • Review schedule or measure fidelity for minutes of each intervention session, number of days per week, and total number of sessions. |
| | • Are there sufficient opportunities to respond? | • Observe the number of opportunities to respond. |
| | • Is there sufficient review? | • Review lesson plans for amount of review. |
| Curriculum | • Do the students have the background knowledge or prerequisite skills to access the curriculum? | • Examine permanent products to assess students' prerequisite skills relative to the scope and sequence of curriculum.<br>• Interview interventionist. |
| | • Does the intervention target the needed skill for the students? | • Review focus of curriculum or permanent products and compare to students' needs. |
| | • Do different examples and nonexamples need to be used for the instruction of the skill? | • Review lesson plans for juxtaposition of examples. |
| | • Does the difficulty level of the materials match the group instructional level (that is, frustrational, instructional, or independent)? | • Review permanent products for accuracy to calculate instructional level of the group.<br>• Review lesson plans relative to group's instructional level. |
| Environment | • Does the behavioral support need to be adjusted to be more supportive?<br>• Is there sufficient classroom management? | • Observe the amount of feedback or acknowledgment provided.<br>• Observe any routines or structures in the intervention.<br>• Review lesson plans for teaching related to behavioral support or classroom management. |
| | • Do students feel connected to the teacher or each other? | • Interview or observe students during intervention. |
| | • Can adjustments be made to motivate students' learning? | • Observe level of engagement or interview interventionist to assess engagement. |
| Learner | • Is the instructional setting and design of the plan taking into account the right students' needs or characteristics? | • Interview learners or interventionist.<br>• Observe intervention. |

**Figure 5.18: Example questions and ways to assess them for group problem analysis.**

### D. Result: Working for More Than 75 Percent

We illustrated examining a bar graph where all the students have the same goal to calculate what percentage of students the intervention is working for (see figure 5.16, page 170). If the data are graphed on a line graph or when students have different goals, examine each student's data and determine whether students are meeting their goals or not. To determine whether students are meeting their goals, take the median datapoint of the last three datapoints and compare that against the goal line. Ask if the datapoint is above or below the goal line. If it is above, then the intervention is working. If the datapoint is below, then the intervention is not working for the student. Calculate the total percentage of students who the intervention is working for, and if it's more than 75 percent of students, then answer question 3 from figure 5.14 (page 168).

As an example for when an intervention is working for most students, we've displayed the progress of four students receiving academic Tier 2 intervention supports in reading in figure 5.19. By looking at the students' growth compared to the goal line, three of the four students are above the goal line (Chad, Lauren, and Adalyn),

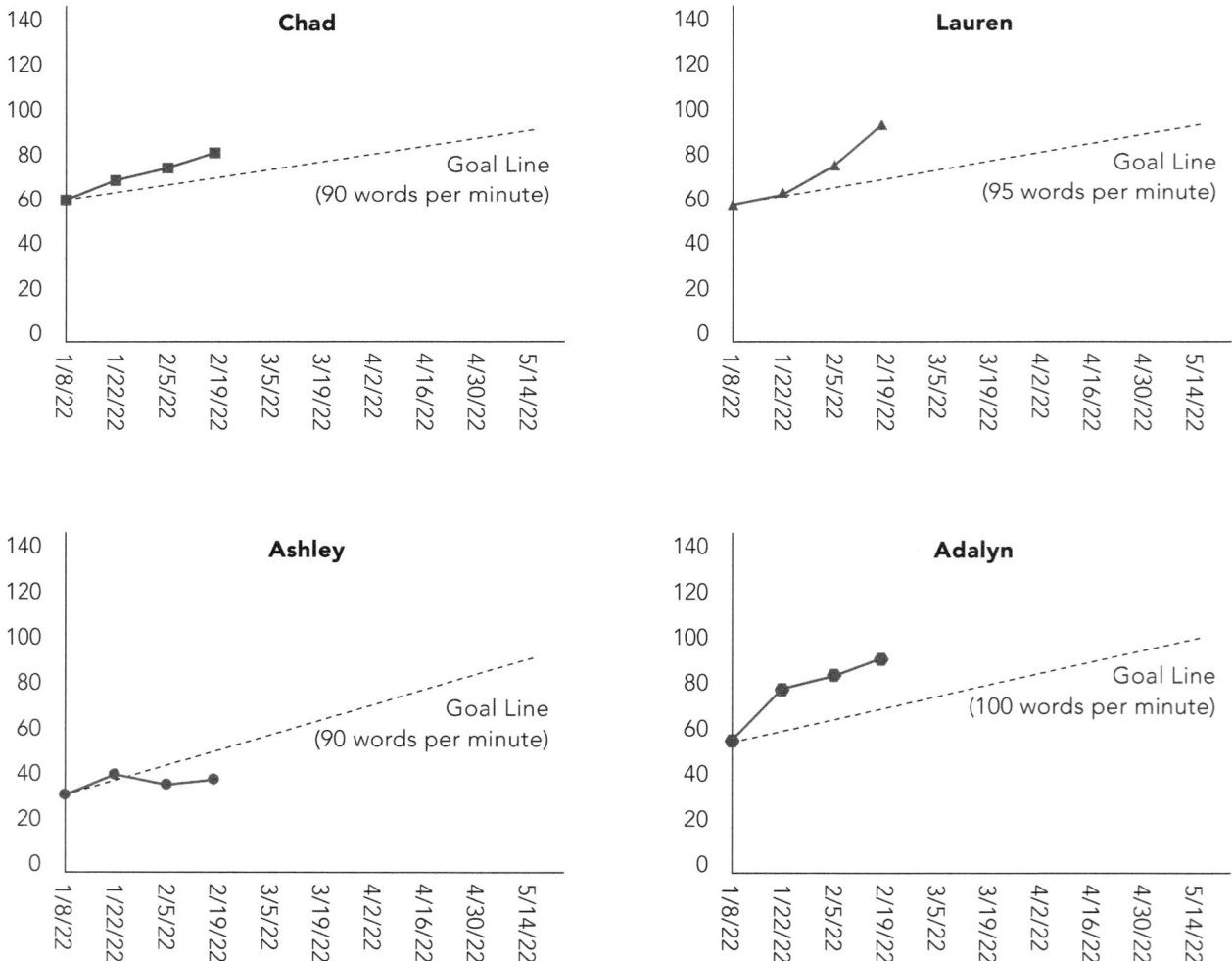

Figure 5.19: Progress of students in a Tier 2 intervention.

which is 75 percent. With 75 percent of the group successful, we can conclude that over-all, Tier 2 supports are effective for these students.

### 3. Ask, "Which Students Is the Intervention Working For? Which Students Is It Not Working For?"

Now that we know the intervention is being implemented with fidelity and it's bene-fiting most students (as seen in the examples in figure 5.19), we can turn our attention to the individual students. Additionally, keep in mind the number of datapoints and weeks of the intervention. We recommend not making decisions about changes to inter-ventions unless there are eight or more datapoints and at least twelve to fourteen weeks of intervention (Norman & Christ, 2016; Van Norman, 2021). These are general guide-lines, but the more datapoints and longer the use of intervention, the greater the chance of accurate decisions (Van Norman, 2021).

As mentioned previously, to determine which students the intervention is working for and not working for, analyze the data visually and compare the current growth against the student's goal line. Compare the median datapoint of the last three datapoints against the goal line. If the median datapoint is above the goal line, then the student is making positive growth and educators can discuss fading or discounting the student's support. If the datapoint is below the goal line, then we suggest adjusting or intensifying the inter-vention through individual problem analysis.

#### E. Action: Identify Students With Median Datapoint Above Goal Line

When looking at progress-monitoring graphs for students in the intervention, identify those students with the median of their last three datapoints above the goal line. For exam-ple, in figure 5.20, Judipe's median datapoint is 90 words per minute. They have reached their goal of 90 words per minute and have been receiving the intervention for over two months. In their case, it would be reasonable to fade out or discontinue the interven-tion. In figure 5.21 (page 174), we recommend ways to remove or fade an intervention.

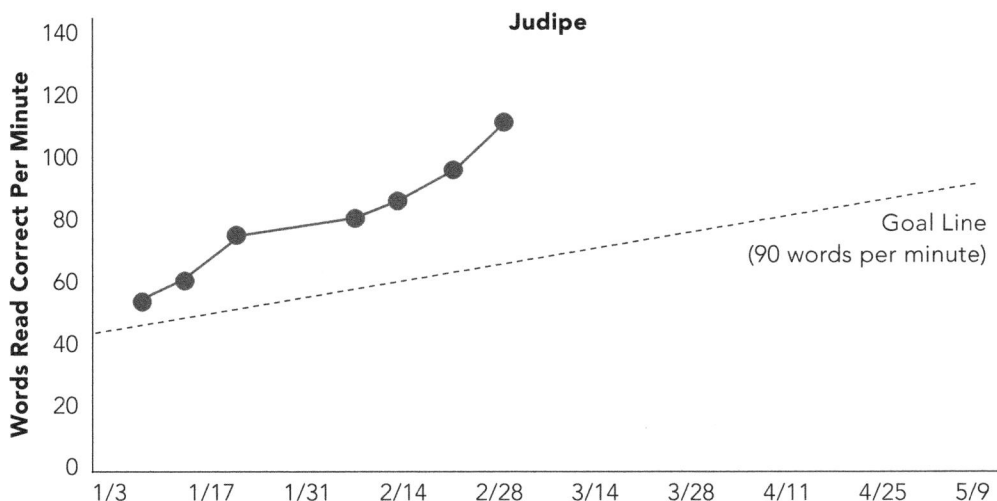

**Figure 5.20: Progress-monitoring graph of a student receiving Tier 2 intervention.**

| Domain | Example Ways to Fade |
|---|---|
| Instruction | • Reduce the dosage of the intervention, such as increasing the group size, reducing the number of sessions, or decreasing the lengths of the sessions.<br><br>• Increase the time between a response and feedback; alternatively, change the level of feedback.<br><br>• Adjust the explicit instruction or guided practice for the student by adjusting the amount of modeling, review, or opportunities to respond that are provided. |
| Curriculum | • Remove the intervention time, but continue to provide daily or weekly check-ins during core instruction to ensure the skills taught in the intervention session transfer to core instruction.<br><br>• Shift the focus of the intervention to the next stage in the instructional hierarchy. |
| Environment | • Reduce the frequency, nature, or amount of acknowledgment or reinforcement.<br><br>• Remove the intervention time, but progress monitor the student more frequently for two weeks to ensure skills sustain. |
| Learner | • Celebrate the "graduation" of the intervention with the student, and make a plan for seeking help or ensuring the student uses the learned skills moving forward. |

**Figure 5.21: Example ways to fade a Tier 2 intervention across instruction, curriculum, and environment.**

### F. Action: Identify Students With Median Datapoint Below Goal Line

When looking at the progress-monitoring graphs, also identify those students with the median of their last three datapoints below the goal line. For example, Leon (see figure 5.22) has a median datapoint well below the goal line. Students who score below the goal line will need some individual problem solving, and we recommend first checking that fidelity is high for that particular student. Although fidelity of the intervention may be high for the group overall, perhaps that particular student has been disengaged or absent, and thus hasn't received the intervention as intended. Educators can review attendance records or examine any engagement data gathered (such as the information captured in the example in figure 5.12, page 167, the generic fidelity tool). If the fidelity is low for that student, resolve the lack of fidelity and continue with the intervention.

If fidelity data are high (that is, the student has received the intervention as intended), determine whether the student needs additional problem solving at Tier 2 or whether they should receive Tier 3 supports. Students who have scored well below the goal line (such as Leon), received a previous iteration of Tier 2, or have received Tier 2 supports for twenty weeks may need intensive supports (Vaughn

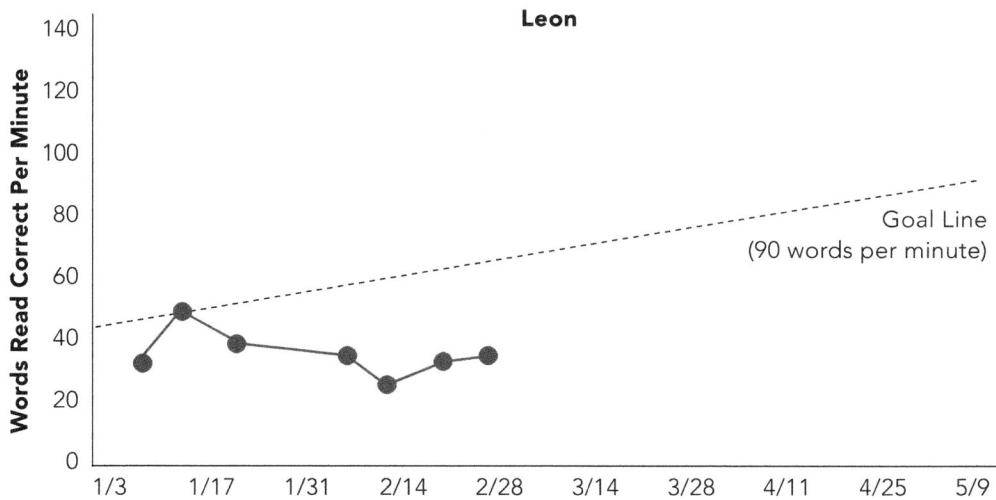

**Figure 5.22: Progress-monitoring graph of a student with median datapoint below the goal line.**

et al., 2012). Educators make these decisions on a case-by-case basis, but they should have school and district policy or guidelines to help make those decisions. Keep in mind that the changes for students may vary depending on the extent to which their scores fall below the goal line. For example, in figure 5.23, Heron is just below the goal line, so she may be a good candidate for increasing the dosage or intensity of the Tier 2 intervention. Leon is well below the goal line, so they may need more substantial changes, perhaps even more intensive supports (that is, Tier 3). See page 184 for a reproducible with questions and ways to answer them for problem solving at Tier 2 for an individual student; you can also examine the information in the next chapter as well.

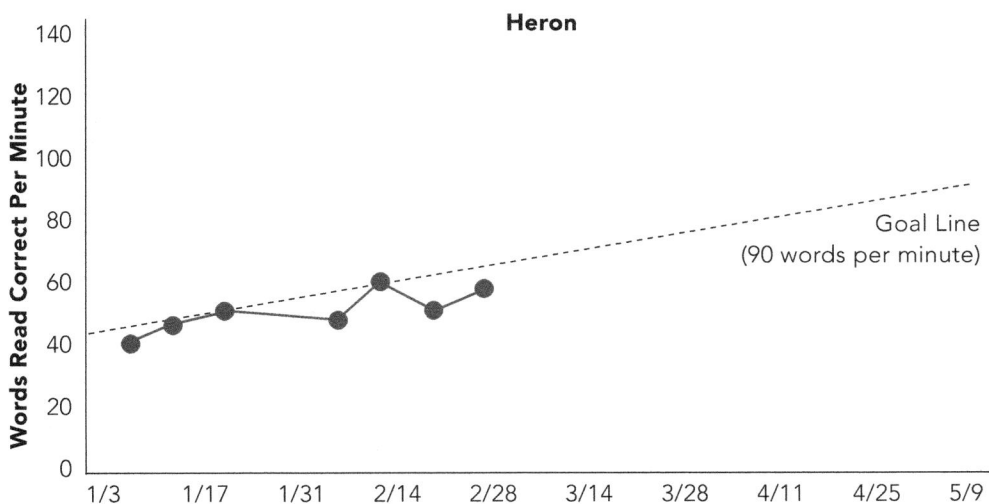

**Figure 5.23: Progress-monitoring graph for a student just below goal line.**

## Tier 2 Team Roles

Our recommendation is that each grade level or department has its own Tier 2 team that coordinates and provides Tier 2 interventions (in fact, it may be very similar to your Tier 1 team). There may be different structures in various schools based on the size of the school or interventions possible (for example a smaller rural school may just have one teacher per grade level; thus, teachers across grade levels may meet and discuss the data for interventions), but we describe a team for a given grade level that oversees interventions for its students.

Regardless of the specific team structure, the purpose of the Tier 2 team is to oversee all aspects of Tier 2. The team is responsible for reviewing screening data and conducting risk verification to determine who may need support, determining which interventions to provide students, gathering and reviewing progress-monitoring data (or both), and determining when and what adjustments to make to the intervention. Tier 2 teams may even actually provide the intervention, as the interventionists or teachers providing the interventions are typically members of these teams. Although there may be individual members or smaller task groups to conduct the aforementioned tasks, a Tier 2 team should do the following.

- Analyze screening data to identify students who need support.
- Determine the instructional need of students who require support and identify an intervention (that is, use the placement protocol and intervention matrix).
- Determine groups for interventions.
- Analyze (and in some cases, gather) progress-monitoring data.
- Make adjustments to Tier 2 interventions.
- Communicate with parents and staff regarding students receiving Tier 2.
- Recommend Tier 3 supports when appropriate.

When forming a Tier 2 team, consider which educators should make up the team and how to conduct team meetings.

### Members

The members may vary, but at a minimum, the Tier 2 team should include the general education teachers of the students whose data are being examined. Although teachers may have oversight of an intervention time to create groups and provide interventions for students, leadership or administration can also be present for any larger decisions needed. Further, additional support staff or interventionists may be a part of the team. Because part of the team's function is to identify who needs support, we're less concerned about members' titles and more focused on their role on the team. This team will need access to screening data, knowledge of Tier 2 interventions, and the skills to review and analyze progress-monitoring data.

Team members will need to communicate well with staff, family, and students, particularly those who are receiving Tier 2 interventions. Certain interventions will likely need a coordinator or contact person with expertise on the intervention.

### Meetings

When thinking about Tier 2, there are two different types of meetings: (1) initial placement and (2) review meetings. During *initial placement* meetings, the team will review screening data and risk-verification data to place students into interventions (steps 1 to 3 of the problem-solving model). In contrast, during *review meetings*, the team will analyze fidelity and progress-monitoring data to make adjustments to intervention groups (step 4 of the model). For each meeting, we offer general guidelines for before, during, and after the meetings in figure 5.24.

---

**Before Meetings**

- Gather the necessary data for the meeting, including screening data, progress-monitoring data, and fidelity data.
- Ensure any progress-monitoring data are graphed visually and organized by groups or interventions.

**During Meetings**

- Follow the steps of the problem-solving model.
- Document changes to interventions.

**After Meetings**

- Implement changes needed to the interventions or for students.
- Notify parents, teachers, and other personnel as appropriate.

---

**Figure 5.24: Guidelines for before, during, and after Tier 2 meetings.**

## Common Roadblocks and Possible Solutions

Next, we discuss common roadblocks that may occur with Tier 2 and data-based decision making. These roadblocks include how to handle more than 20 percent of students needing intervention, when staff want to individualize at Tier 2, when data are not organized to facilitate decision making, and how to handle the many tasks that a Tier 2 team must take on.

### More Than 20 Percent of Students Need Intervention

Often, schools will find that more than 20 percent of their students score within an at-risk range, thus posing the issue of more students needing intervention than the school has capacity to support. When schools have this many students needing intervention, first they'll want to examine how they can adjust the core instruction to support all or most students since this indicates a systemwide issue (see chapter 3, page 73; Harlacher et al., 2015; McIntosh & Goodman, 2016). In doing so, they can maximize the number of students they can reach and create a more efficient MTSS, but when most students appear at risk, then the core instruction needs to be adjusted to meet their needs. The next step is to prioritize the students who can be served within interventions. One option is to identify 20 percent of the students with the lowest scores and offer intervention for them. Keep in mind, the relative intensity of Tier 2 may be more robust since students will have scored at a higher risk level. A factor that plays into this is the amount of resources that are available. We recommend that schools provide intervention to their most needy students and within the limits of their resources (for example, time and personnel) to ensure they create an effective Tier 2 system. This highlights the importance of the core instruction. If 40 percent of students score at risk and need intervention, but only 20 percent of students will receive additional intervention, one can see how the core instruction needs to be adjusted to meet the needs of the other 20 percent of students who did not receive intervention. Here, schools will need to be creative and flexible as they work to ensure their instruction across MTSS can meet the needs of their students.

### Staff Wanting to Individualize at Tier 2

Although some frameworks, particularly older response to intervention approaches, have used individual problem solving at Tier 2 (Greenwood et al., 2008), this is not a highly touted approach because of its lack of efficiency (Barnes & Harlacher, 2008; McIntosh & Goodman, 2016). The time and heavy use of resources necessary to intensify at Tier 2 often don't make sense because we know that a standard intervention provided at Tier 2 is more cost effective and efficient. Also, as mentioned, 70–80 percent of students respond to a standard intervention and do not need additional intervention beyond that (Hawken et al., 2021; Vaughn et al., 2010). Therefore, schools can save time, money, and resources by identifying students quickly and providing a standardized, evidence-based intervention at Tier 2 (Zumeta-Edmonds et al., 2019). As outlined in this chapter, using a placement protocol can help educators make accurate, educated attempts at matching students' needs to an intervention. If unsuccessful at Tier 2, then educators can use intensive assessment and individual problem solving for Tier 3 supports.

### Lack of Data Organization to Facilitate Decision Making

One common barrier occurs when teams or educators meet to look at data that are not in graph form. Progress-monitoring data are best viewed in graph form because this allows educators to see student performance over time and quickly compare it in relation to a goal line. We've seen teams or educators examine their data organized as a table, which renders quick decision making nearly impossible. Progress-monitoring data should always be graphed, and screening data should be organized such that it's quick to identify which risk category a student is in (for example, color coded, rank ordered, or numerically ordered from low scores to high scores). If a team can organize the data prior to meeting, then team members can spend their time analyzing the data during the meeting rather than finding or organizing them. The role of the data coordinator on the team can be to bring the organized data to the team meeting.

### Overwhelming Amount of Team Tasks for Tier 2

There are quite a few tasks for a Tier 2 team to handle, including analyzing screening data, using a placement protocol, looking at fidelity data, examining progress-monitoring data (perhaps even collecting it), and overseeing movement within groups. Quite the list of tasks! That said, we understand the need for flexibility. Team structures and roles for a Tier 2 team are not rigid. Divide up the tasks among the team members or consider using just one person for some of the tasks. For example, one person can examine screening data and identify students who need risk verification. That person can bring the list to the team to divide up conducting risk verification. Or perhaps other staff members are asked to do some tasks, such as gathering progress-monitoring data. Similarly, one person can examine group performance and bring to the team meeting the list of students who need their intervention adjusted. There is no rigid structure for team roles or division of labor, so work with what's best for your site. Because there are decision rules and placement protocols, the team can trust that educators are using data in the manner it's agreed on.

## Summary

For Tier 2, educators use the problem-solving model by first asking which students are at risk. Using screening data and risk verification, educators can identify which students need Tier 2 supports. They then use the placement protocol to identify an appropriate intervention for them. The placement protocol creates an efficient process, as educators and teams can look at data quickly and see which intervention will likely address that need (there's no need to gather extensive additional data, as the placement protocol outlines what pattern of data indicates which instructional need, which is connected to an intervention used by the school). After implementing the intervention , educators examine fidelity data and progress-monitoring data to determine whether the fidelity of the intervention is sufficient and whether it's working for a given student. Further, they examine whether the Tier 2 intervention is effective as a whole (that is, for the majority of students), which dictates whether group problem solving is needed for all students, or whether individual problem solving is needed. In the next chapter, we apply the problem-solving model to Tier 3 for individual students.

# Tier 2 Worksheets for Problem-Solving Model

## Summary of Problem Solving at Tier 2

| Step | Action | Key Questions | Tasks |
|------|--------|---------------|-------|
| 1 | Problem Identification | • Which students are at risk? | • Identify risk level.<br>• Conduct risk verification for those at risk. |
| 2 | Problem Analysis | • What is each student's instructional need? | • Use the placement protocol to identify key instructional need. |
| 3 | Plan Identification and Implementation | • What intervention addresses that need? | • Confirm placement into the intervention.<br>• Select a goal and progress-monitoring tool.<br>• Select a fidelity tool. |
| 4 | Plan Evaluation | • Is the fidelity at least 90 percent?<br>• Is the intervention effective overall?<br>• Which students is the intervention working for? Which students is it not working for? | • Examine fidelity.<br>• Examine overall effectiveness.<br>• Examine individual student progress. |

┌─ **Step 1: Problem Identification** ─

┌─ **Step 1: Problem Identification** ─────────────────────────────────┐

1. Identify student's risk level based on universal screening. Refer to your screener's risk categories to initially identify those at risk.

2. Of those who scored below the expected criterion, conduct risk verification. Use the following worksheet or another means to capture students' scores.

└──────────────────────────────────────────────────────────────────┘

### Risk-Verification Worksheet

| Name | Initial Screening Score: _____ | Risk-Verification Measure 1: _____ | Risk-Verification Measure 2: _____ | Intervention Needed? |
|------|------|------|------|------|
|  |  |  |  |  |
|  |  |  |  |  |
|  |  |  |  |  |
|  |  |  |  |  |
|  |  |  |  |  |
|  |  |  |  |  |

Write the name of students who scored below the expected criterion in their respective row and enter scores from two other measures. Flag for intervention each student who has two of three scores that fall below the expected criterion.

┌─ **Step 2: Problem Analysis** ──────────────────────────────────────┐

3. Identify the instructional need of each student who needs Tier 2 supports by using the placement protocol for your school.

└──────────────────────────────────────────────────────────────────┘

### Placement Protocol Template

| If the Student Scored: | And | And | And | Then the Instructional Need Is: | Provide: |
|------|------|------|------|------|------|
|  |  |  |  |  |  |
|  |  |  |  |  |  |
|  |  |  |  |  |  |
|  |  |  |  |  |  |
|  |  |  |  |  |  |

Enter information based on your district or school's placement protocol.

## Step 3: Plan Identification and Implementation

4. Confirm the intervention by communicating with relevant staff and family members.

5. Identify a goal for each student (for example, expected benchmark criterion for next benchmark period) and a fidelity tool to measure each intervention.

6. Document which students are receiving which intervention in the following table.

### Intervention Grouping for Tier 2

| Student | Tier 2 Intervention | Goal | Fidelity Tool |
|---------|--------------------|------|---------------|
|         |                    |      |               |
|         |                    |      |               |
|         |                    |      |               |
|         |                    |      |               |

Write each student's name and intervention, along with the goal and fidelity tool. Add more rows as needed.

**Step 4: Plan Evaluation**

7. Evaluate Tier 2 and students' progress using the questions in the following table.

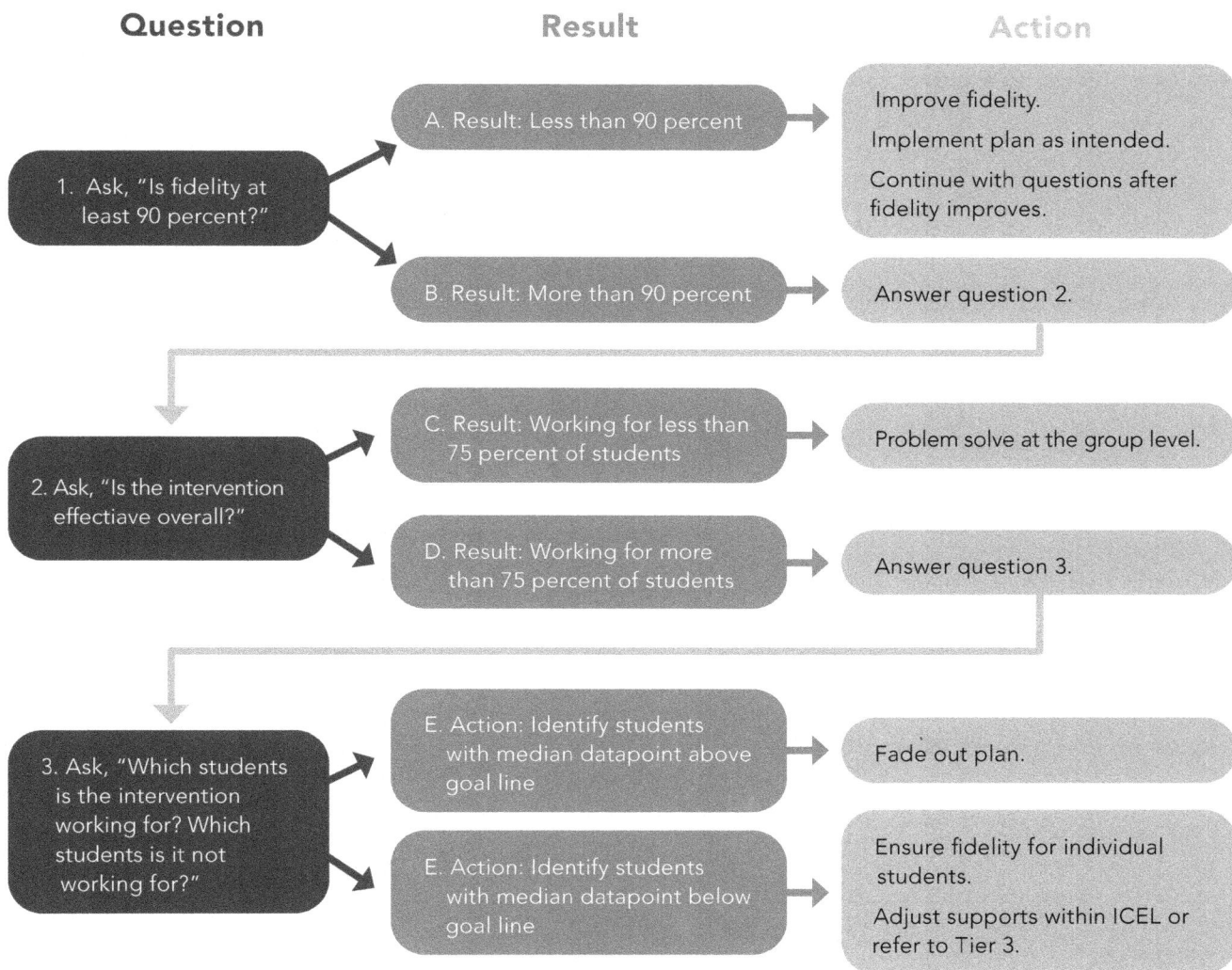

| Question | Result | Action |
|---|---|---|
| 1. Ask, "Is fidelity at least 90 percent?" | A. Result: Less than 90 percent | Improve fidelity. Implement plan as intended. Continue with questions after fidelity improves. |
| | B. Result: More than 90 percent | Answer question 2. |
| 2. Ask, "Is the intervention effectiave overall?" | C. Result: Working for less than 75 percent of students | Problem solve at the group level. |
| | D. Result: Working for more than 75 percent of students | Answer question 3. |
| 3. Ask, "Which students is the intervention working for? Which students is it not working for?" | E. Action: Identify students with median datapoint above goal line | Fade out plan. |
| | E. Action: Identify students with median datapoint below goal line | Ensure fidelity for individual students. Adjust supports within ICEL or refer to Tier 3. |

# Example Questions to Ask for
# Individual Problem Analysis at Tier 2

| Domain | Questions | Example Ways to Assess |
|---|---|---|
| Instruction | • Has the student attended a sufficient number of sessions?<br>• Is fidelity sufficient for the student? | • Review attendance records.<br>• Review fidelity data or collect fidelity data on engagement. |
| | • Was the instruction explicit enough for the student (for example, sufficient modeling, guiding practice, and feedback)? | • Observe aspects of explicit instruction for that student. |
| | • Does the student have sufficient opportunities to respond? | • Observe opportunities to respond for that student, including accuracy of those responses. |
| Curriculum | • Does the student have the background knowledge or prerequisite skills to access the curriculum? | • Examine permanent products to assess student's prerequisite skills relative to the scope and sequence of curriculum.<br>• Interview interventionist. |
| | • Does the intervention target the needed skill for the student? | • Review focus of curriculum or permanent products and compare to student's needs. |
| | • Does the difficulty level of the materials match the student's instructional level (that is, frustrational, instructional, or independent)? | • Review permanent products for accuracy to calculate instructional level for the student.<br>• Review lesson plans relative to student's instructional level. |
| Environment | • Does the behavioral support need to be adjusted to be more supportive? | • Observe the amount of feedback or acknowledgment provided to the student.<br>• Review lesson plans for teaching related to behavioral support or classroom management. |
| | • Does the student feel connected to the teacher or other students? | • Interview or observe the student during intervention. |
| | • Can adjustments be made to motivate student's learning?<br>• How is the student's engagement or motivation during the intervention? | • Observe level of engagement or interview interventionist to assess engagement.<br>• Review fidelity data or observe student during intervention. |
| Learner | • Are there cultural or linguistic factors not being considered for the student? | • Review student's records or previously gathered data.<br>• Interview student, teachers, or family. |
| | • Is the instructional setting and design of the plan correctly taking into account the student's needs or characteristics? | • Interview student or interventionist.<br>• Observe intervention. |

# CHAPTER 6

# Data-Based Decision Making at Tier 3 for Individual Students

Tier 3 consists of individualized and intensive supports designed for students with serious and ongoing needs. It's focused on interventions for students based on their specific and individual needs. It requires the most comprehensive resources and energy within the school (McIntosh & Goodman, 2016).

Tier 3 is highlighted by a few features, including the following (McIntosh & Goodman, 2016; Zumeta-Edmonds et al., 2019).

- Individualized support based on the data-based needs of the student

- Intensive support relative to previous tiers

- The most explicit instruction on the skill that the student hasn't mastered yet

- The most time to practice the targeted skills and more frequent opportunities to respond

- The most frequent feedback on skill performance

- The smallest instructional setting (usually a group size of no more than three students)

- The most communication with the home setting

In this chapter, we apply the problem-solving model to Tier 3. We discuss each step, including the key questions listed in figure 6.1 (page 186) and tasks for each step. Following our discussion of the problem-solving model, we then share how to structure a team to use the model for Tier 3. We also include common roadblocks

| Step | Action | Key Questions | Tasks |
|------|--------|---------------|-------|
| 1 | Problem Identification | • Which students are most at risk?<br>• Which students are not making sufficient growth? | • Identify risk level and determine need for Tier 3.<br>• Examine progress-monitoring data and determine need for Tier 3. |
| 2 | Problem Analysis | • What is the student's instructional need?<br>• Why is the student not making adequate growth? | • Review previously gathered information.<br>• Select a hypothesis.<br>• Use RIOT/ICEL to confirm the hypothesis. |
| 3 | Plan Identification and Implementation | • What adjustments to instruction, curriculum, and environment can improve the student's skills? | • Identify factors to adjust within the instruction, curriculum, and environment.<br>• Select a goal and progress-monitoring tool.<br>• Select a fidelity tool. |
| 4 | Plan Evaluation | • What is the fidelity of the plan?<br>• Is the plan working for the student? | • Evaluate fidelity.<br>• Evaluate progress-monitoring data. |

**Figure 6.1: Key questions for use of the problem-solving model at Tier 3.**

and solutions for using the model at Tier 3. Further, we provide worksheets at the end of the chapter (page 217) to guide educators or teams as they conduct problem solving at the Tier 3 level.

## Problem Identification

In this step, educators use the problem-solving model at Tier 3 to identify those students who are at risk and need the most intensive supports offered by the school. Educators will not only consider screening data to determine who needs Tier 3 supports but also progress-monitoring data for some students when making a determination. As such, educators define the problem at this level by either the gap between the student's performance compared to a criterion *or* as the gap between the student's current growth compared to the expected growth from a Tier 2 intervention.

### *Identify Risk Level: Which Students Need Intensive Supports?*

We discussed using screening data to identify students who are at risk in chapter 5 (page 151), and the same concepts apply here. For Tier 3, educators are determining whether students are in such dire risk that they need intensive supports right away.

Examine the screening data and identify those students who are within the severe or well below benchmark range and then conduct risk verification (as described in chapter 5, page 151). For example, in figure 6.2, we list several ninth-grade students from an incoming class who scored within a severe-risk range based on a spring mathematics assessment. Additional information was gathered to conduct risk verification and to make decisions about the provision of Tier 3 supports. As illustrated in figure 6.2, Eleanor, Chidi, and Jason are identified for Tier 3, whereas Tahani is not.

| Name | Screening Assessment in Mathematics | Risk-Verification Measure 1 | Risk-Verification Measure 2 | Intervention Needed? |
|------|-------------------------------------|-----------------------------|-----------------------------|----------------------|
| Eleanor | Severe Risk | Some Risk | Severe Risk | Yes, Tier 3 |
| Chidi | Severe Risk | Some Risk | Severe Risk | Yes, Tier 3 |
| Jason | Severe Risk | Severe Risk | Severe Risk | Yes, Tier 3 |
| Tahani | Severe Risk | Low Risk | Low Risk | No |

Each student who has two of three scores in the severe-risk range is a candidate for Tier 3.

**Figure 6.2: Risk verification for Tier 3.**

### *Examine Progress-Monitoring Data: Which Students Are Not Making Sufficient Growth?*

Educators can also examine progress-monitoring data from students who have received Tier 2 supports. Additionally, they analyze fidelity data and other relevant information such as the length of Tier 2 supports or the number of Tier 2 iterations in determining whether a student should receive Tier 3 supports. To analyze progress-monitoring data, ask questions regarding the length of time the student has received the intervention, the fidelity of that intervention, and the student's growth rate. Remember that Tier 2 interventions are typically provided for ten to twenty weeks, and after twenty weeks there is a diminishing return for students (Vaughn et al., 2012). Further, if students haven't made progress in two iterations of Tier 2, then providing Tier 3 supports is likely warranted. Use the questions in figure 6.3 (page 188) as a guide. Although it may be tempting to provide Tier 3 supports without answering the questions in figure 6.1 (page 186), they're important to ensure data-based decisions and avoid an over-expenditure or misuse of resources.

If the intervention has been provided for a sufficient time or number of iterations (for example, twelve to twenty weeks; Vaughn, Wanzek, & Murray, 2012) and if the fidelity data indicate it was provided as intended (over 90 percent fidelity), then examine the growth and determine whether the student will reach the goal in a reasonable amount of time with the current intervention or whether

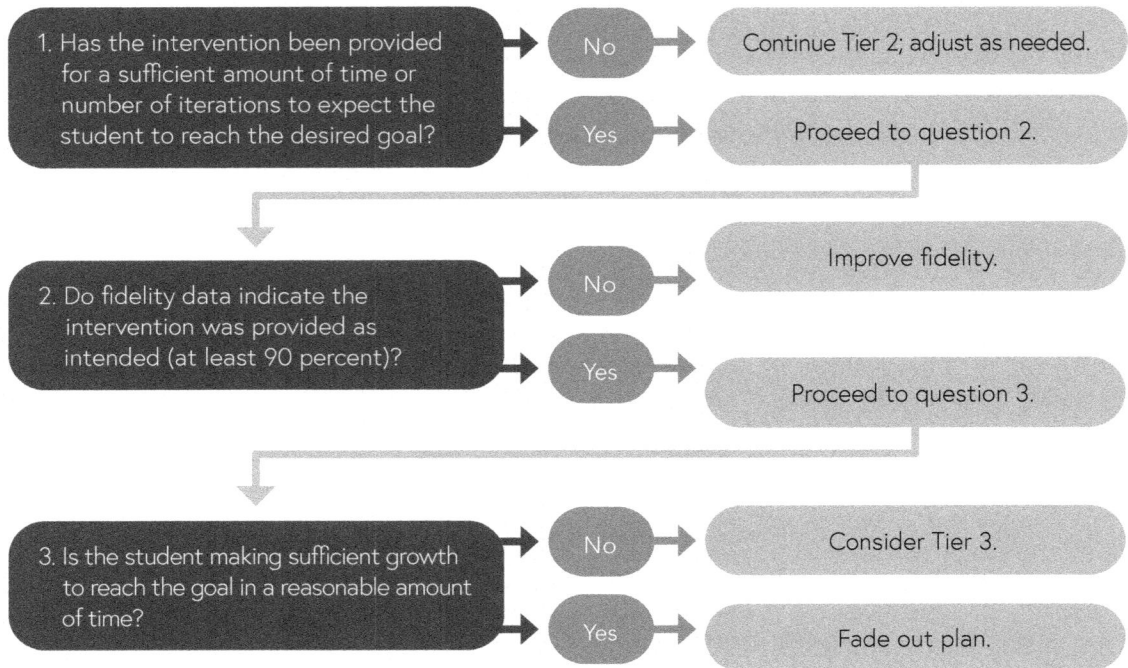

**Figure 6.3: Problem identification when analyzing progress-monitoring data for Tier 3.**

Tier 3 is needed. For example, consider the student's growth in figure 6.4. The student received two iterations of Tier 2 over a period of sixteen weeks, yet they still were not going to reach their goal. As a result, the problem was the gap between their current growth and growth needed to reach their goal; the decision was made to provide Tier 3 supports.

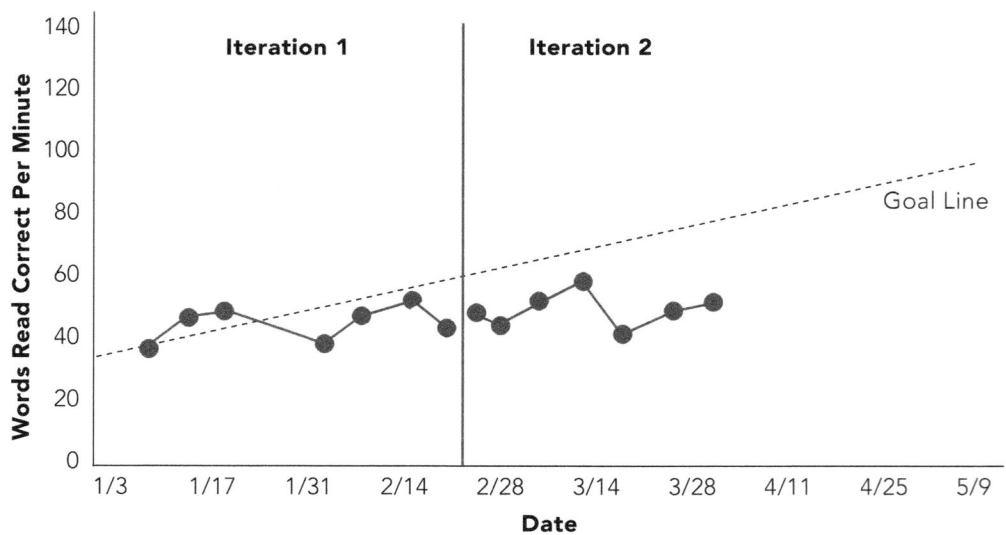

**Figure 6.4: Example graph for a student receiving a Tier 2 intervention.**

Following identification or confirmation that a student requires intensive supports at Tier 3, educators can identify what support that student needs in the next step, problem analysis.

## Problem Analysis

In this step, educators explore hypotheses about why students need additional support or why their current support isn't benefiting them. Educators use the RIOT/ICEL matrix to explore various aspects of the instructional environment and the needs of the student (see figure 2.6, page 54). Educators identify a hypothesis and gather information that either confirms or disconfirms it. If confirmed, educators can proceed to develop a plan to resolve the issue, but if it's disconfirmed, they gather additional information and explore additional hypotheses. Thus, problem analysis is an iterative process conducted until educators find a hypothesis.

When exploring hypotheses, keep in mind there is no set order or standard way to explore them. Rather, educators will explore the most reasonable or obvious hypothesis based on the student. We recommend checking if the intervention matches the instructional need of the student. If the intervention doesn't match the instructional need of the student (for example, the student needs mathematics computation instruction but is receiving mathematics application instruction), then adjust the focus of the intervention. If the intervention does match the student's instructional need, then we suggest exploring the intensity of the instruction and other general dimensions within the instruction and environment. Here we offer a way to organize and analyze information for problem analysis: first, review previously gathered and existing information, then select a hypothesis, use RIOT/ICEL to confirm the hypothesis, and summarize problem analysis before moving to the next step.

### Review Previously Gathered and Existing Information

Begin by examining the previously known or gathered information to determine the student's instructional need or why the student is not making adequate growth. There is likely a fair amount of data already gathered to review, particularly if the student has been receiving interventions previously. Use a template such as the one in figure 6.5 (page 190) to organize the information. (We have provided example information in figure 6.5, but a blank template is included in the reproducible "Tier 3 Worksheets for Problem-Solving Model" on page 217.) This can help you consider the broad hypotheses and areas to examine when exploring hypotheses.

### Select a Hypothesis

After reviewing the previously gathered or existing data, consider what could be a reasonable hypothesis for the student. In figure 6.6 (page 191), we offer some general hypotheses to consider. This is not an exhaustive list of possible hypotheses,

| Area | General Hypothesis | Summary of Relevant Information |
|------|--------------------|---------------------------------|
| Instruction | Is the instruction evidence based, explicit, and intense enough for the student? | • There is a high rate of responses for students, but it's unclear how accurate students are with those responses.<br>• There are twenty-five minutes of Tier 2 time provided four days per week in reading. |
| Curriculum | Does the curriculum match the needs of the student? Does the student have the prerequisite skills to access the curriculum successfully? | • Student is in acquisition stage with phonics, based on analysis of recent screening data.<br>• It's unclear what specific needs student has in phonics. |
| Environment | Does the environment support learning in a positive, proactive way? | • There's a lack of high rate of praise and no clear expectations for classroom and instructional setting. |
| Learner | Does the instruction, curriculum, and environment consider the student's unique characteristics? | • Student's culture matches the predominant culture in school.<br>• Student has no second language needs. |

**Figure 6.5: Example summary of previously known or gathered information.**

but we've organized key ones across instruction, curriculum, environment, and the learner (Burns, 2021; Christ & Arañas, 2014). Determine whether one of the hypotheses makes sense for the student and consider whether additional information is needed to confirm the hypothesis. If none of those hypotheses apply, identify a different one to begin.

### Use RIOT/ICEL to Confirm the Hypothesis

With a hypothesis identified, determine whether the gathered information is sufficient to confirm the hypothesis or whether you need additional information to confirm it. Consult the RIOT/ICEL matrix in chapter 2 (page 54) and determine any additional information that is necessary, or consider the information listed in figure 6.6 under the Possible Areas to Assess column. In this section, we offer data collection methods to consider, depending on the hypothesis selected, concerning instruction, curriculum, environment, or learner and student engagement. Keep in mind that hypothesis exploration can be an iterative process, as you may gather data, disconfirm a hypothesis, select a different hypothesis, and gather more data until you confirm a hypothesis.

| Domain | Hypothesis | Possible Areas to Assess | Possible Instructional Need |
|---|---|---|---|
| Instruction | The student hasn't had sufficient instruction. | ▪ Examine explicitness, dosage, and intensity of instruction.<br>▪ Observe rate of opportunities to respond in relation to accuracy and corrective feedback.<br>▪ Calculate minutes of instruction and consider whether it's sufficient for student's needs. | ▪ Provide additional instruction, modeling, and feedback on the skills to perform the task. |
| | The student needs more practice with the skill. | ▪ Review lesson plans or permanent products for amount of repetition and skill review the student has received. | ▪ Provide more repetition, practice, fluency instruction or application of the skill. |
| Curriculum | The task is too hard, or the student lacks the prerequisite skills to perform the task. | ▪ Assess skills along the instructional hierarchy, including prerequisite skills, and compare results to scope and sequence of the intervention.<br>▪ Conduct survey-level assessment.<br>▪ Conduct error analysis. | ▪ Teach prerequisite skills or background knowledge needed to perform the task.<br>▪ Increase explicitness of instruction to ensure learning of prerequisite skills.<br>▪ Adjust focus or supplement intervention to teach prerequisite skills. |
| Environment | The environment isn't supportive or accommodating of certain student characteristics. | ▪ Interview student, staff, or family for student characteristics or information to inform environment and instruction.<br>▪ Observe instruction for student needs.<br>▪ Examine use of effective classroom management. | ▪ Explicitly adjust setting to accommodate the student characteristics.<br>▪ Adjust or improve use of effective classroom management strategies. |
| Learner | The student lacks sufficient motivation to perform the skill. | ▪ Examine behavioral support in the environment and use of engagement strategies.<br>▪ Review behavior-management expectations during instruction and intervention times.<br>▪ Review materials to see if they're culturally and developmentally appropriate. | ▪ Adjust motivation, engagement, or reinforcement strategies. |

**Figure 6.6: Possible hypotheses to explore at Tier 3.**

### Instruction

If the hypothesis is that the instruction is insufficient or that there's a mismatch between the student's need and the instruction provided, observing the instruction is warranted. You can observe instruction for elements of explicitness, such as the amount of guided instruction and modeling. We recommend observing instruction for the number of opportunities to respond, the student's accuracy of responses, and whether the teacher provides praise or corrective feedback to the student following an opportunity to respond. We suggest opportunities to respond because they're an indication of the intensity of the instruction, and their accuracy can indicate whether the student is mastering the material (Harlacher & Whitcomb, 2022; Haydon, MacSuga-Gage, Simonsen, & Hawkins, 2012; Simonsen et al., 2021). In figure 6.7, we offer a general observation checklist that an educator could use to observe the instruction or interventions provided to the student. Admittedly, gathering all these data may take some skill and practice with observing instruction to accurately gather the information. We've illustrated example data in figure 6.7 (also see the reproducible "Tier 3 Worksheets for Problem-Solving Model" on page 217).

These data in figure 6.7 indicate a rate of 3.2 opportunities to respond per minute, with feedback provided at a rate of 1.9 per minute or for 59 percent of the responses. Students generally need eight to twelve opportunities to respond during small-group direct instruction, and four to six responses in larger group settings, such as whole-class instruction. Further, students with intensive needs should receive feedback (either praise or corrective feedback) for at least 80 percent (and ideally 100 percent) of their responses. Students should also be accurate at least 80 percent of the time with new material and at least 90 percent with review material or previously taught material (Archer & Hughes, 2010; Gunter et al., 2004; Harlacher, 2015; Haydon et al., 2012; MacSuga-Gage & Simonsen, 2015; Simonsen et al., 2021; Simonsen & Myers, 2015). We generally recommend at least four to six opportunities to respond in Tier 1 instruction, six to eight during Tier 2 supports, and eight to twelve during Tier 3 supports (Harlacher et al., 2014).

### Curriculum

When educators hypothesize that the intervention had the wrong focus or that the student lacks the prerequisite skills or background knowledge to access the intervention, it's helpful to determine where the student's skills actually are. Educators can use diagnostic assessments to accurately assess the specific skills that students have mastered (for example, multiplication facts from 0–7) and those that they have not (multiplication facts from 8–9). Examples of diagnostic assessments include phonics inventories, the Reading Rockets Phonemic Awareness Assessment (see https://bit .ly/46VwUZn), the Northwest Evaluation Association Measures of Academic Progress (www.nwea.org/map-growth), and the Renaissance Star assessment (www.renaissance .com/products/star-assessments). It's helpful to determine where a student's skill is along the instructional hierarchy of skills being taught, as the student's mastery of

**Directions:** Observe instruction for ten minutes. If longer, use additional sheets or add rows to the figure. For each opportunity the teacher provides the student to respond, mark an ✘ in the checkbox in the first column. If the opportunity to respond is correct, color in the box. In the Feedback: Praise or Corrective? column for that opportunity to respond, if the student receives corrective feedback, then place a check mark in the corresponding box for that opportunity to respond. If the student receives praise or acknowledgment, then place a plus sign in the corresponding box. If the student receives neither praise nor corrective feedback, place a dash.

Date __11/6__   Setting __Classroom__

Time __9:35–9:45__   Task __Observed small-group, core instruction__

| Minute | Opportunities to Respond (OTRs) | Feedback: Praise or Corrective? |
|:---:|:---:|:---:|
| 1 | ■ ■ □ □ □ □ □ □ □ □ <br> □ □ □ □ □ □ □ □ □ □ | ⊞ ⊞ □ □ □ □ □ □ □ □ <br> □ □ □ □ □ □ □ □ □ □ |
| 2 | ✘ ■ ■ ■ ✘ □ □ □ □ □ <br> □ □ □ □ □ □ □ □ □ □ | ☑ ⊞ ⊞ ☑ □ □ □ □ □ □ <br> □ □ □ □ □ □ □ □ □ □ |
| 3 | ■ ■ ■ ■ ✘ □ □ □ □ □ <br> □ □ □ □ □ □ □ □ □ □ | ⊞ ⊞ ⊟ ⊞ ⊟ □ □ □ □ □ <br> □ □ □ □ □ □ □ □ □ □ |
| 4 | ■ ■ ■ ■ □ □ □ □ □ □ <br> □ □ □ □ □ □ □ □ □ □ | ⊞ ⊟ ⊞ ⊞ □ □ □ □ □ □ <br> □ □ □ □ □ □ □ □ □ □ |
| 5 | ■ ✘ □ □ □ □ □ □ □ □ <br> □ □ □ □ □ □ □ □ □ □ | ⊞ ⊟ □ □ □ □ □ □ □ □ <br> □ □ □ □ □ □ □ □ □ □ |
| 6 | ■ ✘ ✘ □ □ □ □ □ □ □ <br> □ □ □ □ □ □ □ □ □ □ | ⊞ ⊟ ⊟ □ □ □ □ □ □ □ <br> □ □ □ □ □ □ □ □ □ □ |
| 7 | ■ ✘ □ □ □ □ □ □ □ □ <br> □ □ □ □ □ □ □ □ □ □ | ⊞ ⊟ □ □ □ □ □ □ □ □ <br> □ □ □ □ □ □ □ □ □ □ |
| 8 | ■ ■ ■ ■ □ □ □ □ □ □ <br> □ □ □ □ □ □ □ □ □ □ | ⊞ ⊟ ⊟ □ □ □ □ □ □ □ <br> □ □ □ □ □ □ □ □ □ □ |
| 9 | ■ ✘ ■ □ □ □ □ □ □ □ <br> □ □ □ □ □ □ □ □ □ □ | ⊞ ⊟ ⊞ □ □ □ □ □ □ □ <br> □ □ □ □ □ □ □ □ □ □ |
| 10 | ■ ✘ ✘ □ □ □ □ □ □ □ <br> □ □ □ □ □ □ □ □ □ □ | ⊞ ⊟ ⊟ □ □ □ □ □ □ □ <br> □ □ □ □ □ □ □ □ □ □ |
| **Average or Totals** | 3.2 OTRs per minute with 69 percent accuracy | Feedback provided 59 percent of the time (1.9 per minute) |

**Figure 6.7: Observation form for instruction.**

the skill impacts the type and focus of instruction for that student (Burns, 2021). We discuss the instructional hierarchy in chapter 2 (page 41), so we refer you back to that section for a review. In figure 6.8, we offer a general set of questions to identify where a student's mastery of a skill falls. Please note that we limit the table to just the first three stages of the skill, as the fourth stage (adaptation) is less targeted in Tiers 2 and 3 (Burns, 2021; Parker & Burns, 2014).

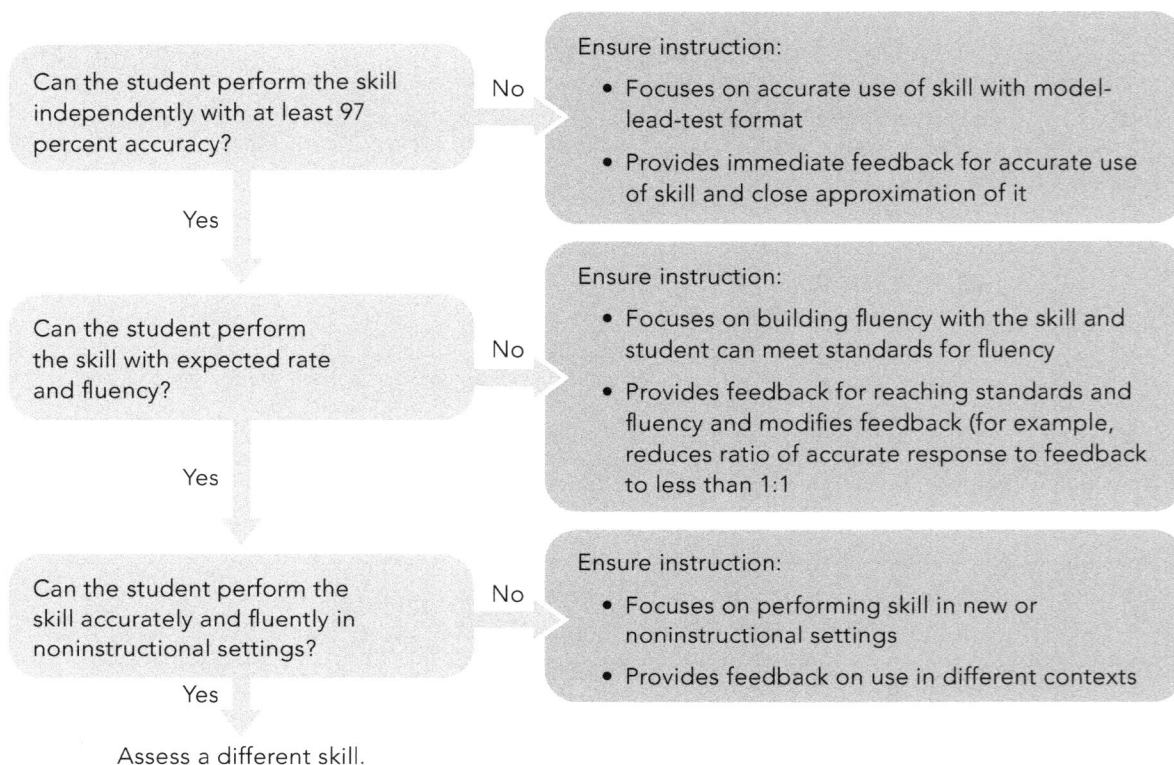

| | | |
|---|---|---|
| Can the student perform the skill independently with at least 97 percent accuracy? | **No** → | **Ensure instruction:**<br>• Focuses on accurate use of skill with model-lead-test format<br>• Provides immediate feedback for accurate use of skill and close approximation of it |
| ↓ Yes | | |
| Can the student perform the skill with expected rate and fluency? | **No** → | **Ensure instruction:**<br>• Focuses on building fluency with the skill and student can meet standards for fluency<br>• Provides feedback for reaching standards and fluency and modifies feedback (for example, reduces ratio of accurate response to feedback to less than 1:1) |
| ↓ Yes | | |
| Can the student perform the skill accurately and fluently in noninstructional settings? | **No** → | **Ensure instruction:**<br>• Focuses on performing skill in new or noninstructional settings<br>• Provides feedback on use in different contexts |
| ↓ Yes | | |
| Assess a different skill. | | |

**Figure 6.8: Application of the instructional hierarchy for a given skill.**

Two options we highlight for determining whether students have mastered skills are (1) survey-level assessment and (2) error analysis.

### Survey-Level Assessment

One option when exploring where the student's skills fall within the instructional hierarchy is a survey-level assessment. A *survey-level assessment* is a process in which educators administer academic probes or brief assessments to students to determine their instructional level in a content area. The educator administers brief probes, such as curriculum-based measurement, and determines the student's proficiency on that probe. Then the educator tests backward in grade levels until they find the level at which the student performs within an instructional level, which can be generally defined as scoring 93–97 percent on the assessment (Harlacher et al., 2013; Parker & Burns, 2014). Survey-level assessment is used often for elementary-aged students, but it can also be used for older students when assessing basic skills (Christ & Arañas, 2014).

A survey-level assessment allows an educator to determine whether the student's skills are within the instructional level described previously, frustrational level, or independent level. Students benefit from interventions typically when they target and build on skills within the instructional level rather than the independent or frustrational levels (Burns, 2021; Burns et al., 2010; 2014; Harlacher et al., 2013).

As an example, the data in figure 6.9 show the administration of oral reading fluency probes for a fourth grader. To reach the instructional level, the student should read both accurately and fluently for a given grade level, based on the end-of-year criterion. Under each Passage column, the educator documents the student's rate, errors, and accuracy. The Median column is the median score across those three passages. The Criterion column lists the expected criterion for that level. As illustrated, the educator tested backward, starting with the student's grade level until the student met the criterion for independence level (that is, above 97 percent accuracy and above expected rate). Here, the student met criteria for an independent level with second-grade material and at an instructional level with third-grade level.

| | Passage 1 | Passage 2 | Passage 3 | Median | Criterion | Instructional Level |
|---|---|---|---|---|---|---|
| Level 4 | 70 words correct per minute/ 7 errors 91 percent accuracy | 63/5 93 percent | 64/6 91 percent | 64 91 percent | 77 | Frustrational |
| Level 3 | 85/6 93 percent | 77/1 99 percent | 85/5 94 percent | 85 94 percent | 53 | Instructional |
| Level 2 | 98/3 97 percent | 95/3 97 percent | 100/3 97 percent | 98 97 percent | 30 | Independent |

Note: When below the expected rate, less than 93 percent accuracy is frustrational range, 93–97 percent is instructional range, and above 97 percent is independent range.

**Figure 6.9: Example results of a survey-level assessment in reading.**

*Error Analysis*

Another option for identifying what skills students have mastered or not mastered is to conduct an error analysis on the student's work (Harlacher et al., 2013; Hosp et al., 2014). Because this is Tier 3, educators will want nuanced information for the given content area. For example, knowing a student needs instruction in phonics is often not enough information for Tier 3; rather, educators need to know what specific vowel sounds or letter blends in which the student needs instruction.

The use of diagnostic data can ascertain this, as well as analyze a student's error patterns. By counting and categorizing the errors a student makes, educators can tailor the instruction to target and strengthen those missing skills.

To analyze errors, gather at least fifty errors that a student makes and group the errors into categories based on the content area. For example, if analyzing mathematics fact errors, group them into the type of mathematics fact (for example, addition and subtraction) or common steps for mathematics facts (for example, borrowing and carrying over). Educators can also analyze the errors and form the categories as they count the type of errors made, such as determining the number of times a student has misread a suffix when reading. Educators can also analyze the errors made against common skills for that content area (for example, sight words, misses beginning sound, misses ending sound, short vowels, and long vowels). Regardless of the error-analysis approach, the goal is to identify patterns of errors made by the student, which the teacher can then target during instruction. We recommend exploring the following websites to learn more about different techniques and worksheets for error analysis.

- National Center on Intensive Intervention's Example Diagnostic Tools table, which includes links for error analysis (https://bit.ly/3O3634N)
- IRIS Center: Error Analysis for Reading (https://bit.ly/3pY9aTH)
- WestEd's Doing What Works: Systematic Analysis of Student Errors protocol (https://dwwlibrary.wested.org/resources/104)
- WestEd's Doing What Works: Reading Skills Error Analysis Sheet (https://dwwlibrary.wested.org/resources/317)

### Environment

When evaluating whether the environment is supportive for students' needs, educators will want to interview them to see what needs they have and the extent to which they perceive the environment supports them. Educators can also interview staff (for example, the intervention teacher and the homeroom or classroom teacher) and family members as well. Here are example questions to use when interviewing students.

- What do you like most about school?
- Which subjects do you find enjoyable or easy? Which ones are difficult?
- What is challenging about school for you?
- If you could change something about school to make it better for you, what would you change?
- What in school is helpful for you?
- How do your teachers help you with learning? What are some things they do that are not helpful for learning?

In addition, we suggest observing the instruction and looking for the presence of effective classroom management strategies, including the rate of praise to redirects or constructive criticism. Classrooms with at least five praise statements to one redirect are associated with higher academic outcomes and less instances of behavioral disruptions or unexpected behavior (Cook et al., 2016; Harlacher, 2015; Reinke, Herman, & Stormont, 2013). Educators can observe whether the praise is general or behavior specific. *General praise* is praise that indicates something is positive (for example, "Great job!"), but behavior-specific praise precisely acknowledges what the student did well and offers feedback (for example, "You worked slowly and diligently. That's very responsible of you"; Harlacher, 2015; Simonsen & Myers, 2015). In figure 6.10, we have included a template with example data that you can use to observe praise in an educational setting and calculate the ratio of praise to redirects for a student. To assess classroom management, teachers can complete the Classroom Management Observation Tool (CMOT; Simonsen et al., 2020) form

**Directions:** Observe instruction for ten minutes. Draw a tally mark for each instance of general praise, behavior-specific praise, and redirects. For the fifth instance in a minute, slash across the four tally marks to create a group of five. Use the formula at the end to calculate the ratio of praise to redirects.

Date __2/12__     Setting __Small group__

Time _1:30 p.m._     Task Observed __Literacy instruction (Tier 2)__

| Minute | General Praise | Behavior-Specific Praise (BSP) | Total Praise (General and BSP) | Redirects |
|:---:|:---:|:---:|:---:|:---:|
| 1 | ‖ | │ | 3 | │ |
| 2 | | │ | 1 | |
| 3 | | | 0 | │ |
| 4 | ‖ | │ | 3 | |
| 5 | │ | ‖│ | 4 | |
| 6 | ‖ | ‖‖ | 6 | |
| 7 | ‖ | 卅 | 7 | │ |
| 8 | │ | ‖‖ | 4 | ‖ |
| 9 | | ‖│ | 3 | │ |
| 10 | | │ | 1 | ‖ |
| Totals | 10 | 23 | 33 | 8 |
| Average/ Minute | 1 | 2.3 | 3.3 | 0.8 |
| Ratio of Praise to Redirects (Total Praise/Total Redirects) | | | 4.12:1 | Aim for at least 5:1 ratio |

**Figure 6.10: Observation template for praise.**

*Visit **MarzanoResources.com/reproducibles** for a free reproducible version of this figure.*

(see the reproducible "Classroom Management Observation Tool [CMOT]" on page 223), or an observer can use the questions in figure 6.11 to rate the presence of classroom management practices (the teacher can also complete these questions rather than an observer). Readers can find additional information on effective classroom management at the Center on PBIS (2021; https://bit.ly/3toT5rq).

| Question | Rating |
|---|---|
| Are there three to five common classroom expectations that are explicitly taught to students? | Yes   No   Not Observed |
| Are routines taught to students for them to get their needs met (for example, asking for help, asking for a restroom break, or turning in assignments)? | Yes   No   Not Observed |
| Are students regularly acknowledged when they display the classroom expectations or prosocial skills? | Yes   No   Not Observed |
| Are there a variety of methods to respond and correct instances of errors or unwanted behavior? | Yes   No   Not Observed |
| Are there a variety of methods used to build relationships among students and between the teacher and students? | Yes   No   Not Observed |
| Are there a variety of methods used to actively engage students during instruction? | Yes   No   Not Observed |
| Are there high rates of opportunities for students to respond? | Yes   No   Not Observed |

**Figure 6.11: Questions for classroom management.**

*Visit **MarzanoResources.com/reproducibles** for a free reproducible version of this figure.*

### Learner

If there are questions about motivation and the level of student engagement, interviewing students for their perspective is important (in fact, it's probably ideal to always interview students and get their perspective). You can use the questions shared previously and add questions about interests and preferences that students have, such as the following.

- What sort of things do you enjoy doing in your free time?
- What are some of your favorite interests, such as music artists, games, or movies?
- When you do well in school, how do you like to be rewarded?

- When you do well in school, what would you want from your teachers? From your classmates?

- Do you like to work in groups or alone?

- Do you prefer private recognition or public recognition when you do well?

- What makes it hard to stay interested in school?

- What would motivate you more in school?

- What subjects or people in history would you like to learn more about in school?

We also suggest evaluating the products and materials used during instruction for their cultural and developmental alignment with the student's background and interests. For example, do the stories they're reading feature characters that are similar to them? Do the topics they're writing about or solving mathematics problems for align with their interests or culture? Additionally, educators can administer a student interest or reinforcement survey (see an example for elementary-aged students at https://bit.ly/3pVQnZc). We offer an example of the survey for secondary students on page 225.

Additionally, educators can interview the student, staff who work with the student, and family members to identify the unique needs and perspectives of the student. They can examine what the student specifically needs or unique characteristics that would impact learning, such as vision needs or the presence of disabilities. As part of assessing learners, we also recommend including questions about the student's needs, background for any disabilities or historical needs that may have been missed (for example, visual needs or auditory or hearing issues), and other characteristics that may inform instruction (for example, the student has an anxiety disorder and requires space to use breathing skills to manage anxiety).

### *Summarize Problem Analysis*

Once you've gathered information confirming a hypothesis about why a student isn't progressing or why the problem is occurring, proceed to develop a plan during the next step. Capture the results of problem analysis using a form similar to figure 6.12 (page 200). The reproducible version is available on page 219 as part of the worksheets at the end of this chapter.

## Plan Identification and Implementation

Here, educators will devise a plan to resolve the issue. This involves identifying factors to adjust within instruction, curriculum, and the environment, thinking through considerations when creating the plan, selecting a goal and progress-monitoring tool, selecting a fidelity tool, and creating a communication plan.

| Instruction<br>What instructional factors are contributing to the problem? | Curriculum<br>What curricular factors are contributing to the problem? |
|---|---|
| Slightly slow pacing, as the rates of responses during Tier 2 intervention block are less than 6 per minute (4.5 responses per minute)<br><br>Pacing is good in core (5.6 responses per minute in large group for class) | Student has not mastered some prerequisite content, as student struggles with multidigit operations (85 percent mastery on probes) and steps for algebraic formulas (50 percent accuracy)<br><br>Amount of practice and repetition embedded in lesson plans is limited |
| Environment<br>What environmental factors are contributing to the problem? | Learner<br>What learner factors are contributing to the problem? |
| High rates of praise and feedback (5.5 to 1 ratio of praise to redirects)<br><br>Schoolwide expectations have been taught and reviewed monthly | High attendance, native English speaker<br><br>Meeting benchmarks in other subject areas |

| Hypothesis (mark in following list) |
|---|
| ☐  The student hasn't had sufficient instruction.<br>☐  The student needs more practice with the skill.<br>☑  The task is too hard, or the student lacks the prerequisite skills to perform the task.<br>☐  The environment isn't considering certain student characteristics.<br>☐  The student isn't motivated to perform the skill.<br>☐  Other: |

| What data confirm the hypothesis? |
|---|
| The low accuracy with skills from assessments, and the limited practice and review opportunities within lesson plans |

*Source: © Oregon Response to Instruction and Intervention, n.d.a. Adapted with permission.*

**Figure 6.12: Template for capturing problem-analysis results.**

### *Identify Factors to Adjust Within Instruction, Curriculum, and the Environment*

Identify factors to adjust that will address the hypothesis from step 3. We offer factors to adjust in figures 6.13, 6.14 (page 202) and 6.15 (page 202) grouped across instruction, curriculum, and the environment. (Note that there aren't learner factors to change; rather, the changes in instruction, curriculum, and environment address the needs of the learner).

| Instruction |
|---|
| **Dosage** |
| ☐ Increase minutes per session (for example, from twenty to thirty minutes per session). |
| ☐ Increase frequency of sessions (for example, from two days per week to four days or add double dose). |
| ☐ Increase total sessions (for example, intervention extended from a six-week course to ten weeks). |
| ☐ Add additional time to interventions or supports (for example, add a fifteen-minute intervention block, add before- or after-school time, or decrease time between review of card). |
| ☐ Change intervention facilitator. |
| ☐ Reduce group size. |
| ☐ Include strategies or select an intervention with a stronger evidence base or higher effect sizes than what is being used. |
| **Delivery or Explicitness** |
| ☐ Ensure clarity of directions and that simple, direct language is used. |
| ☐ Increase opportunities to respond. |
| ☐ Ensure clear error correction procedures and corrective feedback to increase accuracy of responses and opportunities to respond. |
| ☐ Ensure appropriate scaffolding. |
| ☐ Adjust pacing of instruction. |
| ☐ Adjust model-lead-test format to ensure accurate responses. |
| ☐ Modify instruction to support transfer of skills the student learns to other formats and contexts. |

**Figure 6.13: Instruction factors to adjust for designing plans.**

*Visit **MarzanoResources.com/reproducibles** for a free reproducible version of this figure.*

### Think Through Considerations When Creating Plans

Developing plans for students with intensive needs is complex and nuanced, so as you identify factors to adjust for support, here are some things to think about.

- **Anchor the plan around the skill:** You can anchor the plan around the skill or skills for which the student needs teaching while also adjusting the instruction, curriculum, and environment to support teaching of those skills. We suggest using a teach-prompt-response framework when identifying skills that students need (Harlacher & Whitcomb, 2022). We offer a general template to use with example information in figure 6.16.

| Curriculum |
| --- |
| ☐ Add metacognitive and comprehension strategies. |
| ☐ Make strategies more conspicuous with strategies or tools. |
| ☐ Ensure appropriate placement of student within the sequence of skills. |
| ☐ Modify sequence or order of skills to ensure a logical progression. |
| ☐ Adjust examples and nonexamples of content. |
| ☐ Ensure judicious review, systematic cumulative review, or both. |
| ☐ Adjust amount of practice; ensure spaced practice. |
| ☐ Activate background knowledge more (ensure students have necessary background knowledge and skills for the solution strategies). |
| ☐ Ensure the support targets the student's full set of academic skill deficits (ensure coordination with Tier 1 and Tier 2). |
| ☐ Ensure interventions do not address skills the student has already mastered. |

**Figure 6.14: Curriculum factors to adjust for designing plans.**

*Visit **MarzanoResources.com/reproducibles** for a free reproducible version of this figure.*

| Environment |
| --- |
| ☐ Change setting to reduce distractions. |
| ☐ Reteach or reinforce behavioral expectations. |
| ☐ Reteach or teach self-regulation or executive functioning skills. |
| ☐ Reteach or teach routines or procedures. |
| ☐ Ensure precorrection and prompting targets are taught skills. |
| ☐ Adjust reinforcement or ensure reinforcement for academic engagement. |
| ☐ Modify use of general praise to be behavior-specific praise. |
| ☐ Increase praise to a 5:1 ratio of positive statements to corrective feedback. |
| ☐ Modify materials to align with student's interests and background. |

**Figure 6.15: Environment factors to adjust for designing plans.**

*Visit **MarzanoResources.com/reproducibles** for a free reproducible version of this figure.*

| Factor | Description | Plan |
|---|---|---|
| Teach | What skills are being taught or targeted for the student to master? | Reading comprehension |
| Prompt | What prompting strategies can ensure the student uses the taught skills accurately?<br><br>What prompts will discourage inaccurate use of the skills? | Verbal prompting to use the "Click or Clunk" strategy and a visual bookmark on the student's desk of the "Click or Clunk" strategy<br><br>The teacher will remind the student not to rush through reading prior to beginning. The teacher will ask one to two questions about the text throughout instruction to ensure the student is reading and understanding the text. |
| Response | How will use of the skill be reinforced or acknowledged?<br><br>What corrective strategies can be used to address errors? | Each time the student uses the strategy, they mark a checkmark on their tracking sheet.<br><br>Teacher will observe and provide correction when the student uses the skill, using corrective feedback. |

**Figure 6.16: Template for plans for teaching skills.**

- **Coordinate across the day:** When developing Tier 3 plans, be sure to plan for and consider the entire day. Imagine an exercise plan to get healthy and in shape; you may work out for thirty minutes once a day, but there's a remaining twenty-three-and-a-half hours in a day to also consider for getting healthy and in shape, such as cross training or sensible diet choices. Similarly, don't put all your eggs into one basket of intervention time; rather, use the entire day and other areas of instruction. For example, if the intervention time is addressing phonics skills, then other parts of the day can address other skills that the student needs to master (for example, Tier 3 addresses phonics, Tier 2 addresses phonics and fluency, and Tier 1 addresses vocabulary and reading comprehension).

- **Address each issue identified:** For every issue identified within instruction, curriculum, and the environment, identify a way to address it during this step. This creates a multifaceted plan. Further, when considering changes in instruction, curriculum, and the environment, try to identify the simplest, smallest changes that would lead to the most robust effect. Generally, the use of a high rate of opportunities to respond and high rates of behavior-specific praise are two cost-effective methods for intensifying instruction (Harlacher, 2015; Simonsen et al., 2021; Simonsen & Myers, 2015). We also suggest exploring the effect sizes from John Hattie's (2023) research. Visit the Visible Learning site (https://bit .ly/3DouBjP) for a list of 252 strategies and factors ranked according to student achievement levels.

- **Use the gradual release model:** When exploring hypotheses, it may be helpful to think of a gradual release model. Is the skill sufficiently modeled to the student with clear directions? Is there sufficient guidance as the student applies the skill? Is the instruction supportive for when the student models the skill? Explore each aspect of the model-lead-test format and see if there are improvements within that sequence.

- **Keep thinking simple:** For students who made some growth but are still below their goal, increasing intensity may be the simplest way to improve student performance. Consider the explicitness and dosage factors in figure 6.13 (page 201).

### *Select a Goal and Progress-Monitoring Tool*

Setting goals for students with intensive needs is a nuanced process. Many programs have rates of growth, pathways of progress, and zones of growth to help determine specific goals for students. We offer guidance here, but the key issue is to set a goal so the student catches up to peers or to grade-level expectations.

As in chapter 5 (page 151), we suggest selecting a goal and progress-monitoring tool together because the goal will inform how to measure progress toward the goal. Educators can select a goal based on the grade-level standard or low-risk criterion. However, because part of the issue for some students is their slow growth, it may be more suitable to select the goal based on average growth rates and multiply that by 1.5 (Bailey & Weingarten, 2022). Multiplying by 1.5 may seem like a lot of growth to expect, but keep in mind these students are also receiving your most intensive supports and therefore they should have the most growth.

In figure 6.17, we offer sample average growth rates per week for reading, mathematics, and writing. We suggest using local norms when possible, but we provide the average rates here as a starting point. You can calculate the goal by taking the student's current score (the baseline or observed performance) and adding the product of multiplying the growth rate by 1.5 by the number of weeks of intervention:

$$\text{Baseline or Observed Performance} + [(\text{Average Growth Rate} \times 1.5) \times \text{Number of Weeks}] = \text{Goal}$$

For example, for a fourth grader who is reading thirty-five words correct per minute, the average growth rate is 1.2 words correct per minute. If intervention is twenty weeks, then the student's goal would be $35 + [(1.2 \times 1.5) \times 20] = 71$ words correct per minute.

| Grade | Words Correct per Minute (Reading)[a] | Correct Digits (Mathematics Computation) | Correct Applications (Mathematics Applications) | Correct Writing Sequences[b] |
|---|---|---|---|---|
| 1 | 1.9 | 1.58–1.77[b*] | 0.79–0.84 | – | 0.29–0.34 |
| 2 | 1.6 | 1.10–1.20[b] | 0.64–0.68 | 0.40–0.45 | 0.38–0.44 |
| 3 | 0.9 | 1.09–1.19[b] | 0.89–0.96 | 0.24–0.28 | 0.33–0.44 |
| 4 | 1.2 | 0.86–0.96[b] | 0.87–0.94 | 0.16–0.20 | 0.30–0.39 |
| 5 | 0.8 | 0.89–0.99[b] | 0.51–0.61 | 0.09–0.11 | 0.33–0.42 |
| 6 | 0.3 | 0.72–0.81[b] | 0.40–0.48 | 0.17–0.20 | 0.44–0.54 |
| 7 | – | 0.67–0.75[b] | 0.34–0.42 | 0.22–0.25 | 0.24–0.32 |
| 8 | – | 0.53–0.60[b] | 0.26–0.32 | 0.12–0.14 | 0.24–0.27 |

Note: [a] = Weekly growth rate from Hasbrouck & Tindal, 2017

[b] = Average rates of growth (fifth percentile) for students who score in an average range on their initial screening measure

* = Winter to Spring growth

*Source: AIMSweb, 2012; Hasbrouck & Tindal, 2017.*

**Figure 6.17: Average rates of growth from fall to spring with curriculum-based measurement for reading, mathematics, and writing.**

Select a progress-monitoring tool that measures the skills you're teaching and that will provide sensitive and responsive data. We discuss selecting a tool in chapters 1 (page 15) and 5 (page 151), but as a reminder, select a tool that meets criteria for progress monitoring and measures the targeted skills.

### Select a Fidelity Tool

In figure 6.18 (page 206), we provide an example fidelity measure to use during intervention times. In addition, we recommend gathering fidelity data for students throughout the day, such as attendance or engagement data in core instruction. In doing so, you'll have a more complete view of students' fidelity to their overall instruction and supports. As discussed in chapter 5 (page 151), you can use additional fidelity tools, such as checklists or observation forms of the interventions, if you do not use the example in figure 6.12 (page 200).

### Create a Communication Plan

One final piece of Tier 3 is to ensure people understand who to communicate the plan to. Often this includes families, the staff working with the students, and the students themselves. Determine who is going to communicate which information,

| Datapoint | Was the Student Present? | Was the Student Engaged? | | | Was the Intervention Implemented as Intended? | | | Duration or Frequency | Was the Quality of the Intervention Delivery High? | | |
|---|---|---|---|---|---|---|---|---|---|---|---|
| 1 | ☐ Y   ☐ N | ☐ 3 | ☐ 2 | ☐ 1 | ☐ 3 | ☐ 2 | ☐ 1 | | ☐ 3 | ☐ 2 | ☐ 1 |
| 2 | ☐ Y   ☐ N | ☐ 3 | ☐ 2 | ☐ 1 | ☐ 3 | ☐ 2 | ☐ 1 | | ☐ 3 | ☐ 2 | ☐ 1 |
| 3 | ☐ Y   ☐ N | ☐ 3 | ☐ 2 | ☐ 1 | ☐ 3 | ☐ 2 | ☐ 1 | | ☐ 3 | ☐ 2 | ☐ 1 |
| 4 | ☐ Y   ☐ N | ☐ 3 | ☐ 2 | ☐ 1 | ☐ 3 | ☐ 2 | ☐ 1 | | ☐ 3 | ☐ 2 | ☐ 1 |
| 5 | ☐ Y   ☐ N | ☐ 3 | ☐ 2 | ☐ 1 | ☐ 3 | ☐ 2 | ☐ 1 | | ☐ 3 | ☐ 2 | ☐ 1 |
| TOTAL | | | | | | | | | | | |

Note: To use this form, record fidelity at least once per week. Choose a day randomly and record the information within the table. Use a different day each week to gather fidelity data. Calculate a total percentage score for each dimension. Add rows as needed.

Legend: 3 = highest rating, 1 = lowest rating

Source: © National Center on Intensive Intervention, n.d.d. Adapted with permission.

**Figure 6.18: Generic fidelity tool.**

Visit **MarzanoResources.com/reproducibles** for a free reproducible version of this figure.

and outline the plan for everyone. Use a template or a method to document the plan with the decisions made, such as the one in figure 6.19. A reproducible version is available on page 220 as part of the worksheets at the end of the chapter.

## Plan Evaluation

Once educators have implemented the plan, they can then review the plan's implementation and effectiveness. As with Tier 2, educators start by asking about the fidelity of the intervention or plan, ensuring that the student received the plan as intended (that is, is it at least 90 percent?). Then, they examine the progress-monitoring data to determine the student's growth (see the questions to use for plan evaluation in figure 6.20, page 208)—in other words, is the plan working?

### Ask, "What Is the Fidelity of the Plan?"

Gather the fidelity data and calculate a score to represent fidelity. With Tier 3, it's helpful to analyze different dimensions of fidelity and not just one omnibus score to get a full picture. For example, the fidelity tool in figure 6.21 (page 208) provides data on several fidelity dimensions, including the student's exposure to the intervention or plan (that is, attendance; column A), student engagement (column B), adherence to the plan (column C), dosage of the plan (column D), and quality of the delivery of the plan (column E). For a given column, calculate a total

| Instructional Plan for Student | | | | |
|---|---|---|---|---|
| Domain | Adjustments to support learner | Who is responsible? | When and where? | How often? |
| Instruction | Increase rate of responding and immediate corrective feedback | Mr. Hems <br> Mrs. Cornish | Intervention block; core instruction | Four days per week |
| | Provide more modeling and explicit instruction for prerequisite skills | Mr. Hems | Intervention block | Two days per week |
| Curriculum | Increase practice with prerequisite skills by embedding additional problems | Mrs. Cornish | Core instruction | Four days per week |
| Environment | No changes | | | |

| Monitoring Plan | | |
|---|---|---|
| Progress-monitoring tool and goal | Who is responsible? | How often? |
| Curriculum-based measurement in mathematics computation with multidigit problems | Mr. Hems | Once per week |
| Fidelity tool | Who is responsible? | How often? |
| Self-report using checklist | Mr. Hems, Mrs. Cornish | Once per week |

| Communication Plan | | |
|---|---|---|
| How will the plan be communicated to relevant staff? | Who is responsible? | How often? |
| One-on-one discussion with Mr. Hems and Mrs. Cornish | Ms. Benez | Once |
| How will the plan be communicated to the family and student? | Who is responsible? | How often? |
| Email and meeting | | |

| Additional Notes |
|---|
| Ms. Benez will check in after one week to identify any issues and bring them to the team. Mr. Santino will create the self-report for the fidelity tool checklist based off previous plans. |

*Source: © Oregon Response to Instruction and Intervention, n.d.a. Adapted with permission.*

**Figure 6.19: Template for Tier 3 communication plan.**

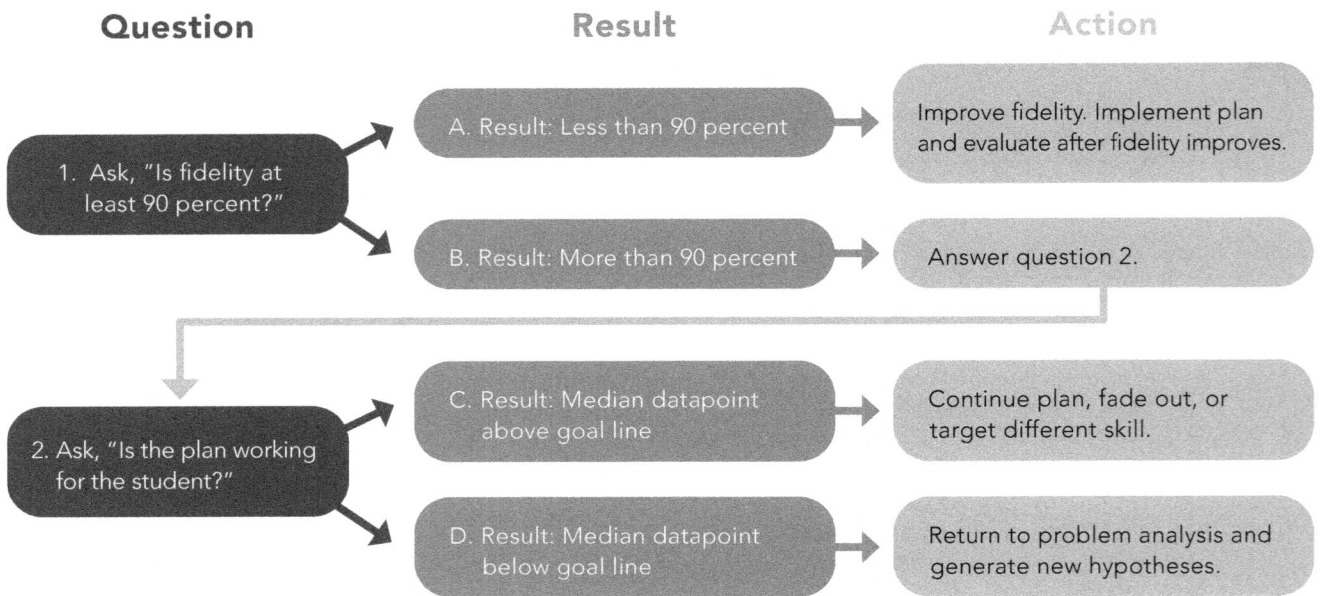

**Figure 6.20: Plan evaluation for Tier 3.**

| Datapoint | Was the Student Present? | Was the Student Engaged? | Was the Intervention Implemented as Intended? | Duration or Frequency | Was the Quality of the Intervention Delivery High? |
|---|---|---|---|---|---|
| 1 | ☑Y  ☐N | ☑3  ☐2  ☐1 | ☑3  ☐2  ☐1 | 25/30 | ☑3  ☐2  ☐1 |
| 2 | ☑Y  ☐N | ☐3  ☑2  ☐1 | ☑3  ☐2  ☐1 | 30/30 | ☑3  ☐2  ☐1 |
| 3 | ☑Y  ☐N | ☑3  ☐2  ☐1 | ☑3  ☐2  ☐1 | 28/30 | ☑3  ☐2  ☐1 |
| 4 | ☑Y  ☐N | ☐3  ☐2  ☑1 | ☑3  ☐2  ☐1 | 25/30 | ☐3  ☑2  ☐1 |
| 5 | ☑Y  ☐N | ☑3  ☐2  ☐1 | ☑3  ☐2  ☐1 | 30/30 | ☑3  ☐2  ☐1 |
| **TOTAL** | 5/5 = 100 percent | 12/15 = 80 percent | 15/15 = 100 percent | 138/150 = 92 percent | 14/15 = 93 percent |

*Source: © National Center on Intensive Intervention, n.d.d. Adapted with permission.*

**Figure 6.21: Example of a completed fidelity tool for an individual student.**

percentage and judge that percentage against a 90 percent threshold (for example, in figure 6.21, student engagement was 80 percent).

We recommend a few specific questions to ask to analyze the nuances of fidelity. Ideally, all of these would be at least 90 percent fidelity.

- Was the intervention provided as intended (that is, adherence)?
  - ◆ If fidelity data are below 90 percent, problem solve improving delivery of intervention.
  - ◆ If fidelity data are above 90 percent, then ask the following question.
- Is the quality of the intervention sufficient?
  - ◆ If fidelity data are below 90 percent, problem solve quality of delivery of intervention.
  - ◆ If fidelity data are above 90 percent, then ask the following question.
- Was the student engaged?
  - ◆ If fidelity data are below 90 percent, problem solve ways to increase student engagement.
  - ◆ If fidelity data are above 90 percent, then ask if the plan is working for the student (that is, analyze progress-monitoring or outcome data).

If the fidelity is less than 90 percent, problem solve around fidelity and ensure the intervention is implemented as intended. Consider the following question to improve fidelity.

- Do the staff need more training or coaching in providing the plan?
- Would an increase in communication or clarity of the plan improve fidelity?
- Are the staff resistant to aspects of the plan?
- Can the plan be simplified or streamlined to improve fidelity?
- Do the gathered data reflect the fidelity of the plan?

With low fidelity, improve fidelity and continue the intervention before judging the student's growth. If the fidelity is above 90 percent, then you can conclude the intervention is being provided as intended and then evaluate the student's growth.

### Ask, "Is the Plan Working for the Student?"

Examine the progress-monitoring data and analyze the last three datapoints. Find the median datapoint and compare that against the student's goal line.

- If the median datapoint is above the goal line, determine if the plan should continue, if it should be faded out, or if a different skill should be targeted and measured for the intervention (for example, the student has mastered a skill, so a new skill can be targeted). For fading the plan, examine figure 5.13 (page 167) for ways to fade or reduce support.
- If the median datapoint is below the goal line, return to problem analysis and generate hypotheses as to why the student isn't progressing. Analyze instruction, curriculum, and environment, including aspects of core instruction (don't limit your analysis to just the intervention time). In figure 6.22 (page 210), we offer considerations when conducting further problem analysis.

| Domain | Questions | Example Ways to Assess |
|---|---|---|
| Instruction | • Has the student attended a sufficient amount of sessions? | • Review attendance records or data similar to column A in figure 6.11 (page 198).<br>• Review fidelity data or collect fidelity data on engagement. |
| | • Was the instruction explicit enough for the student? | • Observe aspects of explicit instruction for that student.<br>• Interview student for understanding of content during instruction. |
| | • Does the student respond accurately to a sufficient number of opportunities to respond? | • Observe opportunities to respond for that student, including accuracy of those responses and feedback provided to the student. |
| Curriculum | • Does the student have the background knowledge or prerequisite skills to access the targeted skill? | • Examine permanent products to assess student's prerequisite skills relative to the scope and sequence of curriculum.<br>• Interview interventionist. |
| | • Is core instruction and other targeted support coordinated well with Tier 3? | • Observe instruction in core and other interventions.<br>• Review curriculum or focus of other instruction provided to student. |
| | • Does the intervention target the needed skill for the student? | • Review focus of curriculum or permanent products and compare to student's needs. |
| | • Does the difficulty level of the materials match the student's instructional level? | • Review permanent products for accuracy to calculate instructional level for the student.<br>• Review lesson plans relative to student's instructional level. |
| Environment | • Does the behavioral support need to be adjusted to be more supportive? | • Observe the amount of feedback or acknowledgment provided to the student. |
| | • Can adjustments be made to motivate student's learning?<br>• How is the student's engagement or motivation during the intervention? | • Observe level of engagement or interview interventionist to assess engagement.<br>• Review fidelity data or observe student during intervention. |
| Learner | • Are there cultural or linguistic factors not being considered for the student? | • Review records of the student or previously gathered data.<br>• Interview student, teachers, or family. |
| | • Is the instructional setting and design of the plan correctly taking into account the student's needs or characteristics? | • Interview student or interventionist.<br>• Observe intervention. |

**Figure 6.22: Considerations for further problem solving at Tier 3.**

For plan evaluation, teams can use the table in figure 6.23 to capture their decision making and next steps.

| Plan Evaluation | |
|---|---|
| What is the fidelity data source and score? | |
| What is the progress-monitoring data source and score? | |
| What are the next steps for the student? Discuss evidence and rationale for the choice.<br><br>☐ Continue plan<br><br>☐ Adjust plan<br><br>☐ Fade out plan | Evidence and rationale: |
| What adjustments, if any, does the plan need? | |
| Instruction | |
| Curriculum | |
| Environment | |
| Additional notes: | |

**Figure 6.23: Tier 3 plan evaluation and next steps template.**

## Tier 3 Team Roles

Our recommendation is that a specialized, multidisciplinary team should oversee Tier 3 supports (this team may be called various names within schools, but it is the team that meets to discuss individual students and plan their support). This team is responsible for overseeing and helping to coordinate the development and provision of Tier 3 supports. This team will assist staff or make decisions about students' needs for Tier 3 supports, but it will also help design and coordinate implementation of Tier 3, including monitoring its impact. Specifically, this team will do the following.

- Analyze screening data and progress-monitoring data to identify students who need intensive supports.

- Develop or assist in identifying what Tier 3 support is appropriate for a given student (for example, conduct problem analysis and help develop the plan).
- Analyze (and, in some cases, gather) progress-monitoring data as they relate to student growth in Tier 3.
- Make adjustments or coordinate adjustments to Tier 3 interventions.
- Ensure communication with parents and staff regarding students receiving Tier 3 supports.

Schools should consider members to include in the Tier 3 team as well as when and how to meet.

### Members

The team should include a few key members. First, an administrator who has decision-making authority should be on the team so they can adjust resources, schedules, or other issues within the school. Because this team deals with students who have the most intensive needs, the team will need members who have expertise or experience working with students with such needs. That isn't to say this team is your special education team or that students receiving Tier 3 supports are exclusively the same as students receiving special education services; rather, this team should have expertise in how to adjust instruction to support students with ongoing, chronic needs. In particular, the team will want someone with content expertise in behavior theory and behavioral supports within school. The team will also want people with content expertise in academic areas, including literacy and mathematics at a minimum, as well as people with expertise in instruction and factors related to positive student achievement. Note that teams can have people with content expertise in more than one area; one team member may have expertise in both literacy and instruction, for example. Finally, we suggest someone with data expertise to create graphs and provide interpretation.

### Meetings

This Tier 3 team is responsible for making decisions about who needs Tier 3 supports, including planning the support and analyzing and reviewing student progress. This team will meet on an ongoing basis to review data to make decisions about who needs Tier 3 supports (problem identification), as well as to review progress-monitoring data and fidelity data (plan evaluation). The team will also need to meet at times, either as a whole team or as a subcommittee, to evaluate information to design and plan Tier 3 supports (problem analysis and plan identification and implementation). In such scenarios, we suggest ad hoc members meet with key staff, such as those who work with students, and family or community members who work with the students (when appropriate). These ad hoc meetings take place as needed with a short-term goal of planning the intervention and communicating with key personnel regarding the intervention (for example, staff, families, and administrators). Thus, we recommend that Tier 3 meetings occur weekly or biweekly and focus on reviewing data to make decisions about students receiving Tier 2 supports. Ad hoc meetings with key personnel can form and meet weekly on a temporary basis to design and plan Tier 3 supports, and once their work is done (for example, problem analysis is completed and a plan is created and implemented), they can disband and turn the monitoring of the plan over to the larger Tier 3 team. For each meeting, we offer general guidelines for before, during, and after the meetings in figure 6.24.

---

**Before Meetings**

- Gather the necessary data for the meeting, including screening data, progress-monitoring data, and fidelity data.
- Ensure any progress-monitoring data are graphed visually and organized for the student.

**During Meetings**

- Follow the steps of the problem-solving model.
- Document changes to interventions.

**After Meetings**

- Implement changes needed for the student.
- Notify parents, teachers, and other personnel as appropriate.

---

**Figure 6.24: Guidelines for before, during, and after Tier 3 meetings.**

## Common Roadblocks and Solutions

Next, we discuss the common roadblocks that teams may face with planning for Tier 3 and possible solutions. These roadblocks include a student being significantly below grade level, infeasibility of holding separate Tier 2 and Tier 3 meetings, coordination of all three tiers, and the challenge of addressing multiple needs of students with limited resources.

### Progress Monitoring When a Student Is Significantly Below Grade Level

When students are performing significantly below grade level, selecting a tool that measures grade-level performance may not be sensitive enough to pick up on the changes in their skills. For example, imagine an eighth-grade student who reads at a fifth-grade level. Measuring weekly using a probe at the eighth-grade level would be less sensitive to growth in the student's skills on a week-to-week basis, particularly compared to probes at a fifth- or sixth-grade level. For such situations, we suggest setting goals for the student's instructional level (for example, fifth grade) and monitoring toward both the instructional level and the student's grade level. We recommend measuring progress toward the instructional goal on at least a weekly basis and then also measuring progress toward a grade-level goal on a monthly or biweekly basis. In doing so, educators can have information on a global and more nuanced scale.

### Infeasibility of Holding Separate Tier 2 and Tier 3 Identification Meetings

It's probably easier and more efficient to identify students who may need Tier 2 supports than those who need Tier 3 supports from the results of universal screening and risk verification in one meeting or by looking at the data collectively. You can have one team or even one or two people work together to analyze the screening data and make a list of students who may need Tier 2 or Tier 3 supports. (Recall that students who score just below the benchmark may need Tier 2 and those who score well below may need Tier 3.) Flag these students before the meeting and then focus on risk verification or intervention placement in the meeting. Additionally, teams can start their Tier 3 problem solving at the end of a Tier 2 meeting for students who score well below criterion or have had multiple rounds of Tier 2 intervention.

### Lack of Clarity on Whether Students Should Receive All Three Tiers

Many teachers ask, "Do students receive all three tiers?" The honest answer is that it depends. Students should receive the level of support throughout their day that they need to be successful. For some, this may be a heavy plan of Tier 1, Tier 2, and Tier 3. For others, it may be Tier 1 with some accommodations and a Tier 3 time. Educators will want to identify the student's needs and gaps and then create a plan that addresses each of them without reducing access to critical core instruction. All levels of support should be coordinated to ensure the student's plan is comprehensive. Further, educators will want to make sure that they're not supplanting core instruction to provide intervention time (therein creating additional gaps in the students' skills).

### The Challenge of Addressing Multiple Needs of Students With Limited Resources

A difficult challenge with students receiving Tier 3 supports is the amount of needs they have, which is compounded by limited resources in many settings. There is no singular answer to this question, but we suggest a few things to consider. One is that the student's plan may need to be structured to focus on a priority skill or need initially, and then the plan can be adjusted as the student masters the priority skill. For example, perhaps educators give more attention to the student's literacy skills before mathematics skills. Once the student masters needed literacy skills, educators can adjust the plan to address mathematics skills more. Educators can set up frequent reviews of the student's plan and target a critical skill intensely for

> ## Including Families
>
> It's always critical to involve families as much as possible when providing intensive supports (or any supports) to students. Notify and involve families when their child receives Tier 2 supports. We encourage including them as much as possible, but at the minimum, inform families when their child receives supports. Provide them with regular updates on their child's progress. For Tier 3, families are more involved, as they can offer more detailed input and involvement in the planning and, if possible, the delivery of the supports. We encourage schools to meet with the families while planning Tier 3 supports. If they're unable to attend meetings, we recommend at least getting their input ahead of time. Although most supports will take place during school hours, any family support or involvement to enhance or supplement the school support can be very beneficial. Schools should collaboratively plan support with families, and ask them how they can support or enhance the student's plan.

a few weeks, rather than creating a catchall plan that they leave alone for several weeks or months at a time.

A second consideration is to anchor the student's interventions on the academic support they're receiving and to then provide behavioral support that aligns with the development or learning of academic skills. Sometimes, a student may receive an academic intervention and then separate behavior interventions. For example, a student may have a thirty-minute mathematics intervention and then a separate thirty-minute intervention for social skills and then perhaps another academic intervention time. This separation of academics and behavior can limit the integration of skills, use a lot of resources, and inadvertently create silos or make communication difficult (McIntosh & Goodman, 2016). If educators focus on interventions for academic skills and then provide behavioral support to support academic skills, this could align and create efficient use of resources.

Finally, schools will simply need to engage all the key personnel involved with the student and be creative. We hate to use the adage *think outside of the box*, but educators will need to be creative and willing to do things differently (even very differently). Can the schedule be changed? Can families accommodate different drop-off or pickup times to allow additional instructional time? Can educators adjust roles to have more personnel available to support students? Can the school use online learning to enhance the staff's skills to work with certain students? Certain school structures may limit what can be done, so we offer the notion to change those school structures.

## Summary

At Tier 3, educators begin the problem-solving model by asking which students are at severe risk and require intensive supports. They do this by examining screening data and using risk verification to identify students scoring within a severe range, and they can use progress-monitoring data to see which students didn't respond to Tier 2 supports and need a more intensive level of intervention. During the problem analysis step, teams explore hypotheses and gather data using the RIOT/ICEL framework. Once they are confident they understand the problem and have data that confirm a hypothesis, they develop an individualized plan in which alterable variables within the instruction, curriculum, and environment are adjusted to support the student. Included in the plan are methods to communicate with the involved personnel, as well as how to measure student progress and fidelity of the plan. The plan is implemented, and educators then examine data to determine the extent to which it worked or not. If the plan is successful, teams can discuss fading out the plan. If not successful, educators continue to problem solve, engaging in an iterative process to ultimately resolve the problem.

# Tier 3 Worksheets for Problem-Solving Model

**Summary of Problem Solving at Tier 3**

| Step | Action | Key Questions | Tasks |
|------|--------|---------------|-------|
| 1 | Problem Identification | • Which students are most at risk?<br>• Which students are not making sufficient growth? | • Identify risk level and determine need for Tier 3.<br>• Examine progress-monitoring data and determine need for Tier 3. |
| 2 | Problem Analysis | • What is the student's instructional need?<br>• Why is the student not making adequate growth? | • Review previously gathered information.<br>• Select a hypothesis.<br>• Use RIOT/ICEL to confirm the hypothesis. |
| 3 | Plan Identification and Implementation | • What adjustments to instruction, curriculum, and environment can improve the student's skills? | • Identify factors to adjust within the instruction, curriculum, and environment.<br>• Select a goal and progress-monitoring tool.<br>• Select a fidelity tool. |
| 4 | Plan Evaluation | • What is the fidelity of the plan?<br>• Is the plan working for the student? | • Evaluate fidelity.<br>• Evaluate progress-monitoring data. |

## Step 1: Problem Identification

1. Identify students' risk level based on universal screening. Refer to your screener's risk categories to initially identify those at risk.

2. Of those who scored below the expected criterion, conduct risk verification. Use the following worksheet or another means to capture students' scores.

3. Also examine progress-monitoring data to determine student's need for Tier 3. Use the following table to examine the data.

### Risk-Verification Worksheet

| Name | Initial Screening Score: _____ | Risk-Verification Measure 1: _____ | Risk-Verification Measure 2: _____ | Intervention Needed? |
|------|------|------|------|------|
| | | | | |
| | | | | |
| | | | | |
| | | | | |
| | | | | |

Write the name of each student who scored below the expected criterion in the respective row and enter scores from two other measures. Flag for intervention each student who has two of three scores that fall below the expected criterion.

### Analyzing Progress-Monitoring Data for Tier 3 Identification

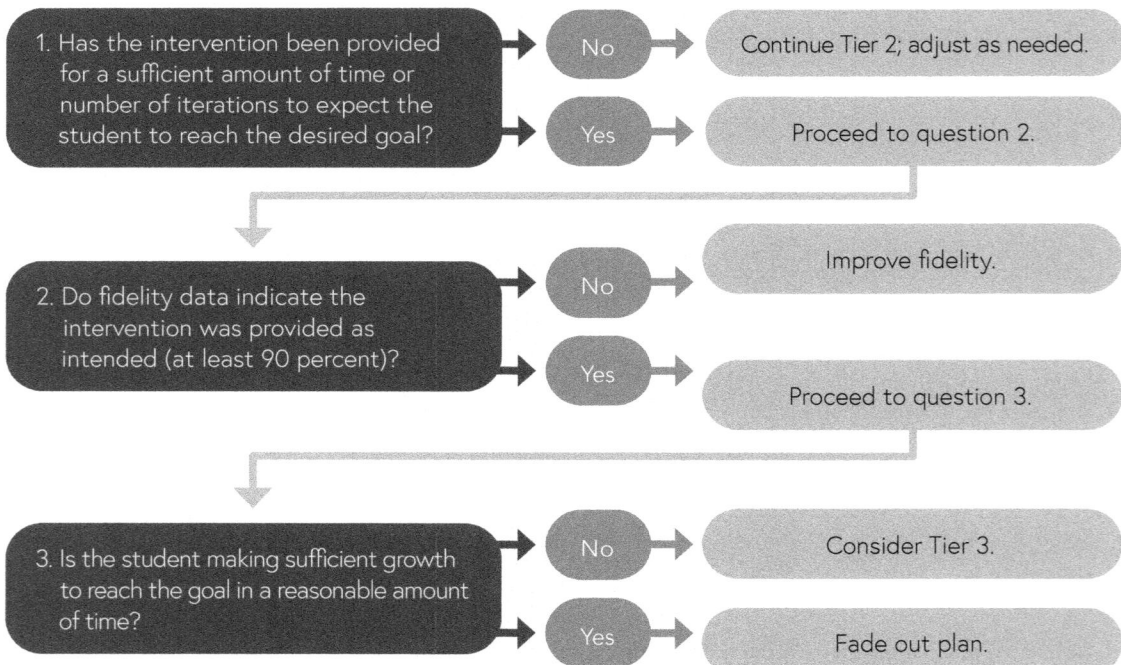

1. Has the intervention been provided for a sufficient amount of time or number of iterations to expect the student to reach the desired goal?
- No → Continue Tier 2; adjust as needed.
- Yes → Proceed to question 2.

2. Do fidelity data indicate the intervention was provided as intended (at least 90 percent)?
- No → Improve fidelity.
- Yes → Proceed to question 3.

3. Is the student making sufficient growth to reach the goal in a reasonable amount of time?
- No → Consider Tier 3.
- Yes → Fade out plan.

**Step 2: Problem Analysis**

4. Review previously gathered information about the student and capture it in the following table.

5. Select a hypothesis and then gather additional information as needed using RIOT/ICEL. Gather and review information until a hypothesis is confirmed using the following template.

## Summary of Previously Known and Gathered Information

| Area | General Hypothesis | Summary of Relevant Information |
|---|---|---|
| Instruction | Is the instruction evidence based, explicit, and intense enough? | |
| Curriculum | Does the curriculum match the needs of the student? Does the student have the prerequisite skills to access the curriculum successfully? | |
| Environment | Does the environment support learning in a positive, proactive way? | |
| Learner | Do the instruction, curriculum, and environment consider the student's characteristics? | |

## Template for Capturing Problem-Analysis Results

| **Instruction** What instructional factors are contributing to the problem? | **Curriculum** What curricular factors are contributing to the problem? |
|---|---|
| | |
| **Environment** What environmental factors are contributing to the problem? | **Learner** What learner factors are contributing to the problem? |
| | |

| **Hypothesis:** |
|---|
| ☐ The student hasn't had sufficient instruction. ☐ The student needs more practice with the skill. ☐ The task is too hard, or the student lacks the prerequisite skills to perform the task. ☐ The environment isn't considering certain student characteristics. ☐ The student isn't motivated to perform the skill. ☐ Other: |
| **What data confirm the hypothesis?** |
| |

*Source: © Oregon Response to Instruction and Intervention, n.d.b. Adapted with permission.*  page 4 of 7

### Step 3: Plan Identification and Implementation

6. Outline a plan to support the student by identifying factors within the instruction, curriculum, and environment to adjust.

7. Identify a goal, progress-monitoring tool, fidelity tool, and communication strategy for the plan.

**Template for Plan**

| Instructional Plan for Student | | | | |
|---|---|---|---|---|
| Domain | Adjustments to support learner | Who is responsible? | When and where? | How often? |
| Instruction | | | | |
| Curriculum | | | | |
| Environment | | | | |

| Monitoring Plan | | |
|---|---|---|
| Progress-monitoring tool and goal | Who is responsible? | How often? |
| | | |
| Fidelity tool | Who is responsible? | How often? |
| | | |

| Communication Plan | | |
|---|---|---|
| How will the plan be communicated to relevant staff? | Who is responsible? | How often? |
| | | |
| How will the plan be communicated to the family and student? | Who is responsible? | How often? |
| | | |

| Additional Notes |
|---|
| |

*Source: © Oregon Response to Instruction and Intervention, n.d.b. Adapted with permission.*

## Step 4: Plan Evaluation

8. Evaluate the student's Tier 3 plan using the questions in the following table. Capture information in the additional table.

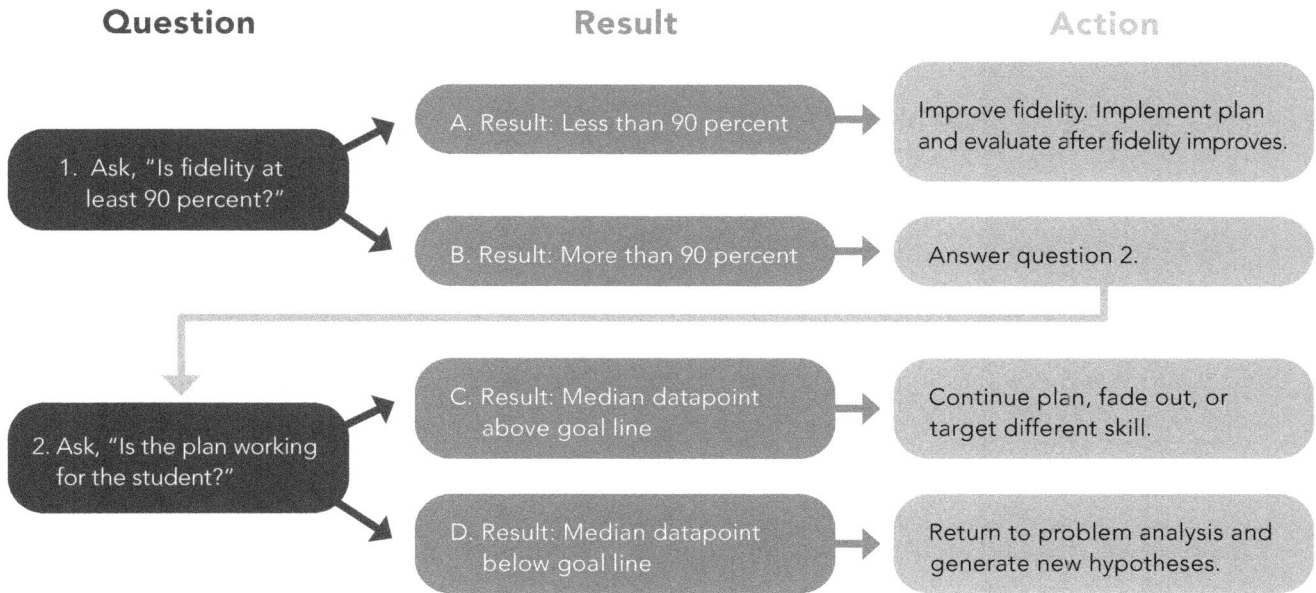

| Question | Result | Action |
|---|---|---|
| 1. Ask, "Is fidelity at least 90 percent?" | A. Result: Less than 90 percent | Improve fidelity. Implement plan and evaluate after fidelity improves. |
| | B. Result: More than 90 percent | Answer question 2. |
| 2. Ask, "Is the plan working for the student?" | C. Result: Median datapoint above goal line | Continue plan, fade out, or target different skill. |
| | D. Result: Median datapoint below goal line | Return to problem analysis and generate new hypotheses. |

| Plan Evaluation |
|---|
| What is the fidelity data source and score? |
| What is the progress-monitoring data source and score? |

| What are the next steps for the student? Discuss evidence and rationale for the choice.<br><br>☐ Continue plan<br>☐ Adjust plan<br>☐ Fade out plan | Evidence and rationale: |
|---|---|
| What adjustments, if any, does the plan need? ||
| Instruction | |
| Curriculum | |
| Environment | |
| Additional notes: ||

## Reference

Oregon Response to Instruction and Intervention. (n.d.b). *Intervention audit form.* Accessed at www.oregonrti.org/s/ Intervention-Audit-Form.docx on June 25, 2023.

# Classroom Management Observation Tool (CMOT)

**Overview:** The CMOT includes two components: (1) **observation items**, which have been validated for informing decisions about relative strengths and needs with positive and proactive classroom management, and (2) a **checklist** of empirically supported practices to look for periodically.

**Instructions:** Complete observation items routinely to inform decisions about professional development, and complete checklist periodically to check presence or absence of empirically supported practices.

Educator _____ Observer _____ Date _____

Grade Level _____ Content Area _____ Time Start _____ Time End _____

Instructional Activity:

Group Size: ☐ Whole Class     ☐ Small Group

## CMOT Observation Items

Assess implementation of positive and proactive classroom management practices.

| **Positive and Proactive Classroom Management Practices** *Please complete this portion after observing an educator for a minimum of fifteen minutes of instruction.* | **1** Disagree strongly | **2** Disagree somewhat | **3** Agree somewhat | **4** Agree strongly |
|---|---|---|---|---|
| 1. The educator effectively engaged in active supervision of students in the classroom (that is, moving, scanning, interacting).[a] | 1 | 2 | 3 | 4 |
| 2. The educator effectively provided most or all students with opportunities to respond and participate during instruction.[b] | 1 | 2 | 3 | 4 |
| 3. The educator effectively provided specific praise to acknowledge appropriate student academic and social behavior.[c] | 1 | 2 | 3 | 4 |
| 4. The educator provided more frequent acknowledgment for appropriate behaviors than inappropriate behaviors (+ to − ratio). | 1 | 2 | 3 | 4 |

[a]Effective **active supervision** includes systematic scanning, unpredictable movement, and interactions spread across students.

[b]Effective **opportunities to respond** provide opportunities for various numbers of students using various opportunity and response modalities.

[c]Effective **specific praise** names the behavior and is contingent, genuine, and contextually and culturally appropriate.

page 1 of 2

### CMOT Checklist

Periodically check for evidence of the following effective classroom management practices.

| Check for Evidence of Classroom Structure and Expectations |
| --- |
| 1. The educator posted a schedule for the day, the class activity, or both. ☐ Yes   ☐ No |
| 2. The educator posted three to five positively stated behavioral expectations in the classroom. ☐ Yes   ☐ No |
| 3. The physical arrangement of the room was appropriate for the activity.[d] ☐ Yes   ☐ No |
| 4. The educator developed routines for the day, the class activity, or both.[e] ☐ Yes   ☐ No |
| 5. The educator taught[f] and prompted[g] three to five positively stated behavioral expectations. ☐ Yes   ☐ No |
| 6. The educator selected and implemented additional consequence strategies, if appropriate, to support student behavior.[h] ☐ Yes   ☐ No |

[d]**Physical arrangement** (seating assignments, furniture arrangement, and so on) is designed to maximize structure and minimize distraction.

[e]Students demonstrate fluency with **routines**, educator provides lesson plans, educator references previously taught routines, or a combination.

[f]Students demonstrate fluency with **expectations**, educator lesson plans, educator references previously taught expectations, or a combination.

[g]Effective **prompts** are delivered before a behavior is expected and make it more likely for students to engage in appropriate behavior for the given activity and environment.

[h]**Additional consequence strategies** may include classroom systems to acknowledge appropriate behavior or consequences to respond to inappropriate behavior; effective implementation is consistent, systematic, and accompanied by behavior-specific feedback.

*Source: Simonsen, B., Freeman, J., Kooken, J., Dooley, K., Gambino, A. J., Wilkinson, S., et al. (2020).* Classroom Management Observation Tool (CMOT). *Accessed at https://nepbis.org/classrooms-data-tools-resources on October 5, 2023. © Northeast Positive Behavior Interventions and Supports. Reprinted with permission.*

# Interest Inventory for Secondary Students

Use these questions to gauge student interest or discern what may motivate them during school.

1. What would you like to be when you graduate?

2. What are some of your hobbies? What do you like to do for fun?

3. Are there activities or after-school clubs that you're involved in?

4. What is your favorite:

    a. Movie?

    b. Book?

    c. Television or streaming show?

    d. Website?

    e. Music or artist?

    f. Food?

    g. Candy?

5. Favorite subject in school? Why?

6. Least favorite subject in school? Why?

7. Who is your favorite adult in the school?

8. How do you like to be recognized or rewarded?

# Epilogue

Data literacy is a critical issue for schools. Educators can be buried in data, even though they have a plethora of tools available to them. As stated by National Center on Intensive Intervention researchers Kristin Ruedel, Laura Berry Kuchle, & Tessie Bailey (2021), it's helpful to think about three broad questions when developing a data system.

First, ask why you are gathering the data. Do staff members understand the purpose behind the data they're gathering? If they do not, then perhaps the staff need training on why they're using the data. If you're unsure why you're gathering the data, consider whether those data need to be collected.

Second, analyze your data systems to ensure they are accessible to staff. Are they user friendly? Do they illustrate the data clearly for staff? We discussed graphing data in chapter 2 (page 41) for ease of decision making, but schools will want to make sure teams and educators have ready access to data and that they can use that data easily during meetings.

Third, consider how well your staff can use the data. This is the focus of our book. Within this book, we outlined the use of the problem-solving model at each tier of MTSS. In doing so, we aimed to make data-based decisions practical and clear for educators. By illustrating the model across all tiers, we show the versatility of the model because it can be applied to systems, groups of students, and individual students. We have aimed to focus on how to use data well.

Finally, we'll add that our intention is to provide a structure to use data efficiently and effectively. We have outlined suggestions and provided forms and templates, but we caution educators not to get too hung up on using them to the detriment of decision making. Rather, use these forms and guides as a template to begin, and feel empowered to change them to meet your needs. It's always best to keep your focus not on completing a form but instead on making sensible and unbiased decisions for students.

# References

Acadience Learning. (2021). *Benchmarks and composite score*. Accessed at https://acadiencelearning.org/wp-content/uploads/2021/11/Acadience-Reading-K-6-Benchmark-Goals-handout_2021_color.pdf on June 25, 2023.

AIMSweb. (2012). *AIMSweb ROI growth norms*. Accessed at www.illuminateed.com/wp-content/uploads/2017/01/ROI_Norm_Tables1.pdf on June 25, 2023.

Albers, C. A., & Kettler, R. J. (2014). Best practices in universal screening. In P. L. Harrison & A. Thomas (Eds.), *Best practices in school psychology: Data-based and collaborative decision making* (pp. 121–131). Bethesda, MD: National Association of School Psychologists.

Alnaim, M. (2018). The impact of zero tolerance policy on children with disabilities. *World Journal of Education*, *8*(1), 1–5.

American Psychological Association Zero Tolerance Task Force. (2008). Are zero tolerance policies effective in the schools? An evidentiary review and recommendations. *American Psychologist*, *63*(9), 852–862.

Anderson, C., & Borgmeier, C. (2007). *Efficient functional behavior assessment: The Functional Assessment Checklist for Teachers and Staff (FACTS)*. Accessed at www.pbis.org/resource/efficient-functional-behavior-assessment-the-functional-assessment-checklist-for-teachers-and-staff-facts on October 4, 2023.

Anderson, C. M., & Borgmeier, C. (2010). Tier II interventions within the framework of school-wide positive behavior support: Essential features for design, implementation, and maintenance. *Behavior Analysis in Practice*, *3*(1), 33–45. http://dx.doi.org/10.1007/BF03391756

Archer, A., & Hughes, C. (2010). *Explicit instruction: Effective and efficient teaching*. New York: Guilford Press.

Ardoin, S. P., Christ, T. J., Morena, L. S., Cormier, D. C., & Klingbeil, D. A. (2013). A systematic review and summarization of the recommendations and research surrounding curriculum-based measurement of oral reading fluency (CBM-R) decision rules. *Journal of School Psychology*, *51*, 1–18.

Ardoin, S. P., & Daly, E. J. III. (2007). Introduction to the special series: Close encounters of the instructional kind—How the instructional hierarchy is shaping instructional research 30 years later. *Journal of Behavioral Education*, *16*(1), 1–6.

Ball, D. L., & Forzani, F. M. (2011). Building a common core language for learning to teach: And connecting professional learning to practice. *American Educator*, *35*(2), 17–39.

Bailey, T. R., Colpo, A., & Foley, A. (2020). *Assessment practices within a multi-tiered system of supports* (Document No. IC-18). Accessed at https://ceedar.education.ufl.edu/wp-content/uploads/2020/12/Assessment-Practices-Within-a-Multi-Tiered-System-of-Supports-2.pdf on June 25, 2023.

Bailey, T. R., & Weingarten, Z. (2022). *Strategies for setting high-quality academic individualized education program goals*. Accessed at https://intensiveintervention.org/sites/default/files/NCII-SetAcademicIEPGoals508.pdf on June 25, 2023.

Barnes, A., & Harlacher, J. (2008). Clearing the confusion: Response to intervention as a set of principles. *Education and Treatment of Children*, *31*, 417–431.

Bottani, J., Duran, C. A. K., Pas, E. T., & Bradshaw, C. P. (2019). Teacher stress and burnout in urban middle schools: Associations with job demands, resources, and effective practices. *Journal of School Psychology*, *77*, 36–51.

Brown-Chidsey, R., & Bickford, R. (2015). *Practical handbook of Multi-Tiered Systems of Support: Building academic and behavioral success in schools*. New York: Guilford Press.

Burns, M. K. (2011). Matching math interventions to students' skill deficits: A preliminary investigation of a conceptual and procedural heuristic. *Assessment for Effective Intervention*, *36*(4), 210–218.

Burns, M. K. (2021). Intensifying reading interventions through a skill-by-treatment interaction: What to do when nothing else worked. *Communiqué*, *50*(4), 30–32.

Burns, M. K., Appleton, J. J., & Stehouwer, J. D. (2005). Meta-analytic review of responsiveness-to-intervention research: Examining field-based and research-implemented models. *Journal of Psychoeducational Assessment*, *23*, 381–394.

Burns, M. K., Codding, R. S., Boice, C. H., Lukito, G. (2010). Meta-analysis of acquisition and fluency math interventions with instruction and frustration level skills: Evidence for a skill-by-treatment interaction. *School Psychology Review*, *39*(1), 69–83.

Burns, M. K., Karich, A. C., Maki, K. E., Anderson, A., Pulles, S. M., Ittner, A., et al. (2013). Identifying classwide problems in reading with screening data. *Journal of Evidence-Based Practices for Schools*, *14*(2), 186–204.

Burns, M. K., Riley-Tilman, T. C., & VanDerHeyden, A. (2012). *RTI applications, volume 1: Academic and behavioral interventions*. New York: Guilford Press.

Burns, M. K., & Symington, T. (2002). A meta-analysis of pre-referral intervention teams: Student and systemic outcomes. *Journal of School Psychology*, *40*, 437–447.

Burns, M. K., VanDerHeyden, A. M., & Zaslofsky, A. F. (2014). *Best practices in delivering intensive academic interventions with a skill-by-treatment interaction*. Accessed at https://www.academia.edu/29718851/Best_Practices _in_Delivering_Intensive_Academic_Interventions_With_a_Skill_by_Treatment_Interaction on June 25, 2023.

Center on MTSS. (n.d.). *Tier 2 identification procedures*. Accessed at https://mtss4success.org/resource/tier-2 -identification-procedures on June 25, 2023.

Center on MTSS. (2022a). *Communication with and involvement of all staff*. Accessed at https://mtss4success.org /sites/default/files/2022-02/MTSS_Com-w-Staff.pdf on June 25, 2023.

Center on MTSS. (2022b). *MTSS infrastructure and support mechanisms*. Accessed at https://mtss4success.org/sites /default/files/2022-02/MTSS-Infrastructure.pdf on June 25, 2023.

Center on PBIS. (2021). *Supporting and responding to student's social, emotional, and behavioral needs: Evidence-based practices for educators*. Accessed at www.pbis.org/resource/supporting-and-responding-to-behavior-evidence-based -classroom-strategies-for-teachers on October 4, 2023.

Chaparro, E. A., Horner, R., Algozzine, B., Daily, J., & Nese, R. N. T. (2022). *How school teams use data to make effective decisions: Team-Initiated Problem Solving (TIPS)*. Accessed at www.pbis.org/resource/how-school-teams-use -data-to-make-effective-decisions-team-initiated-problem-solving-tips on October 4, 2023.

Christ, T. J., & Arañas, Y. A. (2014). Best practices in problem analysis. In P. Harrison & A. Thomas (Eds.), *Best practices in school psychology VI: Data-based and collaborative decision making* (pp. 87–98). Bethesda, MD: National Association of School Psychologists.

Christ, T. J., & Silberglitt, B. (2007). Estimates of the standard error of measurement for curriculum-based measures of oral reading fluency. *School Psychology Review*, *36*(1), 130–146.

Christ, T. J., Zopluoglu, C., Monaghen, B. D., & Van Norman, E. R. (2013). Curriculum-based measurement of oral reading: Multi-study evaluation of schedule, duration, and dataset quality on progress monitoring outcomes. *Journal of School Psychology, 51*(1), 19–57.

Coffey, S. E., Stallworth, L., Majors, T., Higgs, K., Gloster, L., Carter, Y., et al. (2018, March 6). *Using the cluster support team and Multi-Tiered Systems of Support to provide wraparound services in a large urban school district.* Accessed at https://digitalcommons.georgiasouthern.edu/nyar_savannah/2018/2018/18/ on June 25, 2023.

Collins, A., & Harlacher, J. (2023). *Effective bullying prevention: A comprehensive schoolwide approach.* New York: Guilford Press.

Cook, C. R., Grady, E. A., Long, A. C., Renshaw, T., Codding, R. S., Fiat, A., et al. (2016). Evaluating the impact of increasing general education teachers' ratio of positive-to-negative interactions on students' classroom behavior. *Journal of Positive Behavior Interventions, 19*(2), 1–11.

Crone, D. A., & Horner, R. H. (2015). *Building positive behavior support systems in schools: Functional behavioral assessment* (2nd ed.). New York: Guilford Press.

Daly, E. J., Lentz, F. E., & Boyer, J. (1996). The instructional hierarchy: A conceptual model for understanding the effective components of reading interventions. *School Psychology Quarterly, 11*(4), 369–386.

Daly, E. J., & Martens, B. K. (1994). A comparison of three interventions for increasing oral reading performance: Application of the instructional hierarchy. *Journal of Applied Behavior Analysis, 27*(3), 459–469. https://doi.org/10.1901/jaba.1994.27-459

Deno, S. L. (1985). Curriculum-based measurement: The emerging alternative. *Exceptional Children, 52*, 219–232.

Deno, S. L. (2003). Developments in curriculum-based measurement. *The Journal of Special Education, 37*(3), 184–192.

Deno, S. L. (2016). Data-based decision making. In S. R. Jimerson, M. K. Burns, & A. M. VanDerHeyden (Eds.), *Handbook of response to intervention: The science and practice of multi-tiered systems of support* (2nd ed.; pp. 9–28). New York: Springer.

Doğan, S., & Adams, A. (2018). Effect of professional learning communities on teachers and students: Reporting updated results and raising questions about research design. *School Effectiveness and School Improvement, 29*(4), 1–26.

Donegan, R. E., Wanzek, J., & Al Otaiba, S. (2020). Effects of a reading intervention implemented at differing intensities for upper elementary students. *Learning Disabilities Research & Practice, 35*(2), 62–71.

Donohoo, J. (2017). *Collective efficacy: How educators' beliefs impact student learning.* London: Sage.

Dowhower, S. (2006). Repeated reading revisited: Research into practice. *Reading & Writing Quarterly, 10*(4), 343–358.

Drummond, T. (1994). *The Student Risk Screening Scale (SRSS).* Grants Pass, OR: Josephine County Mental Health Program.

DuFour, R., DuFour, R., Eaker, R., Many, T. W., & Mattos, M. (2016). *Learning by doing: A handbook for Professional Learning Communities at Work* (3rd ed.). Bloomington, IN: Solution Tree Press.

Dunlap, G., Iovannone, R., Kincaid, D., Wilson, K., Christiansen, K., Strain, P. S., et al. (2010). *Prevent-teach-reinforce: The school-based model of individualized positive behavior support.* Baltimore, MD: Brookes.

Feuerborn, L., Wallace, C., & Tyre, A. D. (2013). Gaining staff support for schoolwide positive behavior supports: A guide for teams. *Beyond Behavior, 22*(2), 27–34.

Filderman, M. J., Toste, J. R., Didion, L. A., Peng, P., & Clemens, N. H. (2018). Data-based decision making in reading interventions: A synthesis and meta-analysis of the effects for struggling readers. *The Journal of Special Education, 52*(3), 174–187. https://doi.org/10.1177/0022-46691879001

Fish, R. E. (2017). The racialized construction of exceptionality: Experimental evidence of race/ethnicity effects of teacher's interventions. *Social Science Research, 62*, 317–334.

Fixsen, D. L., Naoom, S., Blase, K., Friedman, R., & Wallace, F. (2005). *Implementation research: A synthesis of the literature.* Accessed at https://nirn.fpg.unc.edu/resources/implementation-research-synthesis-literature on October 5, 2023.

Fletcher, J., Lyon, R., Barnes, M., Stuebing, K., Francis, D., Olson, R., et al. (2002). Classification of learning disabilities: An evidence-based evaluation. In R. Bradley, L. Donaldson, & D. Hallahan (Eds.), *Identification of learning disabilities* (pp. 185–250). Mahwah, NJ: Erlbaum.

Frederick, S. (2005). Cognitive reflection and decision making. *Journal of Economic Perspectives, 19(4),* 25–42.

Freeman, J., Sugai, G., Simonsen, B., & Everett, S. (2017). MTSS coaching: Bridging knowing to doing. *Theory Into Practice, 56(1),* 29–37.

Freeman, R., Miller, D., & Newcomer, L. (2015). Integration of academic and behavioral MTSS at the district level using implementation science. *Learning Disabilities: A Contemporary Journal, 13(1),* 59–72.

Fuchs, L., & Fuchs, D. (1986). Effects of systematic formative evaluation: A meta-analysis. *Exceptional Children, 53(3),* 199–208. Accessed at http://infovisualization.pbworks.com/w/file/fetch/93947669/Fuchs%20Feedback%20Article.pdf on October 27, 2023.

Fuchs, L., & Fuchs, D. (2007). *What is scientifically-based research on progress monitoring?* Accessed at https://files.eric.ed.gov/fulltext/ED502460.pdf on June 25, 2023.

Fuchs, L. S., Fuchs, D., Hamlett, C. L., & Stecker, P. M. (2021). Bringing data-based individualization to scale: A call for the next-generation technology of teacher supports. *Journal of Learning Disabilities, 54(5),* 319–333.

Fuchs, L., & Kern, L. (2014, February). *Data rich, information poor? Making sense of progress monitoring data to guide intervention decision* [Webinar]. Accessed at https://intensiveintervention.org/resource/data-rich-information-poor-making-sense-progress-monitoring-data-guide-intervention on June 25, 2023.

Gimpel Peacock, G., Ervin, R. A., Daly, E. J. III., & Merrell, K. W. (Eds.). (2010). *Practical handbook of school psychology: Effective practices for the 21st century.* New York: Guilford Press.

Glover, T. A., & Vaughn, S. (2010). *Supporting all students: The promise of response to intervention.* New York: Guilford Press.

Good, R. H., Gruba, J., & Kaminski, R. A. (2002). Best practices in using dynamic indicators of basic early literacy skills (DIBELS) in an outcomes-driven model. In A. Thomas & J. Grimes (Eds.), *Best practices in school psychology IV* (pp. 699–720). Bethesda, MD: National Association of School Psychologists.

Good, R. H., III, Kaminski, R. A., Cummings, K. D., Dufour-Martel, C., Petersen, K., Powell-Smith, K. A., et al. (2019). *Acadience® reading K–6 assessment manual.* Eugene, OR: Acadience Learning.

Goodman, R. (1997). The strengths and difficulties questionnaire: A research note. *Journal of Child Psychology and Psychiatry, 38(5),* 581–586. https://doi.org/10.1111/j.1469-7610.1997.tb01545.x

Greenwood, C. R., Kratochwill, T. R., & Clements, M. (2008). *Schoolwide prevention models: Lessons learned in elementary schools.* New York: Guilford Press.

Gresham, F. (2002). Responsiveness to intervention: An alternative approach to the identification of learning disabilities. In R. Bradley, L. Donaldson, & D. Hallahan (Eds.), *Identification of learning disabilities* (pp. 467–519). Mahwah, NJ: Erlbaum.

Gunter, P. L., Reffel, J. M., Barnett, C. A., Lee, J. M., & Patrick, J. (2004). Academic response rates in elementary-school classrooms. *Education and Treatment of Children, 27(2),* 105–113.

Hallam, P. R., Smith, H. R., & Wilcox, B. R. (2015). Trust and collaboration in PLC teams: Teacher relationships, principal support, and collaborative benefits. *NASSP Bulletin, 99(3),* 193–216.

Hamilton, L., Halverson, R., Jackson, S., Mandinach, E., Supovitz, J., & Wayman, J. (2009). *Using student achievement data to support instructional decision making* (NCEE 2009-4067). Accessed at https://ies.ed.gov/ncee/wwc/Docs/PracticeGuide/dddm_pg_092909.pdf on June 25, 2023.

Haring, N. G., Lovitt, T. C., Eaton, M. D., & Hansen, C. L. (1978). *The fourth R: Research in the classroom.* Columbus, OH: Merrill.

Harlacher, J. E., Potter, J., & Weber, J. (2015). A team-based approach for improving core instructional reading practices within RTI. *Intervention in School and Clinic, 50*(4), 210–220.

Harlacher, J. E., & Rodriguez, B. J. (2017). *An educator's guide to schoolwide positive behavioral interventions and supports: Integrating all three tiers.* Centennial, CO: Marzano Research.

Harlacher, J. E., Sakelaris, T., & Kattelman, N. (2013). *Practitioner's guide to curriculum-based evaluation in reading.* New York: Springer Press.

Harlacher, J. E., Sanford, A. K., & Nelson, N. J. (2014, May 15). *Distinguishing between Tier 2 and Tier 3 instruction in order to support implementation of RTI.* Accessed at http://rtinetwork.org/essential/tieredinstruction /tier3/distinguishing-between-tier-2-and-tier-3-instruction-in-order-to-support-implementation-of-rti on October 5, 2023.

Harlacher, J. E., & Whitcomb, S. A. (2022). *Bolstering student resilience: Creating a classroom with consistency, connection, and compassion.* Bloomington, IN: Marzano Resources.

Hasbrouck, J., & Tindal, G. (2017). *Oral reading fluency data 2017.* Accessed at www.readnaturally.com/article /hasbrouck-tindal-oral-reading-fluency-data-2017 on June 25, 2023.

Hattie, J. (2023). *Visible learning: The sequel—A synthesis of over 2,100 meta-analyses relating to achievement.* New York: Routledge.

Haydon, T., MacSuga-Gage, A. S., Simonsen, B., & Hawkins, R. (2012). Opportunities to respond: A key component of effective instruction. *Beyond Behavior, 22*, 23–31.

Hawken, L., Crone, D., Bundock, K., & Horner, R. H. (2021). *Responding to problem behavior in schools* (3rd ed.). New York: Guilford Press.

Heartland Area Education Agency 11. (1998). *Technical manual: Academic and social/behavior problem decision making.* Johnston, IA: Author.

Herrera, S., Murray, K., & Cabral, R. (2019). *Assessment of culturally and linguistically diverse students* (3rd ed.). New York: Pearson.

Hintze, J. M., Wells, C. S., Marcotte, A. M., & Solomon, B. G. (2018). Decision-making accuracy of CBM progress-monitoring data. *Journal of Psychoeducational Assessment, 36*, 74–81.

Horner, R. H., Newton, J. S., Todd, A. W., Algozzine, B., Algozzine, K., Cusumano, D., et al. (2018). A randomized waitlist controlled analysis of team-initiated problem solving professional development and use. *Behavioral Disorders, 43*(4), 444–456.

Hosp, J. L. (2008). Best practices in aligning academic assessment with instruction. In A. Thomas & J. Grimes (Eds.), *Best practices in school psychology V* (pp. 363–376). Bethesda, MD: National Association of School Psychologists.

Hosp, J. L., Hosp, M. K., Howell, K. W., & Allison, R. (2016). *The ABCs of curriculum-based evaluation.* New York: Guilford Press.

Howell, K. W., & Schumann, J. (2010). Proactive strategies for promoting learning. In G. Gimpel Peacock, R. Ervin, E. Daly III, & K. Merrell (Eds.), *Practical handbook of school psychology: Effective practices for the 21st century* (pp. 235–253). New York: Guilford Press.

Hubers, M. D., Moolenaar, N. M., Schildkamp, K., Daly, A. J., Handelzats, A., & Pieters, J. M. (2018). Share and succeed: The development of knowledge sharing and brokerage in data teams' network structures. *Research Papers in Education, 33*(2), 216–238.

Hunter, W. C., Elswick, S. E., & Baylot Casey, L. (2018). Efficient wraparound service model for students with emotional and behavioral disorders: A collaborative model for school social workers and teachers. *Children & Schools, 40*(1), 59–61.

Hyson, D. M., Kovaleski, J. F., Silberglitt, B., & Pedersen, J. A. (2020). *The data-driven school: Collaborating to improve school outcomes.* New York: Guilford Press.

International Literacy Association. (2018). *Reading fluency does not mean reading fast.* Accessed at www.literacy worldwide.org/docs/default-source/where-we-stand/ila-reading-fluently-does-not-mean-reading-fast.pdf on June 25, 2023.

IRIS Center. (2021). *How do you know whether an EBP is effective with your children or students?* Accessed at https://iris.peabody.vanderbilt.edu/module/ebp_03/cresource/q4/p08 on November 6, 2023.

Jimerson, S. R., Burns, M. K., & VanDerHeyden, A. (Eds.). (2007). *Handbook of response to intervention: The science and practice of assessment and intervention.* New York: Springer.

Jimerson, S. R., Burns, M. K., & VanDerHeyden, A. (Eds.). (2017). *Handbook of response to intervention: The science and practice of assessment and intervention* (2nd ed.). New York: Springer.

Joyce, B. R., & Showers, B. (2002). *Student achievement through staff development* (3rd ed.). Alexandria, VA: ASCD.

Jung, P.-G., McMaster, K. L., Kunkel, A. K., Shin, J., & Stecker, P. M. (2018). Effects of data-based individualization for students with intensive learning needs: A meta-analysis. *Learning Disabilities Research & Practice, 33*(3), 144–155. ttps://doi.org/10.1111/ldrp.12172

Kahneman, D. (2011). *Thinking, fast and slow.* New York: Farrar, Straus, and Giroux.

Kamphaus, R. W., & Reynolds, C. R. (2015). *BASC-3 Behavioral and Emotional Screening System.* New York: Pearson.

Kelley, H. H. (1950). The warm-cold variable in first impressions of persons. *Journal of Personality, 18*(4), 431–439.

Klute, M., Apthorp, H., Harlacher, J., & Reale, M. (2017, February). *Formative assessment and elementary school student academic achievement: A review of the evidence* (REL 2017-259). Accessed at https://ies.ed.gov/ncee/rel/regions/central/pdf/REL_2017259.pdf on October 5, 2023.

Langley, G. J., Nolan, K. M., Norman, C. L., & Provost, L. P. (2009). *The improvement guide: Practical approach to enhancing organizational performance* (2nd ed.). San Francisco: Jossey Bass.

Linan-Thompson, S., & Vaughn, S. (2010). Evidence-based reading instruction: Developing and implementing reading programs at the core, supplemental, and intervention levels. In G. Gimpel Peacock, R. Ervin, E. Daly III., & K. Merrell (Eds.), *Practical handbook of school psychology: Effective practices for the 21st century* (pp. 274–286). New York: Guilford Press.

MacSuga-Gage, A. S., & Simonsen, B. (2015). Examining the effects of teacher-directed opportunities to respond on student outcomes: A systematic review of the literature. *Education and Treatment of Children, 38*(2), 211–240.

Marchand-Martella, N. E., Ruby, S. F., & Martella, R. C. (2007). *Intensifying reading instruction for students within a three-tier model: Standard-protocol and problem solving approaches within a Response-to-Intervention (RTI) system.* Accessed at http://escholarship.bc.edu/education/tecplus/vol3/iss5/art2 on June 25, 2023.

Marken, A., Scala, J., Husby-Slater, M., & Davis, G. (2020). *Early warning intervention and monitoring system implementation guide.* Accessed at www.air.org/sites/default/files/EWIMS-Implementation-Guide-FINAL-July-2020.pdf on June 25, 2023.

Marston, D. (2002). A functional and intervention-based assessment approach to establishing discrepancy for students with learning disabilities. In R. Bradley, L. Donaldson, & D. Hallahan (Eds.), *Identification of learning disabilities* (pp. 437–447). Mahwah, NJ: Erlbaum.

Marston, D., Muyskens, P., Lau, M., & Canter, A. (2003). Problem-solving model for decision making with high-incidence disabilities: The Minneapolis experience. *Learning Disabilities Research & Practice, 18*(3), 187–200.

Marzano, R. J. (2018). *Making classroom assessments reliable and valid.* Bloomington, IN: Solution Tree Press.

McCray, E. E., Kamman, M., Brownell, M. T., & Robinson, S. (2017). *High-leverage practices and evidence-based practices: A promising pair.* Accessed at https://ceedar.education.ufl.edu/wp-content/uploads/2017/11/HLPs-and-EBPs-A-Promising-Pair-FINAL.pdf *on June 25, 2023.*

McGuire, A., Peterson, A., & Kuchle, L. (2021). *Guiding questions: The FAIR test.* Accessed at https://ncsi-library.wested.org/resources/732 on June 25, 2023.

McIntosh, K., & Goodman, S. (2016). *Integrated multi-tiered systems of support: Blending RTI and PBIS.* New York: Guilford Press.

McLeskey, J., Barringer, M-D., Billingsley, B., Brownell, M., Jackson, D., Kennedy, M., et al. (2017, January). *High-leverage practices in special education.* Arlington, VA: Council for Exceptional Children & CEEDAR Center.

McLeskey, J., Maheady, L., Billinglsey, B., Brownell, M. T., & Lewis, T. (2022). *High leverage practices for inclusive classrooms. New York: Routledge.*

Mega, L. F., Gigerenzer, G., & Volz, K. G. (2015). Do intuitive and deliberate judgments rely on two distinct neural systems? A case study in face processing. *Frontiers in Human Neuroscience, 9*(456), 1–15.

Merrell, K., Ervin, R. A., Gimpel Peacock, G., & Renshaw, T. L. (2022). *School psychology for the 21st century* (3rd ed.). New York: Guilford Press.

Merrell, R. (2016, Feb 15). *How does cognitive bias affect interviewing.* Accessed at https://medium.com/connected-well/how-cognitive-biases-affect-inteviewing-and-hiring-aa1db8750a1b on June 25, 2023.

Metz, A., & Louison, L. (2018). *The hexagon tool: Exploring context.* Accessed at www.schoolmentalhealth.org/media/SOM/Microsites/NCSMH/Documents/Archives/CS-2.11-Hexagon-Tool.pdf on June 25, 2023.

Michigan MTSS Technical Assistance Center. (2021). *Guidance on the Acadience data management effectiveness of instructional support levels report.* Accessed at https://mimtsstac.org/sites/default/files/Documents/TeamsRoles/DataCoordinators/Acadience/6_Guidance%20on%20Effectiveness%20of%20Instructional%20Supports%20report.pdf on June 25, 2023.

Müller-Lyer, F. C. (1889). Optische urteilstäuschungen. In E. Du Bois-Reymond (Ed.), *Archiv für Physiologie* (pp. 263–270). Accessed at www.biodiversitylibrary.org/item/109723#page/12/mode/1up on June 25, 2023.

Myers, D., & Twenge, J. (2021). *Exploring social psychology* (9th ed.). New York: McGraw-Hill.

National Center for Education Statistics. (2022b). *NAEP report card: 2022 NAEP mathematics assessment.* Accessed at www.nationsreportcard.gov/highlights/mathematics/2022 on June 25, 2023.

National Center for Education Statistics. (2022a). *NAEP report card: 2022 NAEP reading assessment.* Accessed at www.nationsreportcard.gov/highlights/reading/2022 on June 25, 2023.

National Center for Systemic Improvement. (n.d.). *The FAIR test.* Accessed at https://ncsi-library.wested.org/resources/732 on June 25, 2023.

National Center on Intensive Intervention. (n.d.a). *Considerations for effective implementation: 5 elements of fidelity.* Accessed at https://intensiveintervention.org/resource/five-elements-fidelity on June 25, 2023.

National Center on Intensive Intervention. (n.d.b). *Ensuring fidelity of assessment and data entry procedures.* Accessed at https://intensiveintervention.org/sites/default/files/DataFidelity_Final508.pdf on June 25, 2023.

National Center on Intensive Intervention. (n.d.c). *Levels of intervention and evidence.* Accessed at https://intensiveintervention.org/tools-charts/levels-intervention-evidence on October 13, 2023.

National Center on Intensive Intervention. (n.d.d). *Student intervention implementation log.* Accessed at https://intensiveintervention.org/sites/default/files/DBI_Weekly_Log_508.pdf on June 25, 2023.

Newton, J. S., Horner, R. H., Algozzine, B., Todd, A. W., & Algozzine, K. M. (2012). A randomized wait-list controlled analysis of team-initiated problem solving. *Journal of School Psychology, 50*(4), 421–441.

Oregon Response to Instruction and Intervention. (n.d.a). *Individual problem solving form.* Hillsboro, OR: Author.

Oregon Response to Instruction and Intervention. (n.d.b). *Intervention audit form.* Accessed at www.oregonrti.org/s/Intervention-Audit-Form.docx on June 25, 2023.

Oregon Response to Instruction and Intervention. (n.d.c). *Sample elementary reading standards of practice.* Accessed at https://docs.google.com/document/d/13yax3gmmafiP6uif6F8GPecERI9qS7HtZ9Q3y5Ey6SM/edit?usp=share_link on July 13, 2023.

Parker, D. C., & Burns, M. K. (2014). Using the instructional level as a criterion to target reading interventions. *Reading and Writing Quarterly, 30*(1), 79–94.

Parker, D. C., Van Norman, E., & Nelson, P. M. (2018). Decision rules for progress monitoring in reading: Accuracy during a large-scale Tier II intervention. *Learning Disabilities & Research, 33*(4), 219–228.

PBISApps. (n.d.). *SWIS summary*. Accessed at https://files.pbisapps.org/pub/pdf/SWIS-Data-Summary-2019-20.pdf on June 25, 2023.

Pierce, J., & Jackson, D. (2017). *Ten steps to make RTI work in your schools*. Accessed at https://mtss4success.org/sites/default/files/2020-07/10-RTI.pdf on June 25, 2023.

Pluymert, K. (2014). Problem-solving foundations for school psychological services. In P. Harrison & A. Thomas (Eds.) *Best practices in school psychology: Data-based and collaborative decision making* (pp. 25–40). Bethesda, MD: National Association of School Psychologists.

Psychology Today. (n.d.). *Intuition*. Accessed at www.psychologytoday.com/us/basics/intuition on June 25, 2023.

Reinke, W. M., Herman, K. C., & Stormont, M. (2013). Classroom-level positive behavior supports in schools implementing SW-PBIS: Identifying areas for enhancement. *Journal of Positive Behavior Interventions, 15*(1), 39–50.

Reschly, D., & Tilly, W. D. III (1999). Reform trends and system design alternatives. In D. Reschly, W. D. Tilly III, & J. Grimes (Eds.), *Special education in transition: Functional assessment and noncategorical programming* (pp. 19–48). Longmont, CO: Sopris West.

Reynolds, C. R., & Kamphaus, R. W. (2015). *Behavior assessment system for children* (3rd ed.). New York: Pearson.

Rhodes, R. L., Hector Ochoa, S., & Ortiz, S. O. (2005). *Assessing culturally and linguistically diverse students: A practical guide*. New York: Guilford Press.

Roach, A. T., Lawton, K., & Elliot, S. N. (2014). Best practices in facilitating and evaluating the integrity of school-based interventions, In P. Harrison & A. Thomas (Eds.), *Best practices in school psychology: Data-based and collaborative decision making* (pp. 133–146). Bethesda, MD: National Association of School Psychologists.

Ruedel, K., Berry Kuchle, L., & Bailey, T. (2021, January). *Essential elements of comprehensive data literacy*. Accessed at https://ncsi-library.wested.org/resources/735 on October 5, 2023.

Ruhl, C. (2021, May 4). *Cognitive bias: How we are wired to misjudge*. Accessed at www.simplypsychology.org/cognitive-bias.html on June 25, 2023.

Sailor, W., Dunlap, G., Sugai, G., & Horner, R. (Eds.) (2009). *Handbook of positive behavior support*. New York: Springer.

Schildkamp, K., Poortman, C. L., Ebbeler, J., & Peters, J. M. (2019). How school leaders can build effective data teams: Five building blocks for a new wave of data-informed decision making. *Journal of Educational Change, 20*, 283–325.

Schwartz, B. (2005). *The paradox of choice*. New York: Harper Perennial.

Serviss, J. (2022, May 13). *4 benefits of an active professional learning community*. Accessed at www.iste.org/explore/professional-development/4-benefits-action-professional-learning-community on October 5, 2023.

Shakman, K., Wogan, D., Rodriguez, S., Boyce, J., & Shaver, D. (2020, October). *Continuous improvement in education: A toolkit for schools and districts*. Accessed at https://ies.ed.gov/ncee/edlabs/regions/northeast/pdf/REL_2021014.pdf on June 25, 2023.

Shih Dennis, M., & Gratton-Fisher, E. (2020). Use data-based individualization to improve high school students' mathematics computation and mathematics concept, and application performance. *Learning Disabilities: Research and Practice, 35*(3), 126–138.

Shinn, M. R. (2008). Best practices in curriculum-based measurement and its use in a problem-solving model. In A. Thomas & J. Grimes (Eds.), *Best practices in school psychology V* (pp. 243–262). Bethesda, MD: National Association of School Psychologists.

Simmons, D. C., Kame'enui, E. J., Harn, B., Coyne, M. D., Stoolmiller, M., Edwards Santoro, L., et al. (2007). *Attributes of effective and efficient kindergarten reading intervention: An examination of instructional time and design specificity*. Accessed at https://pubmed.ncbi.nlm.nih.gov/17713132 on June 25, 2023.

Simonsen, B., Freeman, J., Kooken, J., Dooley, K., Gambino, A. J., Wilkinson, S., et al. (2020). *Classroom Management Observation Tool (CMOT)*. Accessed at https://nepbis.org/classrooms-data-tools-resources on October 5, 2023.

Simonsen, B., & Myers, D. (2015). *Classwide positive behavior interventions and supports: A guide to proactive classroom management*. New York: Guilford Press.

Simonsen, B., Robbie, K., Meyer, K., Freeman, J., Everett, S., & Feinberg, A. (2021, November 2). *Multi-tiered system of supports (MTSS) in the classroom*. Accessed at www.pbis.org/resource/multi-tiered-system-of-supports-mtss-in-the-classroom on October 5, 2023.

Slotnik, W. J., & Orland, M. (2010). *Data rich but information poor*. Accessed at www.edweek.org/ew/articles/2010/05/06/31slotnik. h29.html on June 25, 2023.

Solomon, B. G., Klein, S. A., Hintze, J. M., Cressey, J. M., & Peller, S. L. (2012). A meta-analysis of school-wide positive behavior support. *Psychology in the Schools, 49*(2), 105–121.

Sommers, S. R. (2006). On racial diversity and group decision making: Identifying multiple effects of racial composition on jury deliberations. *Journal of Personality and Social Psychology, 90*(4), 597–612.

Stanovich, K. E. (1986). Matthew effects in reading: Some consequences of individual differences in the acquisition of literacy. *Reading Research Quarterly, 21*(4), 360–407.

Stecker, P. M., Fuchs, L. S., & Fuchs, D. (2005). Using curriculum-based measurement to improve student achievement: Review of research. *Psychology in the Schools, 42*(8), 795–819. ttps://doi.org/10.1102/pits.20113

Stewart, L., & Silberglitt, B. (2008). Best practices in developing academic local norms. In A. Thomas & J. Grimes (Eds.), *Best practices in school psychology V* (pp. 225–242). Bethesda, MD: National Association of School Psychologists.

Stewart, R. M., Benner, G. J., Martella, R. C., & Marchand-Martella, N. E. (2007). Three-tier models of reading and behavior: A research review. *Journal of Positive Behavior Interventions, 9*(4), 239–253. https://doi.org/10.1177/10983007070090040601

Stoiber, K. C. (2014). A comprehensive framework for multitiered systems of support in school psychology. In P. Harrison & A. Thomas (Eds.), *Best practices in school psychology: Data-based and collaborative decision making* (pp. 41–70). Bethesda, MD: National Association of School Psychologists.

Stoiber, K. C., & Gettinger, M. (2016). Multi-tiered systems of support and evidence-based practices. In S. R. Jimerson, M. K. Burns, & A. M. VanDerHeyden (Eds.), *Handbook of response to intervention: The science and practice of multi-tiered systems of support* (pp. 121–142). New York: Springer.

Sugai, G., & Horner, R. H. (2006). A promising approach for expanding and sustaining school-wide positive behavior support. *School Psychology Review, 35*(2), 246–259.

Swain-Bradway, J., Pinkey, C., & Flannery, K. B. (2015). Implementing schoolwide positive behavior interventions and supports in high schools: Contextual factors and stages of implementation. *Teaching Exceptional Children, 47*(5), 245–255.

Szadokierski, I., Burns, M. K., & McComas, J. J. (2017). Predicting intervention effectiveness from reading accuracy and rate measures through the instructional hierarchy: Evidence for a skill-by-treatment interaction. *School Psychology Review, 46*(2), 190–200. https://doi.org/10.17105/SPR-2017-0013.V46-2

Taylor, R. L. (2009). *Assessment of exceptional students: Educational and psychological procedures* (8th ed.). New Jersey: Pearson.

TeachingWorks. (n.d.). *Curriculum resources: High-leverage practices*. Accessed at https://library.teachingworks.org/curriculum-resources/high-leverage-practices on July 6, 2023.

Tichnor-Wagner, A., Wachen, J., Cannata, M., & Cohen-Vogel, L. (2017). Continuous improvement in the public school context: Understanding how educators respond to plan-do-study-act cycles. *Journal of Educational Change, 18*(4), 465–494.

University of Oregon. (n.d.). *Dynamic indicators of basic early literacy skills* (8th ed.). Accessed at http://dibels .uoregon.edu/dibels8 on October 13, 2023.

U.S. Department of Education Office for Civil Rights. (2014, March 21). *Civil rights data collection: Data snapshot— School discipline.* Accessed at https://ocrdata.ed.gov/assets/downloads/CRDC-School-Discipline-Snapshot.pdf on November 6, 2023.

VanDerHeyden, A. M., & Burns, M. K. (2010). *Essentials of response to intervention.* New York: Wiley.

VanDerHeyden, A. M., & Burns, M. K. (2019). Commentary: Improving decision making in school psychology— Making a difference in the lives of students, not just a prediction about their lives. *School Psychology Review, 47*(4), 385–395.

VanDerHeyden, A. M., & Codding, R. (2015). Practical effects of classwide mathematics intervention. *School Psychology Review, 44*(2), 169–190.

VanDerHeyden, A. M., McLaughlin, T., Algina, J., & Snyder, P. (2012). Randomized evaluation of a supplemental grade-wide mathematics intervention. *American Education Research Journal, 49*(6), 1251–1284.

VanDerHeyden, A. M., & Witt, J. C. (2014). *Best practices in can't do/won't do assessment.* Accessed at www.joewitt .org/Downloads/VanDerHeydenBP.pdf on June 25, 2023.

Van Norman, E. R. (2021). The effect of nonlinear growth on the accuracy of curriculum-based measurement of reading decision rules. *School Psychology, 36*(1), 60–68.

Van Norman, E. R., & Christ, T. (2016). How accurate are interpretations of curriculum-based measurement progress monitoring data? Visual analysis versus decision rules. *Journal of School Psychology, 58*, 41–55.

Van Norman, E. R., Nelson, P. M., & Parker, D. C. (2018). Curriculum-based measurement of reading decision rules: Strategies to improve the accuracy of treatment recommendations. *School Psychology Review, 47*(4), 333–344.

Vaughn, S., & Fuchs, L. (Eds.) (2003). Special issue: Response to intervention. *Learning Disabilities Research & Practice, 18*(3).

Vaughn, S., Linan-Thompson, S., Kouzekanani, K., Bryant, D. P., Dickson, S., & Blozis, S. A. (2003). Reading instruction grouping for students with reading difficulties. *Remedial and Special Education, 24*(5), 301–316.

Vaughn, S., Wanzek, J., & Murray, G. (2012). *Intensive interventions for students struggling in reading and mathematics.* Accessed at https://files.eric.ed.gov/fulltext/ED531907.pdf on June 25, 2023.

Vaughn, S., Wexler, J., Barth, A. A., Cirino, P. T., Romain, M. A., Francis, D., et al. (2011). Effects of individualized and standardized interventions on middle school students with reading disabilities. *Exceptional Children, 77*(4), 391–407. https://doi.org/10.1177/001440291107700401

Watkins, C., & Hornak, R. (2022). *What is fidelity?* Accessed at https://nirn.fpg.unc.edu/resources/what-fidelity on June 25, 2023.

Widmeyer, W. N., & Loy, J. W. (1988). When you're hot, you're hot! Warm-cold effects in first impressions of persons and teaching effectiveness. *Journal of Educational Psychology, 80*(1), 118–121.

Youth in Mind. (2022). *Strengths and difficulties questionnaire.* Accessed at www.sdqinfo.org/a0.html on October 13, 2023.

Ysseldyke, J. E., & Christenson, S. L. (1988). Linking assessment to intervention: Enhancing instructional options for all students. In J. L. Graden & J. E. Zins (Eds.), *Educational psychology* (pp. 91–1090). Bethesda, MD: National Association of School Psychologists.

Ysseldyke, J. E., & Marston, D. (1999). Origins of categorical special education services in schools and a rationale for changing them. In D. Reschly, W. D. Tilly III, & J. Grimes (Eds.), *Special education in transition: Functional assessment and noncategorical programming* (pp. 1–18). Longmont, CO: Sopris West.

Zumeta-Edmonds, R., Gandhi, A. G., & Danielson, L. (2019). *Essentials of intensive intervention.* New York: Guilford Press.

# Index

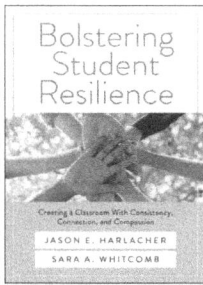

### Bolstering Student Resilience
**Jason E. Harlacher and Sara Whitcomb**
Move beyond the buzzwords surrounding social-emotional learning and focus on three fundamentals for successfully supporting your students. This book illuminates the why behind the work and offers proven strategies for building positive, supportive classrooms.
**BKL063**

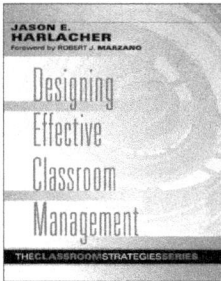

### Designing Effective Classroom Management
**Jason E. Harlacher**
Discover the components of proactive classroom management. With this practical, step-by-step guide, teachers and school administrators will uncover five components that help improve student achievement: create clear expectations and rules, establish procedures and structure, reinforce expectations, actively engage students, and manage misbehavior.
**BKL029**

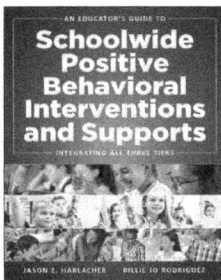

### An Educator's Guide to Schoolwide Positive Behavioral Interventions and Supports
**Jason E. Harlacher and Billie Jo Rodriguez**
Discover how to create an encouraging, productive school culture using the Schoolwide Positive Behavioral Interventions and Supports (SWPBIS) framework. This title includes the authors' personal experiences in applying SWPBIS and explores practical examples of what the elements and tiers of this model look like in practice.
**BKL030**

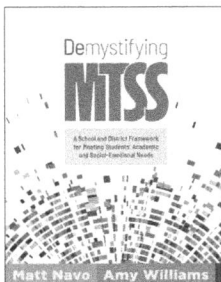

### Demystifying MTSS
**Matt Navo and Amy Williams**
*Demystifying MTSS* distills a complex system into a customizable framework built around four fundamental components. Drawing from research and their experience in building and sustaining effective MTSS, the authors share high-leverage, practical actions school improvement teams can take to ensure all students' diverse needs are met.
**BKF984**

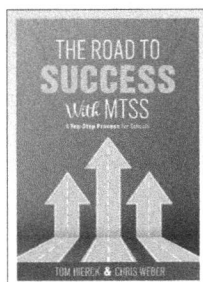

### Road to Success With MTSS
**Tom Hierck and Chris Weber**
Packed with research-based strategies, *The Road to Success With MTSS* is an essential road map for educators beginning their school's multitiered system of supports (MTSS) journey and those who have already come so far and are looking to reflect and reset for success.
**BKG084**

**MARZANO** Resources          Visit MarzanoResources.com or call 800.733.6786 to order.

# Professional Development Designed for Success

Empower your staff to tap into their full potential as educators. As an all-inclusive research-into-practice resource center, we are committed to helping your school or district become highly effective at preparing every student for his or her future.

Choose from our wide range of customized professional development opportunities for teachers, administrators, and district leaders. Each session offers hands-on support, personalized answers, and accessible strategies that can be put into practice immediately.

## Bring Marzano Resources experts to your school for results-oriented training on:

- Assessment & Grading
- Curriculum
- Instruction
- School Leadership
- Teacher Effectiveness
- Student Engagement
- Vocabulary
- Competency-Based Education

**LEARN MORE at** MarzanoResources.com/PD